CRICKET
AT THE
CROSSROADS

CRICKET

AT THE

CROSSROADS

Class, Colour and Controversy from 1967 to 1977

GUY FRASER-SAMPSON

First published 2011 by Elliott and Thompson Limited
27 John Street, London WC1N 2BX
www.eandtbooks.com

ISBN: 978-1-907642-33-3

9 8 7 6 5 4 3 2 1

A CIP catalogue record for this book is available from
the British Library.

Printed in the UK by TJ International
Typset by Envydesign Ltd.

CONTENTS

ACKNOWLEDGEMENTS

To say that the writing of this book has been a labour of love would be an understatement. Being asked to write by a commercial publisher a book about my favourite period of cricket would feature at number two on my fantasy wish list, second only to being asked to join the Test Match Special commentary team. However, this particular fantasy could not have been fulfilled without the help of others, let alone their support and encouragement well above and beyond the call of duty.

Various former England players, including participants in that memorable game at Edgbaston in August 1967 (see Chapter 3), kindly agreed to be interviewed.

Christopher Martin-Jenkins most generously made time available from his impossibly hectic schedule as president of the MCC to offer insight, help and encouragement.

Keith Bradshaw allowed me access to the MCC archives, and Adam Chadwick and Neil Robinson kindly facilitated this.

Frances Edmonds, wife of Phil and a noted author in her own right, introduced me to her daughter Alexandra, who in turn passed me her unpublished dissertation on the socio-political background to the D'Oliveira affair.

Olivia Bays shepherded the book through publication with signal efficiency.

Lorne Forsyth had the vision to see that a book like this could be commercially viable, and the courage to make it happen. That he also has an encyclopaedic knowledge of cricket was a welcome bonus.

Finally, I would like to acknowledge an enormous debt to Remy Kawkabani: true gentleman, true friend.

INTRODUCTION

In 1967 British society was outwardly conventional and conservative. Those attending cricket, or even football matches, did so in a jacket and tie, and gave up their seats on trains and buses on the way home. Yet underneath this hard, polite exterior lay something altogether darker – an implicit belief that one person could be naturally inferior to another (and therefore treated as such) simply on grounds of class, colour, or ethnic background.

For those who were subjected to such a belief, or who took exception to it on grounds of principle, it could easily lead to anger, an anger which would at various times during this story spill out into the open. On two occasions in particular, this anger would swirl around the MCC in its cricketing bastion at Lord's. On each occasion they would ignore it to secure their short-term objectives, but on each occasion, by ignoring it, emerge with their reputation badly dented.

There was also uncertainty born of frustration and confusion. The old ways were being swept away, to the consternation and dismay of some, and the exultation of others. Yet, whichever side of the fence you were on, nobody seemed to know quite what was going to replace them.

There was anger and despair born of the bitter social divisions which had always plagued Britain, perhaps uniquely so. Not for nothing did foreign competitors refer mockingly to the constant labour unrest that paralysed the UK's factories as 'the British disease'. Between 1967 and 1977 over 60 million working days were lost to strikes.

These divisions – between north and south, working class and middle class, 'them' and 'us' – had always been explicit within the game of cricket, with cricketers being classified officially as either 'gentlemen' (amateurs) or 'players' (professionals), and both treated and described differently. The distinction was formally abolished after 1962 and the MCC tour of Australia that winter, managed by no less a personage than His Grace the Duke of Norfolk, was the last to take place under the old system, with the players being accorded different treatment according to whether they were amateurs or professionals, even down to how their names were recorded and to which events they were invited.

There was anger born of a growing recognition that successive governments had badly mismanaged the economy, and yet it was the people who were going to have to pay the bill. This period would see the highest rates of income tax in history, a devaluation of the pound, Britain going bust and having to ask for an IMF bail-out, and retail prices trebling, leaving professional cricketers, already poorly paid in 1967 and without a trade union to argue their cause, dramatically worse off in real terms.

In due course, a sea-change in economic management would come from a grocer's daughter from Grantham, and a sea-change in the fortunes of professional cricketers would come from the grandson of a penniless horse racing punter from Tasmania.

Yet in the meantime, it was in the game of cricket that many of these conflicts and tensions would play themselves out. Of course individual character and personality would play their part, as would both destiny and chance, but underpinning much of what would happen on and off the cricket pitch during the ensuing decade was a strong, ongoing and increasingly resented sense of 'them' and 'us'. During the ten years from 1967 onwards the cricket world would be shaken to the core as the consequences of this division played themselves out. By 1977 both British society and the sport itself would look quite different.

CHAPTER 1

GENTLEMEN AND PLAYERS

It was a sweltering afternoon in 1967 as the England cricket team stepped off a BOAC jet in Barbados and dutifully posed for photos, led by their captain Colin Cowdrey. The beginning of a cricket tour is always aflutter with anticipation. Which newcomer will give glimpses of potential that may be richly fulfilled in the future? Will one of the struggling players find form and confidence simultaneously and leave for home at the end of the tour with their reputation enhanced, and their place in the side secure? It is at this point, of course, that those of a darker imagination will pose the third pertinent question: will one of the established veterans slink moodily onto the plane home, suffering the awkward glances of his fellows, undone by injury or inconsistency, and facing the grim possibility that his Test career may be over?

In respect of this particular team that December afternoon it was the first of these questions that must surely have lain uppermost in the minds of the attending journalists; both those meeting the plane on arrival and those travelling with the team from England, which latter crowd included a certain Brian Close, of whom more shortly. For this was a team chosen consciously to mark a break with the past, featuring a crop of mostly younger players who, it was hoped by the selectors, might form the bedrock of the England team for some years to come. To those who had followed England in recent years it had a somewhat unfamiliar look to it.

The era of Fred Trueman and Brian Statham was over, both having played their last Tests two years previously. John Murray, until recently rated unquestioningly as the best wicketkeeper in the country, was missing. There were some who felt he had been unlucky to be overlooked after his batting heroics against the West Indies in England in 1966, but in truth 1967 had been a wretched year for him.

Missing was the evergreen Tony Lock, one of the best left-arm spinners ever to play the game and who had reinvented himself with a new action and a new county as well as playing first-class cricket for Western Australia. He would therefore have been eligible for selection. However, he was 38 while his obvious like-for-like replacement, Derek Underwood, was just 22, and even *he* did not make the tour, despite his obvious promise.

Missing too was Bob Barber, felt by many to be the natural opening partner for the slower-scoring Geoff Boycott; he had declared himself unavailable because of business commitments. Nor, for the same reason, was there any return of the cavalier Ted Dexter, one of the most exciting batsmen ever to play for England; he had not played a Test since 1965, much to the disappointment of crowds around the world.

This was a team chosen for its blend of experience and youth, then, with the youthful element particularly applicable to the bowlers. The biggest concession to age and experience was Tom Graveney, at 40 the oldest man in the party. He was very much the joker in the pack, having forced his way back into the side in 1966 after a spell in the wilderness, and having played so well since then that it would have been simply unthinkable to leave him out. From the line-up, the selectors hoped and believed, would emerge a cadre of talented players who would form the future core of the side for the next five years or so.

Before the tour party left England, Colin Cowdrey had convened an indoor training session, at which he had laid out what he called a Five Tour Plan, ending with the Ashes series in Australia in 1970–71. He explained to the players that, stealing an idea from football, he expected them to form an ongoing squad from which England sides would be chosen during this period, though, as he admitted, 'one or two of us may fall by the wayside'.[1]

The pairing of Cowdrey, the urbane Home Counties gentleman, and Fred Titmus, the chirpy cockney professional, both of whom were 35, must have seemed to the selectors a match made in heaven, bringing together two complementary individuals who between them could communicate with and inspire any member of the side, no matter what their upbringing or circumstances.

Cowdrey's background was public school and Oxford (both of which he captained), and he made his debut for Kent at the age of 18, moving on to captain them as well. One of the most graceful batsmen of his generation, he married into a wealthy family which enabled him to finance playing cricket as an amateur. Very much an establishment figure, he would end up as one of only two cricketers to be awarded a peerage (the other being Learie Constantine), at the personal instigation of John Major, the former Prime Minister. He was, in short, exactly the sort of cloth from which English cricket liked its captains to be cut, whether at Test or county level.

Titmus, on the other hand, had come up the hard way. Born to working-class parents in a tough area of north London, he was a natural sportsman, playing professional football for Watford and making his debut as a cricketer for Middlesex at the age of just 16. A fine offspinner, he had a trademark arm ball that drifted away towards the slips, so that many of his victims were either caught or stumped by his teammate and close friend, John Murray. A genuine all-rounder, at one stage of his career he achieved the double of 100 wickets and 1,000 runs no less than five times in six seasons. By 1967 he had been captaining Middlesex for three years, and was therefore seen as a natural deputy to Cowdrey, well able to lead the side occasionally should Cowdrey wish to rest himself, or become unavailable through injury. He was a perfect and natural choice as the platoon sergeant of the squad.

It is difficult for a modern reader to appreciate just how tangible and

---

[1] Colin Cowdrey, *M.C.C.: The Autobiography of a Cricketer*, Hodder & Stoughton, London, 1976

significant was the distinction between the amateur and professional cricketer or, as it was more often expressed, gentleman and player. Every season, for example, the gentlemen played at least one first-class fixture against the players, often viewed as a Test trial. On many county grounds the professionals were not allowed to share the same dressing room (or even pavilion) with the amateurs. They were expected to call the amateurs 'sir', and refer to them as 'mister'. Even the way their names were represented on the scorecard made clear their status. As the sixteen-year-old Fred Titmus trudged nervously out onto the Lord's turf to make his debut for Middlesex, it was to the sound of a P.A. announcement regretting that the printers had made an error. 'F.J. Titmus', the announcer said apologetically, 'should read Titmus, F.J.'

The difference had been even more pronounced on tour, when the amateurs had travelled in separate cars and stayed in swanky hotels, dressing for dinner, while the professionals had to put up in boarding houses. For away matches in England the situation could be even more stratified, with the amateurs in one hotel, the professionals in another, but the professional captain on his own in yet another. The image of upstairs, downstairs and the butler's pantry comes strongly to mind.

The distinction was abolished officially in 1962. For some years it had been increasingly difficult to find amateurs who were both wealthy enough to be able to play cricket purely for fun, and good enough to command a place in the side as a player. Even if both these conditions were satisfied, it did not necessarily mean that they would be willing to captain the side. Amateurs often came and went according to business and family commitments; being available to play every match of the season was a different matter. Yet amateur captains were what counties wanted.

'The snobbery was always there,' says England all-rounder Barry Knight. 'Tom Pugh, who took over as Gloucestershire captain from Tom Graveney, was an amateur who could hardly play … pros were pros, amateurs, amateurs, even after 1962. The change was in name only. You always felt they wanted amateur captains.'[2]

---

[2] 'Barry Knight – A Cricketing Odyssey', www.bodacious.com

In truth, there had been many situations where it was apparent to all that the captain was not worth his place in the team as a player, which could and did lead to tension both on and off the field. Even Yorkshire, that most no-nonsense of counties, had suffered, the great left-arm spinner Johnny Wardle being sacked in 1958 after allegedly criticising the amateur captain Ronnie Burnet, a club cricketer who had been plucked from the obscurity of the Bradford League at the age of 39 to be given the job over Wardle's head.

This even occurred at international level. In the winter of 1929–30 there were two simultaneous England tours overseas. One, to New Zealand, was captained by Harold Gilligan (Dulwich College), who despite playing as a specialist batsman achieved a Test average of 17.75 in the series, while the other, to the West Indies, was captained by the Honourable Freddie Calthorpe (Repton and Cambridge), son of Lord Calthorpe and the uncle of cricket commentator Henry Blofeld. Calthorpe also played for England primarily as a batsman, and tabled only a slightly better average: 18.42.

Farce was an occasional alternative to tragedy. In Surrey's eagerness to appoint an amateur captain after the Second World War, they turned to Major Leo Bennett, a good quality club cricketer who captained the BBC's weekend team. Hearing that Major Bennett was currently at the ground paying his membership dues, they buttonholed him and offered him the job. Unfortunately it turned out to be the wrong Major Bennett, but by the time the mistake was discovered it was felt that it was too late to do anything about it. The Surrey committee resolutely refused to admit that he had not in fact been their first choice, and he duly captained the side throughout the 1946 season. Major Nigel Bennett was described by one writer[3] as 'a weak batsman and utterly lost as a county captain'. The Surrey players, however, while doubtless resenting their very poor performance that year, were gracious in their acceptance of his presence, not least, so it was said, because he had an extremely attractive wife who used to attend every game, bringing a waft of perfume and a welcome touch of glamour to the pavilion.

So, the distinction had now been abolished, and at county level most captains were what would have been categorised as professionals under the

---

[3] E.M. Wellings in *Wisden Cricket Monthly*, 1986

old regime; Titmus at Middlesex was a case in point. Yet old habits died hard, and counties still yearned for a well-spoken public schoolboy when they could find one. So too did England and, amazingly, would continue to do so for some decades yet. In recent years their captains of choice had been public schoolboys all: Peter May, Ted Dexter, M.J.K. Smith and Cowdrey himself, who had captained the side sporadically over the years when none of the first three were available, and had finally got the job for himself in 1966, only to lose it after just three matches.

Fred Trueman said:

> Those charged with running the game and selecting England teams... were former schoolboys who went on to Oxford or Cambridge... They looked down on the pros and considered an amateur with a cricket blue from Oxford or Cambridge as a much superior choice when it came to selecting the England team.[4]

M.J.K. Smith had been captain for the first match that summer at Old Trafford where the West Indies attack of Wes Hall, Charlie Griffith, Garry Sobers and Lance Gibbs overwhelmed England, who lost by an innings, Smith scoring just 11 in the match. His opposite number, Sobers, by contrast, scored 161 and then showed yet another side of his all-round brilliance by switching to left-arm spin in England's second innings; he and Gibbs bowled 83 overs between them out of the total of 108.

It was the end for Smith as a captain, though he would be recalled briefly and slightly puzzlingly in 1972. An outstanding all-round sportsman, he was England's last double international (rugby and cricket), but he had never really established himself at Test level, scoring just three centuries in 50 matches, with a batting average of 31. Indeed, playing as he did in an age of talented batsmen, it is difficult to imagine that he would have played anything like 50 Tests had he not been earmarked as captaincy material.

Smith, 'an absent-minded professor'[5] who played in spectacles, was

---

4 Fred Trueman, *As It Was*, Pan Books, London, 2004
5 John Snow, *Cricket Rebel*, Hamlyn, London, 1976

vulnerable against fast bowling, especially early in his innings. Cowdrey says that the selectors were also afraid for his personal safety, as this was an era before helmets, and Smith had problems spotting short-pitched deliveries.[6] So, the selectors now turned to Colin Cowdrey, but he too was to find the brilliant West Indies side more than a handful.

The 1966 Lord's Test was memorable chiefly because it marked the debut of Basil D'Oliveira, the first 'coloured' cricketer to play for England since the 1930s. As so often at Lord's the game was badly affected by the weather, ending in a draw. England achieved a first-innings lead and ran out of time chasing 284 to win in the second innings, ending 87 runs short with four wickets down, led in fine style by a rollicking 126 not out from Colin Milburn. England had been in a position to win the match, only to be denied by a mammoth second-innings undefeated stand of 274 for the sixth wicket between Sobers and his first cousin, David Holford.

Cowdrey himself failed twice with the bat and was heavily criticised in the press for overly defensive tactics, in particular, failing to attack Sobers and Holford before they were set. At least one former England captain felt he was not only defensively minded, but also indecisive, as would be evidenced by his uncertainty after an over-generous (or sporting, depending on your point of view) declaration by Garry Sobers in Trinidad in 1968. Ray Illingworth, the northern professional, says wryly that one of Cowdrey's biggest challenges as captain was deciding whether to call heads or tails.[7]

Trent Bridge was a better game for Cowdrey personally, but another disaster for him as captain, England losing after once again gaining a first-innings lead. Sobers, having been dismissed cheaply, opened the bowling with Wes Hall and took four wickets. Tom Graveney, one of his victims that day, would later say that, with the exception only of Ray Lindwall, Sobers was the bowler he least liked facing throughout his Test career. Sobers the batsman cashed in with 94 in the second innings, but the star of the show was Basil Butcher, who cut the English attack to ribbons in making an unbeaten 209.

---

[6] *M.C.C.* op. cit.
[7] Ray Illingworth, *Yorkshire and Back*, MacDonald, London, 1981

Worse still was to come at Headingley, where West Indies batted first, declared on exactly 500 (Sobers 174), bowled England out, enforced the follow-on and bowled them out again to win by an innings. With the exception only of D'Oliveira, who top-scored with 88, much of England's batting was deeply unimpressive, with Cowdrey again failing twice.

With the series lost, the selectors decided that the time had come for firm action. They dropped the diffident southern amateur Cowdrey and brought in Yorkshire's Brian Close to captain the side, with a young Dennis Amiss receiving his first cap. What followed was little short of cricketing magic. England scored 527 after having at one stage been 166-7, largely thanks to two huge stands. First Tom Graveney put on 217 for the eighth wicket with John Murray, whose batting had been considered a weakness at Test level. Then, still more improbably, the opening bowlers Higgs and Snow put on 128 for the last wicket. With Snow then dismissing both West Indian openers cheaply, this time it was England's turn to win by an innings. After the match Snow and Higgs were asked to pose for the press still holding their celebratory beers. The authorities, scandalised, substituted teacups.

A blunt, combative, northern professional, much loved and admired, Brian Close remains one of cricket's enigmas. His early days were spent in a council house in the working-class suburb of Rawdon, the birthplace of the great Hedley Verity, with two of whose children Close grew up (Verity was killed in Italy during the war). He was an intelligent and hard-working grammar schoolboy who, most unusually in those days, was offered a place at university, which he decided to decline, preferring instead to pursue a sporting career, though he had thought seriously about becoming a doctor.

A good enough footballer to play for Leeds and Arsenal and gain a youth cap for England, he too might have become a double international, but his soccer career was curtailed by a leg injury and the unwillingness of Yorkshire to release him for games which overlapped with the cricket season, so he decided to concentrate solely on cricket. His first season with Yorkshire, 1949, was little short of outstanding, as he became the youngest all-rounder to achieve the double of 1,000 runs and 100 wickets. He was selected to play for the Players against the Gentlemen, which was to prove memorable for more than cricketing reasons. On reaching 50 he was congratulated by the amateurs' wicketkeeper, Billy Griffith, who said 'well played, Brian', to which Close replied 'thank you, Billy'. He was later disciplined and formally reprimanded by the Yorkshire committee for not having addressed him as 'Mr Griffith'.

That same summer he played his first Test match (at Old Trafford against New Zealand), when he was still only 18 years old. He remains the youngest player ever to appear for England.

He was duly selected for that winter's tour of Australia, which proved a personal disaster. Lonely, homesick and struggling with a serious groin injury, he was later to single out some of the senior players, notably Denis Compton, Len Hutton, Cyril Washbrook and skipper Freddie Brown for failing to counsel and support him, accusing him of malingering, and forcing him to play while injured. Ironically, only the Australian captain Ian Johnson was sympathetic to his plight, expressing his concern to Brown (who allegedly referred to Close as a bastard and told Johnson to mind his own business).

The tour set the pattern of Close's Test career. Thereafter he would drift in and out of the side after lengthy intervals, always underachieving (not least by his own high standards), increasingly convinced that there was an 'anti-Close' lobby out to get him, and with controversy rarely far away.

Most famously against Australia in 1961, with England chasing down a total for victory but with Richie Benaud taking wickets regularly from one end with his masterful legspin, Close decided to hit out, and perished in doing so. England lost, and Close was blamed. Many thought the criticism unjust, including Benaud. Close claimed that his tactics were agreed by his captain, Peter May, but the patrician May declined to back him up. Others argued that but for the slow scoring of Raman Subba Row, who took two and a half hours to make less than 50, Close's tactics would not have been necessary. This may have been the reason for May's diplomatic silence. Subba Row (Whitgift School and Cambridge) was a close friend of May (Charterhouse and Cambridge). Close (Aireborough Grammar School) was not.

Close was dropped after just that one Test in 1961 and did not play for England again until 1963. That year he was the hero of one of the classic

Test matches at Lord's where, against the hostile bowling of Charlie Griffith (who broke Cowdrey's arm and in a later series felled Derek Underwood with a blow to the head) and Wes Hall, Close stood up to them in scoring a courageous 70, sometimes advancing down the pitch to meet them, and frequently taking balls on his body. The last over of the match, with Cowdrey emerging from the pavilion with his arm in plaster to allow David Allen to bat out the match for a draw, has passed into cricketing folklore.

Sadly that was the high point of the series for Close. He was steady, scoring three other fifties, but never the century which would have cemented his position in the side, despite being given the chance to play in all five Tests that summer. In fact, that 70 at Lord's would remain his highest Test score. At the end of the series he was quietly dropped, and not heard of again until plucked unexpectedly from county cricket to captain England in that amazing match at the Oval in 1966.

There was no tour that winter, but the following summer, 1967, saw two mini-series, each of three Test matches, against India and Pakistan respectively. Close, the man in possession, captained England to five victories and a draw. Again, though, his own form as a player was indifferent. In six matches, against weak bowling attacks, he scored just 197 runs without once making a 50. As a bowler he was more successful, taking 20 wickets at 20.9, but these figures are flattered by one fine performance against India at Birmingham.

Close himself, in looking back on his career, mused on the possibility of having been cursed with bad luck, on getting out to blinding catches or unplayable deliveries, while the player at the other end was dropped three times and went on to make a century. The truth is probably sadder and more prosaic. As a player, he was probably never quite good enough. This is a harsh judgement, so let us temper it a little.

Brian Close was an outstanding all-rounder in county cricket, particularly in his first few seasons when his fast-medium bowling could be decidedly brisk, and he swung the ball late. He could bowl both seam and spin. He could bat anywhere in the middle order, but was probably a natural number six. He was a fine fielder anywhere, an outstanding close catcher, and a courageous short leg in the days before helmets. Just about anyone who has ever played first-class cricket claims to have been caught by the wicketkeeper following a rebound from Close's forehead.

However, two factors fall to be considered. First, there is a huge gulf between the demands of Test and county cricket, both technical and mental, which many very talented players have failed to bridge over the years; Graeme Hick and Mark Ramprakash would be two recent examples. Many of Close's own contemporaries performed better than he did at Test level without ever becoming established in the England side: Jackie Hampshire (despite scoring a century on debut against the West Indies), Peter Parfitt (who averaged over 40 with the bat against Close's 25), and Phil Sharpe (who also averaged over 40 and was generally reckoned the best slip catcher in the country). So, if he did fail narrowly to make the grade, then he was in good company; these were all very fine players indeed.

Second, while Close's versatility as an almost total all-rounder was his greatest attraction, particularly at county level, perhaps it was also his greatest weakness at Test level. He was a utility player, the jack of all trades, but master of none. In particular he was never quite good enough to justify a place in the side as a batsman, and as he got older his bowling became less effective. Again, let us examine the credentials of this claim.

In a first-class career spanning 28 years and no less than 786 matches, Close never scored a double century. In fact, he was probably rather more effective as a bowler (1,171 wickets at 26.42) than he was as a batsman (34,944 runs at 33.26). In 786 matches he scored 52 centuries. By contrast, in 498 matches Peter Parfitt scored 58, including a double century. That's six more centuries, in only 63% as many games. Yet Parfitt too had pretensions to all-rounder status: but for the perennial presence in the Middlesex side of Fred Titmus, he would undoubtedly have bowled a lot more than he did. He was also a fine slip fielder. Pursuing the comparison, Parfitt only played 37 Tests, spread over an eleven-year period. So, even if Close is right in his contention that he should have played for England more times than he did, he is wrong to feel that he was singled out for special attention. If he was unfortunate, it was in being cursed by the burden of unrealistic expectations at a very young age; the careers of many other promising young all-rounders have since followed a similar trajectory.

There is an extra dimension to Close's game which must be considered, though, if any assessment is to be full and fair. He was an outstanding captain, not just in the technical matters of team selection, field placings and bowling changes, but in his ability to inspire those around him, and in his mentoring of young players. Mike Brearley, who shared these qualities, has pointed out that a captain should really be considered as an all-rounder, and this is fair comment. Whatever the case, it is Close's inspirational captaincy, along with his almost suicidal courage under fire, which will linger in the memory. In a Gillette Cup match in 1973, he took over the wicket-keeping gloves from an injured Jim Parks. Brushing aside suggestions that a younger man should do the job with the claim that he had once been an emergency keeper during a Test, he strapped on the pads. Having fumbled his first few takes, he threw off the gloves and proceeded to keep wicket immaculately to the fast bowlers Hallam Moseley and Allan Jones bare-handed.

Certainly there seems little doubt that in 1967, and for some time thereafter, he was the best man available to captain England. That the distinguished commentator Christopher Martin-Jenkins should have spoken of him as a serious contender as late as 1974[8] speaks volumes.

And so as the 1967 summer progressed, the England selectors found themselves in the position of having selected as captain someone whom they had already discarded as a player, and finding that he had the knack of winning matches. By mid-August, Close himself was looking ahead to the forthcoming winter tour of the West Indies, and was already in preliminary discussions with the selectors about the composition of the touring party. It was at this point, however, that the dread hand of controversy which seemed constantly to hover over Brian Close would reach down and tap him smartly on the shoulder once again.

---

[8] Christopher Martin-Jenkins, *Testing Time*, MacDonald, London, 1974

CHAPTER 2

THE SOCIAL AND POLITICAL LANDSCAPE

As the novelist L.P. Hartley memorably put it, 'the past is another country; they do things differently there'.[9] Anyone looking back from today to the Britain of the 1960s would be struck forcefully by the accuracy of this statement.

Economically, the country was locked into a vicious downward spiral. Knowing that the population was desperate for advances in living standards after the rationing and austerity which had continued after the Second World War, successive governments allowed these to be bought on credit, rather than earned by improvements in productivity. The 1962 film *Live Now – Pay Later* potently evoked the dramatic eruption of consumer debt into people's lives. (In fact, the novel on which it was originally based was much bleaker, featuring a housewife who is forced into prostitution after she falls into debt to a loan shark.)

Economic mismanagement was exacerbated by what became known as the British disease: a combination of incompetent business management and

---

[9] L.P. Hartley, *The Go-Between*, Penguin, London, 2004

militant trade union agitation, brilliantly satirised in *I'm all right, Jack* starring Peter Sellers as the nightmarish shop steward Fred Kite. The Wilson government would be forced to devalue the pound in 1967, signalling the end of the Bretton Woods monetary system which had served the world so well since the war, though this would not be formally abolished until 1971. Though not widely recognised as such at the time, this was in fact an act of enormous significance and could be argued to be the precursor of the modern sovereign debt crisis. Despite the devaluation, Britain would effectively become bankrupt in 1976, with Chancellor of the Exchequer Denis Healey having to go cap in hand to the IMF asking for Britain to be rescued.

Healey, incidentally, also gained notoriety by setting Britain's highest ever rate of income tax (83% on earned income and 98% on investment income), an outrage made possible only by people being effectively locked into the country by exchange controls which made it impossible to transfer money out of the country. Thus, you could live abroad if you liked, but only at the expense of leaving your money behind.

Politically the two main parties offered the public a choice between strident socialism and tired jingoism. Disillusioned members of the Labour Party would later seek 'a third way' by setting up the Social Democratic Party, but at this time the third party, the Liberals, were seen as marginal, with little chance of any success under the 'first past the post' electoral system. Their prospects were not improved when their leader, Jeremy Thorpe, later stood trial for the attempted murder of his gay lover (he was acquitted). This bipolar approach to politics echoed the fascist/communist divide of the 1930s and was hardly conducive to reconciliation between workers and bosses.

For it was the class system which remained at the heart of Britain's social ills, having survived two World Wars, a General Strike and the introduction of commercial television. Middle-class young people would be routed into management jobs regardless of natural intelligence or aptitude. Working-class young people would be expected to leave school at the earliest possible opportunity to take a job in a factory, or clerking in an office. Upper-class people thought work of any kind beneath them, whether they needed the money or not. The impoverished former officer trying to pose as a gentleman, and usually being drawn into rather seedy crime, became a staple of film and fiction.

In cricket, it was reckoned unthinkable for a non-working-class person to be classified as a professional. P.G. Wodehouse, for example, has Psmith rescue Michael Jackson from such an ignominious fate using his ample trust fund as a *deus ex machina*. Though the distinction was officially abolished in 1962, the attitudes behind it survived and flourished throughout the period covered by this book. No professional cricketer would be elected president of the MCC until 2004, 42 years later.

In 1963 Freddie Trueman was fined £50 (a good deal of money in those days) for his off-field behaviour on a tour of Australia managed by the Duke of Norfolk. When he was asked about it by the media, he not unnaturally told the truth, namely that he had been given no explanation about what he was supposed to have done wrong, but had simply received less money than he had been expecting.

Lord's attempted to rescue the situation with a classic piece of political spin, explaining that Trueman had not been fined, but had merely received less than the full amount of his bonus, which was after all discretionary. While outwardly serene, though, the MCC was furious, as a disciplinary file in their archive bears witness. The president of Yorkshire, Sir William Worsley (Eton and Cambridge), Baronet Worsley of Hovingham, past president of the MCC, a Lord Lieutenant of Yorkshire, and father of the Duchess of Kent, was asked to interview Trueman, and his letter to Lord's afterwards[10] drips with resigned condescension.

He reports Trueman as saying: 'I am not a gentleman, and I know that, and I know that my code of behaviour is not always popular with authority …' In despair, he concludes: 'We all know that he is uncouth,and nothing we can do will alter that.'

In a precursor of the Close affair, some (though not nearly as many) members of the public wrote in to complain. One, written by eight Yorkshiremen and dated 20 May, asked: 'Why, now that amateurism has been abolished, must you carry on in this "old school tie" frame of mind?'

---

[10] Sir William Worsley, letter to S.C. Griffith, 16 May 1963

Beyond the game of cricket, the class system would be ruthlessly exploited as a source of amusement. The gentle nonsense humour of the Goons included such characters as Major Bloodnok, a former army officer with an IQ in single figures, and Grytpype-Thynne, a Terry Thomas-type upper-class bounder. Their cultural successors, Monty Python, would famously feature the Upper-Class Twit of the Year race. In between, both social and political issues would be satirised with increasing venom by a whole series of programmes inspired by *That Was The Week That Was*. The British establishment, however, seemed to survive these attacks more or less unscathed.

Race was becoming an increasingly significant factor: Britain, in an era of full employment, had actively encouraged immigrants from Commonwealth locations such as the West Indies to take up low-paid jobs working for the likes of London Transport and the National Health Service. Others came from the Indian subcontinent; still more from East Africa when Idi Amin expelled Uganda's ethnic Indian population in 1972. By this time, racism had become an explosive issue, with Enoch Powell's notorious 'rivers of blood' speech in Birmingham in 1968 splitting the country. He was promptly sacked from the shadow cabinet by Edward Heath, though ironically there were some who credited the lingering afterglow of Powell's popularity with the electorate for Heath's election victory in 1970.

Thus race too became a polarising issue, admitting only of two real choices: either you were racist or you were anti-racist. There did not seem to be any in-between. BBC television were to make an important contribution to the debate through the unlikely medium of a comedy show, *Till Death Us Do Part*, featuring Warren Mitchell as the foul-mouthed racist and all-round bigot Alf Garnett. So effective were Mitchell (a gentle and cultured man in real life) and the scriptwriters in creating the character of Garnett that many members of the public wrote in to complain, not realising that the show was deliberately intended to disgust and repel. The sad truth was that Alf reminded just about everybody of a character in their local pub.

For racism was a feature of British life. Until 1968 landlords could and did display signs that said 'no blacks' or 'no coloureds'. Even ten years later the writer, during a summer job as a student, heard an office manager say to an employment agency 'and I don't want any you can't see in the dark' (in his spare time the man was a Conservative councillor). Yet it was mostly covert, rather than open as it was, for example, in South Africa. When Basil D'Oliveira and his wife moved to Britain they spent some months in a state of confusion, looking for separate buses, and separate entrances to public buildings and cricket grounds. In what might be viewed as an alternative racist joke, it was said that Mike Procter when he first visited London spent three hours waiting for a bus with a white conductor.

Reference to separate buses should serve to remind us that apartheid was being actively practised at this time not just in South Africa, but in various states of the US. In 1968, the year after our story begins, Bobby Kennedy, the man credited with ending that system, was assassinated, as was the great civil rights leader Martin Luther King, sparking race riots across America's southern states.

For 1968 was a year of unrest. In London, protestors mounted a huge demonstration against the Vietnam war in March, which sadly turned violent, in first Trafalgar Square and then Grosvenor Square. Other demonstrations would follow throughout the year. In Paris, students took to the streets aiming at nothing less than the overthrow of their government. In Poland and Czechoslovakia democratic movements were brutally suppressed by the Soviet Union. In Germany, Baader-Meinhof terrorist bombs exploded and a left-wing politician was shot. In Northern Ireland, clumsy police handling of a civil rights march would spark a tragic 30-year period known as 'the Troubles'. Little could anyone have guessed, however, that it would be the game of cricket which would contribute one of 1968's most contentious events, and one of its most lasting controversies.

Another aspect of British life which would be thrown into stark relief by the Close affair was the north–south divide. This was in a way an extension of the class system. Those who had been to public school would speak a standard form of English with a more or less standard accent, regardless of where they lived. Any two people meeting for the first time who spoke in this way would instantly recognise a common bond born of shared experiences such as bad food, cross-country runs and lighting farts in the dormitory. It was for precisely this reason that many people who had not been to public school sought to copy the accent in the hope of being accepted as an honorary member of the club.

Leaving aside this very small segment of the population, however, your accent defined where you had been brought up, and further gradations of the particular accent would also give a clue to your social origins. For many southerners, it was not until the advent of commercial television that they had ever heard a northern accent. A new generation of northern writers arose. Keith Waterhouse, John Braine and Stan Barstow gave life to *Billy Liar*, *Room at the Top*, and *A Kind of Loving* respectively. All made into films, they would build awareness of life north of Watford.

Sometimes, as they will in our story, two of these factors would combine. A southern gentleman would feel himself to be living in a different world from a tradesman living in his own town. Replace the local tradesman with a northern workman and the gulf might seem too great ever to be bridged. Yet this is exactly what various cricketers were called upon to do, with sometimes explosive results.

Essentially, the British people were suffering from a crisis of identity. Since before the Second World War, the grammar schools had offered a way for bright working-class boys to break free of their social origins and compete for management and professional jobs. It was no coincidence, for example, that many of them found their way into the RAF during the war. There were many more technical requirements for those who flew and maintained planes than for those who fought in or supplied, say, the infantry, and so educational skills were at a premium. This did not, however, prevent the other services from looking down on the air force for granting officers' commissions to those of humble birth.

After the war, it became increasingly possible for boys and girls to progress from grammar school to university. Upwardly mobile, they began to form the management pool of the future. The tectonic plates were shifting under the established structures of British society, but nobody could be quite sure where the earthquakes would occur, or when. It was mostly in the new industries, such as the media, where the new wave made most progress, and typically in manufacturing where they made least. Here the British disease raged unchecked, with family background, not ability, conditioning your chances of promotion. In the City too, it was still felt to require a certain type of person to be able to discharge a position of responsibility in a merchant bank or a stockbroking firm. Here, there was often open resentment of grammar schoolboys, who were felt to be too clever by half.

During the same period, and often as part of or immediately after the increase in progression from grammar school to university, there occurred a great regional co-mingling. In the nineteenth century London had seen a huge influx of labourers migrating from the countryside in search of work. In the 1960s it was seeing a similar ingress, but this time it consisted of smart young graduates from the north or (even more unthinkably) Scotland, wearing their BA on one shoulder and their social chip on the other. They were hungry for success, and eager for hard work. They were, in short, the southern middle class's worst nightmare come true.

The crisis of identity had to do with Britain's place in the world too. Though historians disagree on when precisely Britain ceased to be a great power, it was probably at the time of the Washington Naval Treaty in 1922, at the latest. That had not stopped successive British governments continuing to posture on the world stage, a trend that continues to this day. Britain had gone into the Second World War totally incapable of fighting it, and had gone bust within eighteen months, able to continue only as a client of US credit under the thin pretext of Lend Lease. Afterwards, our share of the post-war aid which the US had generously donated to various European countries had been spent not on retooling British industry but on building new houses, and maintaining the ridiculous levels of armed forces around the world which befitted Britain's image of itself as a great power.

It was with the Suez crisis in 1956 that the whole house of cards finally came crashing down. Defied and ridiculed by what Britain saw as a small and backward state, timely military intervention proved impossible, even given the greatly swollen defence budget. When finally Britain was ready to respond, world opinion had moved against her, the so-called 'special relationship' with the US had been exposed as a pathetic delusion on the part of the government (a delusion which nonetheless exists to this day), and Britain and her ally, France, were forced into a humiliating withdrawal.

Along the way Britain and France had been persuaded into an agreement with Israel allowing Israeli forces to invade Egypt, an invasion which was then used as a pretext for Franco-British intervention. It was a shabby, worn-out trick by a shabby, worn-out Britain. A final tragic twist saw Prime Minister Anthony Eden, a man who had won the MC in the trenches of the First World War, and resigned from Chamberlain's cabinet on a point of honour in protest at the appeasement of dictators, lie to the House of Commons about the Israel connection, suffer a nervous collapse, and retire from public life, a last sad relic of the Edwardian Age that was Britain's vanished glory.

Wherever your political sympathies lay, it was impossible now to avoid the inevitable truth that Britain no longer enjoyed anything resembling the power and prestige that she once had wielded. The nation which had once controlled roughly a third of the world was now exposed for what it really was: a small, broke and hopelessly divided island in the Atlantic Ocean. Yet wounded pride and self-delusion persisted in many Britons, not least Alf Garnett, who refused to accept that Britain's great power status had finally been stripped away, revealing some rather grubby underwear.

What did it mean now to be British? How could one be 'British' without that definition including some people over in Northern Ireland with comical accents whose sole objective seemed to be to kill as many of each other as possible? Or people with frankly unintelligible accents in Scotland who seemed to hate the English almost as much as they hated Rangers or Celtic supporters (delete whichever does not apply). Or people with different-coloured skins; surely you had to be white to be British, didn't you?

What did it even mean to be English, now that you knew this to include people speaking what sounded like different languages living in tenement buildings under the shadow of slag heaps? Or people like Alf Garnett whom you found disgusting? Or people with public school accents whom you found insufferably arrogant?

The truth was partly that British society was already much more diverse than most people had ever realised it to be, and that they were slow in coming to terms with this fact. It was partly that it was becoming rapidly more so, given both immigration and social mobility. Alvin Toffler would in 1970 describe 'future shock' – what happens when the rate of change becomes too great for people properly to comprehend it, or assimilate it into their way of thinking.

These profound social and historical influences form the backdrop to our story, so it has been useful to state them explicitly. It was not just British society, but the world of cricket too, which underwent such rapid and significant changes that they can be understood far better in retrospect than they could have been at the time.

As the Warwickshire secretary Leslie Deakins pointed out in 1967, attendance at County Championship matches had dwindled in the space of 20 years by 80% from two and a half million to just half a million. 'We must acknowledge,' he said, 'that we are providing a spectacle that the public does not want.'[11]

The establishment had been sufficiently concerned to ask for various reports to be drawn up outlining what the public *did* want, and there was general agreement both in general and on the specifics.

In general, the public wanted brighter cricket. This would later result in the bonus points system being revised to reward a win more generously, but for some time the situation would remain that it was possible to win as many points for two draws as it was for one win, provided that you gained a first innings lead each time.

'Brighter cricket' nonetheless issued forth constantly as a buzz-phrase, and when Geoff Boycott took nearly ten hours to score 246 against India at Headingley that summer, not only was he pointedly not selected for the 'batsman of the match' prize, but he found himself dropped from the next match as a punishment for slow scoring. Ken Barrington had been dropped

---

[11] Rob Steen, *This Sporting Life – Cricket*, David & Charles, Newton Abbot, 1999

in similar circumstances in 1965, but sadly the selectors soon got tired of paying lip service to the idea of brighter cricket, allowing both over-rates and scoring rates to decline.

More specifically, it seemed that what the public wanted was limited overs cricket. The Gillette Cup, a knockout competition played originally over 65 overs, had been introduced in 1963 and had proved wildly successful. From 1966 it was standardised at 60 overs a side, with a limit of twelve for any one bowler. However, even having included the minnows of the Minor Counties plus Scotland and Ireland, there were only a limited number of these games, since it was a knockout competition. Given the popularity of these games with the public, perhaps something could be organised on a league basis as an even greater money spinner?

At the same time, BBC television was wrestling with a problem of its own. It had been awarded Britain's third television channel, BBC2, in 1964. While initially very successful under its controller (from 1965), David Attenborough, particularly for lavish costume dramas such as *The Forsyte Saga* and for leading edge comedians such as Peter Cooke and Dudley Moore, it had increasingly come under fire for being too highbrow. The BBC badly needed a populist programme, and had actually been flirting with broadcasting cricket on a Sunday afternoon before the required ration of religious broadcasting (the 'God slot') on a Sunday evening.

Sunday was then a rest day in the county programme, but exhibition matches could be arranged for the International Cavaliers, an invitation team not unlike rugby's Barbarians, which would include some recently retired Test cricketers whose backs and knees could safely be trusted over the period of a single afternoon, as well as some big name international players. The emphasis was on fun, big hitting and good-natured sportsmanship. If anything, these games proved even more popular than the Gillette Cup.

Britain in the 1960s was unrecognisable from today in many ways, but at no time was it more different than on a Sunday afternoon. Pubs closed earlier at lunchtime and opened later in the evening. Shops were forbidden by law from opening, and so remained closed. So, usually, did restaurants and cinemas. After listening to *Round the Horne* or *The Navy Lark* on radio after Sunday lunch, a yawning gulf opened up of several hours which could be filled only by the traditional pastimes of arguing with other members of your family, and spying on the neighbours. The Tony Hancock radio show brilliantly portrayed this in an episode entitled simply *A Sunday Afternoon At Home*, written by Ray Galton and Alan Simpson.

At the same time a third interest group, the tobacco industry, were looking for a solution to a problem of their own. With cigarette advertising having been banned on UK television in 1965, how could they keep their various brand names in front of the public?

BBC2 had taken to televising some of the Cavaliers' matches, and it did not take long for the perfect marriage to emerge between the needs of cricket, the needs of BBC2, and the needs of tobacco companies. The John Player League was the first version of cricket ever to be created by television for television. At 40 overs a side, with the bowlers coming off restricted run-ups, it was designed to fit perfectly into the BBC's available time slot on a Sunday afternoon.

It took to the screens in 1969 and the public loved it. Not only did it bring much needed TV and sponsorship revenues into the game, but it encouraged people to turn out on a Sunday afternoon to watch their county side performing under very different conditions. Any batsman who hit a six went into a pool for cash awards at the end of a season. So did any bowler who took four wickets.

The action was hectic and fun. Spectators were guaranteed a result in the course of a single afternoon. Best of all, the bars stayed open all afternoon, and sexy young ladies in miniskirts wandered among the crowd dispensing free John Player cigarettes.

The very success of the Sunday League, as it was popularly known to the dismay of John Player, brought tensions of its own between the progressive elements within the cricket community and the traditionalists. The former saw limited overs cricket as an important part of the way ahead, if only for financial reasons, rather than simply a peripheral bolt-on. The latter saw it as an irrelevant distraction which risked damaging the development of young players by encouraging negative bowling and reckless shot selection. In the event, both would be proved right.

Incidentally, prominent among the traditionalists was Brian Close, who condemned limited overs cricket as 'instant rubbish'. By a sad mischance, some of the leading progressives ended up sitting in judgement upon him as part of an MCC disciplinary committee.

The progressives pointed out that the County Championship was no longer sufficiently financially viable to form the staple offering to the public. The traditionalists asked why nothing had been done to promote the Championship either locally or nationally. For example, could not part of the deal with the BBC have been the provision of a regular weekly feature on the Championship on a Saturday afternoon, just as already happened with soccer?

The progressives, delighted with money flowing into the game's coffers from the Sunday League (from the BBC, John Player, and gate receipts), called for more limited overs cricket. The traditionalists argued that two limited overs competitions were already enough, and that adding a third could not be done without severely cutting back the County Championship schedule.

Interestingly there was no argument at this stage for international limited overs games. The first would happen almost by accident when a Test match was rained off in Melbourne without a ball being bowled in 1971, and owed its arrangement to the spirit of the 'beer match' customarily agreed between village players when a match has finished early. The first deliberately arranged One Day International games were held in 1972, and even then many thought they would simply prove an interesting but brief experiment.

It was the progressives who got their way, of course, as those who champion Mammon against principle always will. 1972 would see the introduction of the Benson & Hedges Cup: different tobacco sponsor, different number of overs, different free cigarettes, different colour miniskirts.

The traditional form of the game would change too, almost beyond recognition. The Sunday rest day would disappear from both Test and County Championship matches. The latter would finally be stretched from three to four days to avoid contrived finishes and encourage the development of young spin bowlers.

The greatest change of all, though, had nothing to do with the structure of the game, but everything to do with the attitude of some of those who played it. In the 1960s, when this story begins, cricket is still played in a spirit of true sportsmanship. Batsmen 'walk' when they know they are out (or at least are supposed to). Fielders do not claim a catch unless they are certain the ball has travelled to them. Players do not show dissent if they disagree with an umpire's decision, though bowlers such as Freddie Trueman are allowed the odd wry comment, such as 'nearly got the bugger that time' after clean bowling a batsmen following two unsuccessful lbw appeals. Most importantly, bouncers are bowled rarely (and never at tail-enders), and are routinely booed by the crowd.

As the decade progresses, the game of cricket undergoes significant change in certain quarters – so significant indeed that it is difficult to argue that what one is witnessing in the end may properly be called 'cricket' at all. Fast bowlers aim deliberately to hit the batsman, and boast of enjoying it when they inflict injury. In the hands of cynical captains who value gamesmanship above sportsmanship, compliant umpires, and cowardly administrators, cricket enters a dark age of a new bodyline. It ceases to be a noble game played hard yet fairly, and becomes something nasty, brutal and ugly. In the process the establishment is tried in the balance and found wanting.

From debonair figures in whites and pads, batsmen evolve into sinister knights with helmets and body armour, a sad comment on the death of cricket. The game has been brutalised. Far from booing when a bowler delivers a bouncer, the crowd roars with pleasure when he hits a batsman. The atmosphere has ceased to be one of sporting appreciation and more closely represents the braying and menace of the film *Rollerball*.

Yet more change is felt in the geopolitics of cricket. In the late 1960s the game is still run very much from Lord's. Indeed, until recently England and Australia have enjoyed weighted voting rights on the International Cricket Council. While these have been given up, the two countries, particularly England, are still able to influence the game through their relative financial position. The English game is profitable, and the poorer nations, particularly the West Indies and Pakistan, rely on lucrative tours of England to boost their coffers.

Yet there is an elephant in the room, obvious to all but mentioned by none. The world of cricket is hopelessly split by South Africa, which practises apartheid and will not admit tours by non-white teams. Consequently they play only England, Australia and New Zealand. This is a sensitive subject, particularly in Australia, which operates a 'whites only' immigration policy. This situation, tacitly tolerated for so long, suddenly falls apart under the pressure of public opinion both in England and other Commonwealth countries, though the establishment fights a stubborn rearguard action.

In time the geopolitical centre of the game will shift eastwards with the growing prosperity and cricketing success of India. Money will change the game for both good and ill. World Series Cricket, at first strenuously resisted by the establishment, will lead to cricketers at every level earning a proper professional income. The growth of betting on cricket matches, particularly in unregulated environments such as India and Pakistan, will eventually lead to scandal and shame for various international players.

That so many innovations could be introduced in such a short period of time is evidence of the pace of change occurring within the game. Nor would this slacken. Sadly, the only thing which would remain constant was the refusal of many members of the cricketing establishment to accept that the British Empire, the Victorian era, the natural superiority of the officer and gentleman, and the unthinking deference of the lower orders had passed away.

Bloodnok and Grytpype-Thynne were still in charge.

CHAPTER 3

THE CLOSE AFFAIR

In August 1967 Yorkshire, under Close, went to Edgbaston to play Warwickshire, led by M.J.K. Smith, in a vital top of the table clash. The match was to become controversial for two reasons, for both of which Close was subsequently blamed. Let us deal with them separately.

First, Close says that as the Yorkshire fielders left the ground for a lunch break, he overheard an insulting remark being made by a spectator. He walked along an empty row to where he thought the remark had come from, laid his hand on the man's shoulder, and asked 'did you say that?', intending 'to reprimand him'. The man said 'no' immediately, whereupon Close apologised and withdrew.[12] Feeling awkward about it, he reported the matter to the Warwickshire secretary, who told him not to worry about it. Close claims that he and the spectator had a drink together after the close of play that day.[13]

Interesting, both Mike (M.J.K.) Smith[14] and Alan (A.C.) Smith, who

---

12 DBC, conversation with the author, 7 May 2011
13 Brian Close, *I Don't Bruise Easily*, MacDonald, 1978
14 MJK, conversation with the author, 18 June 2011

played in the game, have a different recollection: that the incident happened after the end of the match, when a Warwickshire member shouted something very abusive (according to A.C.) at Close, though he cannot remember precisely what was said or done by anybody.[15]

Alan Smith was a great servant of the game, earning six Test caps and being at different times a county captain, an England selector, and head of the TCCB. An amazingly versatile player, he remains the only example of a wicketkeeper taking off his pads to bowl in a first-class match and claiming a hat-trick. It was once said of him that 'as a batsman who bowled a bit, he wasn't a bad wicketkeeper'.

The second incident occurred right at the end of the match when, after interruptions for rain, Warwickshire were chasing 142 in 102 minutes, led by the young and exciting John Jameson. They eventually finished nine runs short, so the match ended in a draw. Much was later made of the fact that Yorkshire had taken 11 minutes to bowl their last two overs, though this period had included the fall of two wickets and two no-balls from Freddie Trueman.

Close recalls that he brought Richard Hutton on for Tony Nicholson, and that Hutton took a practice run-up, at which Close, realising this was sailing rather close to the wind, thought 'oh, bloody hell'. When the umpire asked Hutton what he was doing, Hutton replied that he previously bowled all his overs from the other end. Close shouted at him to bowl straight, because another wicket would ensure that this would be the last over, but he had to shout twice because the crowd were making a lot of noise, and Hutton 'was always a bit dozy'.[16] At this point, umpire Charlie Elliott called out to him to 'get on with it'.

Again the recollections of the two Smiths are a little different. They both remember Trueman being stationed on the boundary at the other end of the ground so that he had a very long walk to his bowling position. A.C., who was the non-striker when Trueman was bowling, is clear that Trueman was bowling no-balls deliberately to try to stop another over from being

---

[15] AC, conversation with the author, 18 June 2011
[16] DBC, conversation with the author, 7 May 2011

bowled, and reports that umpire Elliott decided to give the spirit of the game precedence over the rules. After the first couple, Trueman ran through the crease again as he bowled, and looked back, very surprised, when the umpire failed to call.

'That were a bloody no-ball, Charlie', he protested.

'Get on with it, Freddie', Elliott replied curtly.[17]

As the players left the field, some Warwickshire supporters voiced their displeasure at what they saw as deliberate time-wasting, which had denied Warwickshire an extra over with which the game might have been won. Mike Smith and Close shook hands, Close explaining that Yorkshire had felt they had to fight to the last, and Smith replying that he quite understood.

The controversial ending to the game was, however, splashed all over the next day's papers, and Close found himself summoned to Lord's a few days later to answer for his conduct in respect of the second incident to the executive committee. He pointed out that in the first hour of the final innings Yorkshire had bowled 16 overs despite the participation of three quick bowlers – hardly the conduct of a team looking to waste time. Even in the controversial last hour and 40 minutes, much of which was conducted in a steady drizzle, they bowled 24, which would today be exactly the rate required in Test matches.

When the players came back onto the field for the last ten minutes, after a break for a heavy rainfall, the ground was very wet, which necessitated the ball being dried between each delivery; under the playing conditions of the time this could only be done under the direct supervision of the umpires, rather than by the bowlers as they walked back to their mark. This took up precious extra time. In fact, Yorkshire had, with the tacit consent of the umpires, broken the rules by drying the ball on some occasions as they walked back.

The wet conditions also meant that Close had no choice but to bowl his quicker bowlers, because the spinners could not grip the ball.

The two no-balls and two wickets also took up time, even though the Warwickshire batsmen hastened to the crease. It is entirely possible that

---

[17] AC, op. cit.

these two factors taken together were worth the three or four minutes which an extra over would have given the batting side.

The committee's verdict was unanimous. Yorkshire's conduct had constituted unfair play and was against the best interests of the game. Close personally had been entirely responsible for this conduct, and he was 'severely censured'. This release came just before the final Test match against Pakistan at the Oval, and Close went into the game with a strong sense of foreboding. The day before the match, he went individually to every player in the team and asked them to tell him honestly if he should resign the captaincy. To a man, they said 'no'.[18]

During the match, a Sunday newspaper published a story alleging that during the Warwickshire game Close had attacked a man in the crowd. On the advice of Doug Insole, chairman of selectors, Close chose not to tell his own story but remained silent. He thus never had a chance to answer this charge (which was never made the subject of any formal enquiry or disciplinary hearing), so was never able to present the written statement he obtained from the spectator concerned, a Doug Nicholls from Walsall Wood, which completely vindicated his own version of events.

The article appeared in *The People*, a late and unlamented Sunday newspaper of the populist variety, featuring lurid accounts from three named and photographed spectators who all claimed that Close had pushed through the crowd and given a Warwickshire supporter a good shaking, before being called away into the pavilion by a startled Charlie Elliott. Fred Trueman, it was said, had come hurrying back down from the dressing room to find the spectator and apologise for Close's behaviour, but his victim, 'embarrassed and shocked', had already departed. Just for good measure, *The People* threw in a further 'incident', a lady spectator making the improbable claim that at one point during play Close had been about to run into the crowd 'looking for a punch-up', only to change his mind at the last moment. The article concluded by recording what would today be called the doorstepping of Warwickshire's vice-chairman, who 'was asked if he had reported the collar-shaking incident to the MCC. "I'm

---

[18] Derek Underwood, *Beating the Bat*, Stanley Paul, London, 1975

sorry, old boy, but this is a bloody delicate matter," he said as he stepped into his Mercedes.'

For the record, M.J.K. Smith is adamant that while some confrontation between Close and a member did indeed take place, 'there was no fracas', and that the statements in *The People* were either false or, at least, greatly exaggerated.[19]

It is now common knowledge, however, that this story had no bearing on events. What actually occurred was that three days earlier, on the first day of the final Test, an emergency meeting of the full MCC committee was called. The executive committee's finding was read and noted. Doug Insole then reported, as chairman of the selection sub-committee, that the selectors had met to decide whether, in the light of the statement of censure, they still wished to nominate Close as captain for the West Indies. They had done so unanimously, though the two members who were present almost in *ex officio* capacities (Arthur Gilligan, the president-designate of MCC and Les Ames, the tour manager) had voted 'no'. Thus the result was 4–0 or 4–2 in Close's favour, depending on how you looked at it. Neither Gilligan nor Ames were exactly impartial. Gilligan was related by marriage to Cowdrey's best friend Peter May, while Ames had been Cowdrey's mentor at Kent.

It was at this stage, however, that the knife was slid gently but effectively between Close's ribs.

The executive committee, it was explained, had not examined the 'Close attacks spectator' allegations as part of their formal remit, though 'they had been mentioned' to Close, who had admitted laying hands on a member of the crowd who was 'an innocent bystander'. It was, however, thought proper, the minutes show, that the full committee might wish to take them into account when considering whether to accept the selectors' nomination.

After deliberation, the committee decided 14–4 not to accept the nomination. At this point, Insole put Cowdrey's name forward for consideration, and it was agreed that he be asked to lead the MCC team in the West Indies.

---

[19] MJK op. cit.

This was itself more bizarre than might at first appear. Just three weeks earlier, at the last MCC committee meeting, Insole, on behalf of the selectors, had asked for, and been granted, authority to appoint one of two people captain: Mr D.B. Close, or Mr M.J.K. Smith.

Mike Smith recollects that Insole did indeed contact him to sound him out, and that his response was that he had already told Warwickshire he would be retiring at the end of the season. This must have been between the committee meeting on 2 August and the Yorkshire game a few weeks later. It is always possible, however (the county cricket scene being traditionally a hotbed of gossip), that it was this response which Crawford White got hold of, and passed on to Close. Alternatively it could have been a leak from someone who had been present at the committee meeting. (See below.)

To this day, there are rival explanations for the events of August 1967. To the many who wrote to Lord's in the days leading up to the Emergency Meeting, Close's conduct was beyond the pale, 'not cricket' in the literal sense. Naturally, almost none of these correspondents had actually been at Edgbaston to see what happened, but to be fair a few had been, and did not like what they saw. However, even so, not all of these wanted Close to be deprived of the captaincy. The second wave of letter writing, after the captaincy decision was announced, was almost entirely in favour of Close, with even those who accept that he should have been reprimanded for his conduct at Edgbaston believing that he was still the best man to captain England.

For many, the proceedings seem to have smacked strongly of a pre-agreed device to get rid of Close, and for once a conspiracy theory seems largely consistent with the facts. First, it seems strange that the executive committee should have rejected Close's version of events so totally, particularly without hearing any evidence from either M.J.K. Smith or Elliott. Even if they felt his account was questionable, they could not reject it in the absence of any evidence to the contrary. Yet this is exactly what they appear to have done.

Second, if the committee had indeed been concerned to act in a proper manner then at least two of the five members should have disqualified themselves from participating. One of them had recently published a report of which Close had been publicly critical, while another had earlier taken grave offence to some comments Close had made about the county which he represented (Derbyshire). In such cases, justice must not only be done but be seen to be done. Here neither requirement appears to have been satisfied.

Third, did the facts really constitute 'unfair play'? It was, and has always been an accepted part of cricket that players may attempt, within reasonable limits, to manipulate the clock. One frequently sees a batsman ensuring that the current over will be the last in the session by coming down the pitch to do some gardening, or talk to his partner. Similarly, a few field changes by the captain can achieve the same result. The question of when gamesmanship crosses the line and becomes unfair play is surely one of degree. Given the two wickets and two no-balls (bowled by a fast bowler off a long run), it seems difficult to make out the case here, at least without opposing testimony or evidence of intent, and there is no mention of either. According to Close, none of the other participants were present at the hearing. In fact, one of the Warwickshire players involved, Tom Cartwright, would later say:

The ball was taking an age to get back to the bowler, but it was the sort of thing that was going on in other games at that time. They probably carried it a bit further – but not that much. There was a game the next week against Somerset, and I remember sitting in the dressing room thinking it wasn't that dissimilar.[20]

Incidentally, in 1953 Trevor Bailey had famously bowled his last six overs of the day down the leg side off a long run to prevent Australia from winning a Test match, yet nobody had ever suggested that this was in any way unfair, least of all Doug Insole, his county captain.

More ironically still, Cowdrey in the West Indies would slow over-rates to a funereal pace in the Test matches, shamefully so given that his attack usually contained two spinners. Yet such tactics would go entirely unrebuked.

---

[20] Stephen Chalke, *Tom Cartwright: The Flame Still Burns*, Fairfield, Bath, 2007

Mike Smith says that in the days before the '20 overs in the last hour' rule came in, time-wasting was a fact of life in county cricket, and that everybody did it. Whether Close was indeed guilty of unfair play was therefore a matter of degree. He confirms that Warwickshire made no official complaint to Lord's about what had happened.[21]

Fourth, even if the committee's view was correct, how could they hold Close entirely responsible? If time-wasting had indeed occurred, then it would have needed the connivance of the two bowlers concerned, in which case both Freddie Trueman and Richard Hutton should also have been censured. A further point occurs: would any Lord's committee really believe that the son of Sir Len Hutton could have been capable of such conduct? Yet if he was not, then the case falls apart. In a case of deliberate time-wasting, other than frequent changing of the field, it takes two to tango: the bowler and the captain. One of the spectators wrote to Lord's to complain of 'the antics of Close, *Trueman and Hutton*' (italics added).[22] In fairness, though, as Alan Smith points out, Close was the captain and had he not wanted these things to happen then he could have stopped them.[23]

All of these things tend to suggest a different explanation. Weighed in the balance should also be Close's claim that about a month previously, Crawford White of the *Daily Express* warned him specifically 'they want you out and their own man in. They think you've put the team together, and they don't like it.' As noted above, this could have been based on a leak to White about the committee meeting, or a rumour about Insole approaching Smith; the dates would certainly fit.

It is certainly possible that Close's decided attitude towards selection upset some at Lord's. He had insisted on Illingworth being brought back into the side, for example, and had objected to Colin Milburn on the grounds of his immobility in the field. It is known that he was already in discussions with the selectors about the team which he wanted to take to the West Indies, yet when the team was announced Milburn was pointedly included while Illingworth, equally pointedly, was not.

---

[21] MJK op. cit.
[22] J.P. Tansley, letter dated 21 August 1967
[23] AC op. cit.

Crawford White's words are unsubstantiated hearsay, and would not carry much weight in a court of law, but they are consistent with a darker explanation.

Perhaps the most likely one is that the MCC believed they had created a Frankenstein's monster. They had appointed Close as captain without really wanting to, very much as a fall guy, expecting that he would fail against the West Indies at the Oval as Smith and Cowdrey had done before him. They would then have been able to drop him quietly again during the winter, when there was no tour anyway, go back to one of the Oxbridge boys the following summer, and allow him to establish himself against the comparatively gentle opposition of India and Pakistan.

As Close put it:

[In 1966] The press were hankering after change. I'm sure they only put me in there because they thought I'd go the same way as Cowdrey and Mike Smith. That way they could say 'there you are', and go back to the Oxbridge boys.[24]

Instead, of course, Close had proved consistently successful and they had no valid cricketing grounds on which to change captains. It is therefore entirely possible that they saw the Edgbaston incident as manna from heaven and seized upon it gratefully as the ideal excuse to depose Close. The subsequent newspaper story was simply the icing on the cake, but by then the deed had already been done; the northern professional had served his purpose, and been disposed of. Now the establishment had got the good chap they so desperately craved, the man Close would later describe as 'Cowdrey – yes sir, no sir, three bags full sir'.

While necessarily speculative, this option seems to be the one most consistent with the known facts. If the selectors were perfectly happy with Close as captain before the Edgbaston match, why did they approach Smith? As one writer would later memorably record, Brian Close 'was the last head to topple into the tumbril of the *ancien régime*'.[25]

---

24 *This Sporting Life* op. cit.
25 *This Sporting Life* op. cit.

The Close affair divided the country. John Snow, writing in 1976, bluntly epitomised the views of many:

To me it was a prime example of one person having the 'right' background and the other the 'wrong'. Something which has permeated the game since the early days of Players and Gentlemen.[26]

Close's supporters included the Yorkshire journalist and cricket enthusiast Michael Parkinson, and Prime Minister Harold Wilson who, when asked for his comments by a newspaper, said simply that they were unprintable. Parkinson famously recommended Close not to say he was sorry, as he had nothing for which to apologise (a stance Close maintains to this day), though Yorkshire chairman Brian Sellars appeared to many to cut the ground from beneath Close's feet by writing to the MCC to offer an apology on behalf of Yorkshire County Cricket Club (of which Close was of course captain).

The MCC archives contain a large cardboard box full of letters received from members of the public in August and September 1967. Reading them brings a rather alarming recognition that in British society as a whole, traditional class consciousness was in some cases hardening into something close to class hatred. That the former Conservative Prime Minister Sir Alec Douglas-Home (formerly Earl Home for the uninitiated) was president of the MCC at the time was unfortunate, and presumably for nobody more so than for the Conservative Party.

'A Conservative Worker', writing to ADH (Eton and Christ Church) on 30 August, predicted the affair would lose the Conservatives a million votes: 'Millions of small people see themselves as Close. What you have done rips wide open what you apparently think of us.'

Another sadly anonymous letter, written on 3 September, mocks both 'gentleman Cowdrey' and the MCC itself, and is representative of many, though rather better written than some:

---

[26] *Cricket Rebel* op cit

Close doesn't match up to your social standards. He isn't a member of your little 'magic circle'. He does not have a double-barrelled name, a posh southern accent or a public school upbringing. These, for the MCC, are the first priorities for the English captaincy.

Mrs D. Wood, writing from Lancashire on 4 September puts it simply, but poignantly: 'I am sure you would not have done this to any of your southern gentlemen.'

Interestingly, many questioned whether the full MCC committee should continue to have the right to overrule the selectors. Apparently even at the time it seemed a trifle strange to many for the national cricket side to be picked by four professional cricketers, only for them to be overruled by a group of politicians, generals, air marshals and unemployed peers of the realm. If the committee had listened carefully, they might have heard the faint sound of tumbrils rolling towards them down Wellington Road.

Also interestingly, nobody seemed to have a good word to say for Cowdrey. The main issue, though, for most correspondents, was quite simply: 'who is the best man for the job?' They, unlike the MCC, seemed to draw a clear distinction between Close being disciplined for whatever might have happened at Edgbaston, and losing the captaincy.

Typical is a letter written by a Scottish doctor, living in Oxfordshire, on 30 August:

Close did what he thought right to win, and this must be the real object of any captain. Close has proved himself a very good captain in all the Test matches he has been in charge of, and to me he should still be in charge ... Cowdrey may have the old school tie tied round his neck, maybe too tightly to be able to breathe freely, but he is very slow and does not in any way inspire confidence ... he looks tired, too tired for this job.

It is good to see that amongst all the vituperation and fulmination are not just some well-written, well-argued essays, some running to several pages, but also some classic examples of English humour. One wrote on behalf of the West Indian cricket team to congratulate the MCC on their decision. Another, which reads so well that it might have been written by Peter Cook, and which is signed 'Imperial Echoes', also congratulated the MCC, pointing out: 'We cannot have a man like this in charge, who is determined to win … surely it is better to send out a team of good losers to be laughed at, rather than a team determined to win …'

Many, even the obviously middle class and professional, seemed to believe instinctively that there had been some sort of 'deliberate campaign' or 'vendetta' against Close. Just about every single one implored the MCC to reverse their decision.

Needless to say, they did not, though they clearly did religiously file away every individual letter. So it was that in December 1967 it was the 'gentleman' Colin Cowdrey who stood smiling at the head of his troops as they squinted into the bright Caribbean sunshine, and the 'player' Brian Close who lurked like Banquo's ghost in the press corps.

CHAPTER 4

ENGLAND'S 1967–68 TOUR OF THE WEST INDIES

John Edrich and Colin Milburn were selected as opening batsmen for the West Indies alongside the already established Geoff Boycott. Edrich was a small but powerful left-hander of unflappable temperament. He had famously scored 310 not out against New Zealand in 1965, having been brought into the side only because of injury to other players, but experienced the lowest of lows in the following match when, against South Africa, he was dismissed for a duck in the first innings and then struck a sickening blow on the head by Peter Pollock in the second, taking no further part in the series.

Colin 'Ollie' Milburn was a favourite of crowds everywhere. A big man, and a big hitter of the ball, he attacked the bowling from the very first over and could quickly take a game away from the opposition if he got set. Yet despite his swashbuckling 126 not out against the West Indies in England in 1966, he too had struggled to establish himself, like Edrich playing only two Tests in 1967, with a similar lack of success. The choice of Edrich or Milburn to partner Boycott would not be an easy one.

The middle order batsmen other than Cowdrey were Barrington, Graveney and D'Oliveira. The party appeared to be one batsman light, since if England were to play six batsmen then all these would have to play in every match, with no latitude for injury, rest or loss of form. With neither Barber nor Dexter touring, Cowdrey was the only member of the squad to have played as a 'gentleman' under the old rules. All the others had competed as 'players', or would have done had they been around before 1962.

Ken Barrington was a gritty, resolute batsman, not pretty to watch but entirely dependable, a man who would fight and graft even when clearly out of touch. Notoriously difficult to dismiss, he could be the despair of opposing captains, and had earned the respectful soubriquet of 'the run machine' from his teammates. His slow scoring rate could pose a potential problem, though, particularly with Boycott in the same side (nor were Edrich and Cowdrey renowned as fast scorers). In addition he was a useful legspinner. It is arguable that Barrington was one of the best Test batsmen ever, and it is hard to understand why this is so little recognised. He would end his Test career after playing 82 matches with England's second highest batting average of all time (58.67, bettered only by Herbert Sutcliffe). Even the great Sachin Tendulkar scored fewer runs in his first 82 Tests, and at a lower average.

Tom Graveney was every schoolboy's hero, a graceful batsman playing mainly off the front foot and with one of the most beautiful cover drives the game had ever seen. He was the in-form player, having hardly been able to put a foot wrong since his belated return to the team.

Basil D'Oliveira would in due course become the subject of more media attention than any player ever to play the game – more even than Jack Hobbs or Don Bradman. For the moment, however, his main claim to fame was one of curiosity value, being the first 'coloured' man to play for England since the Nawab of Pataudi Snr in 1933. A solid batsman, he was also a useful slow-medium bowler with a reputation as a partnership-breaker. Brian Close's view that England lacked a genuine all-rounder[27] is only half true when one considers the presence of Barrington, Titmus and D'Oliveira, all of whom could be expected to play in every Test.

---

[27] Brian Close, *The MCC Tour of West Indies 1968*, Stanley Paul, London, 1968

For wicketkeepers, England could call on the experience of Jim Parks (36) and the exciting potential of Alan Knott (21). Knott had played two Tests during 1967, in one of which he conceded not a single bye, but was felt to be a lesser batsman than Parks. Thus, if England had any worries about a long tail, Parks's batting was likely to tip the scales in his favour.

Other than Titmus, England's spin bowling was entrusted to Robin Hobbs and Pat Pocock. Hobbs was a legspinner who had made his debut the previous summer. Playing against both India and Pakistan he took ten wickets in four matches, enough to be labelled promising, but without convincing anyone of his credentials at international level. Pat Pocock was a young offspinner who was most unlikely to feature in the Test side given the presence of Titmus, but was seen as a future Test player, and worth exposing to the atmosphere of international cricket. This came at a price to the overall strength of the squad, however, as it meant there was no room for the vastly more experienced Ray Illingworth, also a useful batsman, nor the young Derek Underwood, whose ability to run through a side on a turning wicket was already earning him his nickname of 'Deadly'.

The quick bowlers were John Snow, Ken Higgs, David Brown and Jeff Jones.

Snow had played a number of matches for England since his debut in 1965, impressing but without ever turning in the sort of match-winning performance that one expects from a great fast bowler. Indeed his main claim to fame so far had been as a batsman, during that heroic last wicket stand with Higgs at the Oval against West Indies in 1966. A moody character who wrote poetry in his more introspective moments, he had a reputation for being difficult for a captain to handle.

Higgs had stepped up from being a county trundler to astonish those who saw him at Test level, seeming to gain a yard of extra pace, and taking wickets while at the same time being difficult to score off. Against the West Indies in 1966 he had taken 24 wickets, and if one adds in the winter tour of New Zealand, in that calendar year he took 41 wickets in eight Tests at an average of just 18.73. At 30, he seemed set fair to be a major part of England's attack for some years to come.

David Brown was a tall man who hit the pitch hard and had a tremendous work rate. Though often used as a stock bowler, he put just as much effort into the last over of the day as the first. He had played for England regularly, but not continually, since 1965; as with Snow, this tour was seen as an opportunity for him to show whether he could make it as a genuine top-class bowler. If he could reproduce the form which impressed everyone who saw him bowl for his county, Warwickshire, then anything could be within his grasp.

Jeff Jones was the slight surprise in the seam bowling line-up, getting in ahead of the likes of John Price of Middlesex and Geoff Arnold of Surrey. Jones probably got the nod because he was a left-armer and thus able to bring variety to the attack.

The opening matches of the tour were unhelpful to the tour selection committee, not least because they were played on poor pitches. Net facilities at most grounds in the Caribbean were also at this time generally unsatisfactory. The main point of interest of this initial period would prove to be England's first brush with two brilliant young opening batsmen: Geoff Greenidge (not to be confused with his more famous namesake Gordon) and Roy Fredericks. It remained a matter of some surprise in the England camp that neither were selected by West Indies during the series.

Once having decided to ignore these two, and plump for the experience of Steve Camacho opening the innings with Seymour Nurse promoted from the middle order, the West Indies side for the first Test more or less picked itself. The tried and tested bowling attack of Hall, Griffith, Sobers and Gibbs was supplemented by the legspin of the all-rounder David Holford, who had famously saved the Lord's Test of 1966 in partnership with his captain and first cousin, Garry Sobers. Rohan Kanhai and Basil Butcher were obvious choices as middle-order batsmen. So too was Deryck Murray as wicketkeeper, particularly since his only serious rival, Jackie Hendricks, had been injured. The only new face in the side would be the tall 23-year-old Clive Lloyd, making his Test debut at home, having played in India the previous year.

There were at least three slight surprises when the England team was announced. The steadiness of Edrich was preferred to the dash of Milburn, despite the latter having made a century before lunch in one of the warm-up games. More controversially perhaps, Brown and Jones were chosen to open the bowling. Cowdrey had doubts whether Snow, who had been in bed with a virus before the team left England, was fully fit, but Higgs, who had played in England's last Test match and done nothing wrong, was surely unlucky to be omitted. D'Oliveira would play as an all-rounder and bat at seven. Parks would bat at six and keep wicket.

England were seen as the underdogs going into the match, with West Indies looking very strong on paper, but by lunchtime, with Boycott and Edrich having weathered the new ball attack of Hall and Sobers, they gained an advantage which they were never to relinquish as the game progressed. A long, grinding century by Barrington and a fluent, graceful one by Graveney took England to the huge total of 568. Cowdrey had batted on into the third day because he thought a draw the most likely result, that his only chance of winning the game was by making West Indies follow on, and that they were quite capable of making 350 in their first innings. In the event, he was to be proved right on all counts.

Despite a glorious century from Clive Lloyd on home debut, and a fighting innings by Kanhai, West Indies, at 363, fell just six short of avoiding the follow-on. A point to note was that in this more chivalrous age, and with West Indies fighting to save the match, Rohan Kanhai 'walked' when caught by Cowdrey in the slips. In tumbling for the catch, Cowdrey had fallen on the ball and so it would have been impossible for the umpire to give the batsman out. Kanhai asked if the catch had been cleanly taken, and on Cowdrey answering 'yes', simply tucked his bat under his arm and walked off.

For once, a good deed did not go unrewarded. In their second innings, West Indies dug in, all of the top six contributing apart from Lloyd, who could be excused a failure after his performance in the first innings. The end of the match was nail-biting stuff, with Sobers and Wes Hall hanging on for the last several overs with only Lance Gibbs to come, but hang on they did, and the match was drawn.

England could take comfort from a good all-round performance with every team member contributing, although it seems slightly strange that in both the first and the second innings Cowdrey gave the legspin of Barrington more overs than that of Hobbs, the specialist bowler. In fact, since Barrington was more than just a part-time legspinner, this raises the question of whether England had been right to play three spinners rather than Snow or Higgs, one of whom might just have got the breakthrough which England so badly needed on the last day.

England had obviously reflected on this when the second Test began in Kingston, Jamaica, with Snow replacing Hobbs. It cannot have been an easy decision. The pitch had been recently relaid, over-watered and over-rolled and nobody could be sure how it was going to behave. There was general agreement after the match that it had not been fit for any form of first-class cricket, generating very variable bounce, which in the event was to prove a boon for the pacy Snow.

It turned out a good toss for Cowdrey to win, for the pitch held together reasonably well for the first day but thereafter deteriorated rapidly. How England must have yearned for the veteran Tony Lock or the young Derek Underwood, either of whom might have proved pretty close to unplayable on such a surface, with their fizzing deliveries.

It was two successive century partnerships early on which laid the foundations for England, first between Edrich and Cowdrey, and then Cowdrey and Barrington. However, Parks and D'Oliveira then both failed and, despite a brief wag of the tail by Titmus and Brown, England were all out for 376. It seemed like a commanding total on this pitch, but nobody could really be sure.

West Indies simply collapsed in their first innings, despite a valiant 34 not out by Clive Lloyd. With some deliveries shooting head high and others scuttling along the ground, John Snow took 7-49 and West Indies were all out for 143.

With two hours left on Saturday, and Sunday, as was customary in those days, being a rest day, Cowdrey opted to enforce the follow-on, despite his three fast bowlers already being close to exhaustion through their efforts to date on what was a very hot day. Nurse chose to counter-attack against tired bowlers when the second innings started, and West Indies closed the day on 81 without loss, still 152 runs behind.

The Monday of the Kingston Test match was to pass into cricketing history, but for all the wrong reasons. Wickets fell steadily in the difficult conditions. Even the great Sobers struggled, being dropped twice in quick succession. The fifth wicket went down when Parks caught Butcher down the leg side off D'Oliveira, and then the trouble started. The crowd, which had been growing increasingly restive with the fall of each West Indies wicket, took such exception to the umpire's decision that they started throwing bottles onto the ground. Courageously, Cowdrey walked up to the fence and began appealing for calm, supported by Sobers who, shouting to make himself heard above the noise, tried to explain that from the non-striker's end he had himself clearly seen Butcher edge the ball.

For a moment it seemed that all might be well. Some of the England fielders started gathering up broken glass in their caps and carrying it to the boundary. Then first one squad of riot police and then another marched onto the playing area, and silently confronted the troubled section of the stands. Lest it might be thought odd to have squads of riot police on duty at a cricket match, it should be explained that similar scenes had been observed at Kingston during previous series.

The sight of the riot police drove the crowd to new heights of fury, and the bottles started coming over the fence more thickly than ever. Cowdrey, entirely understandably, now became concerned for the safety of the players, and led them off the field. As he did so, the police started firing tear gas into the crowd. The breeze quickly spread this across almost the whole ground, and rage turned to panic, with people stampeding away from the affected areas, women and children being trampled underfoot. Brian Close now proved one of the heroes of the hour, twice diving into the crowd from the press box with characteristic bravery, each time picking up a woman who had fallen, and carrying her to safety. The England dressing room, which was largely open to the elements, suffered from the gas particularly badly, the players gasping for breath, wrapping wet towels around their heads, and trying to wash the chemicals out of their smarting eyes. John Snow quickly stripped off and stood doggedly under a shower, which seems to have proved the most effective approach of all.

In cricketing terms, over an hour and a half's play was lost, but the loss to Jamaica and its reputation as a cricketing venue was incalculably greater.

After the chaos subsided it was decided, at Cowdrey's request, to extend play to a sixth day, with 75 minutes of additional time being made available that morning.

When play resumed, England had understandably lost their edge; the effects on the body of tear gas can take hours, or even days, to subside. Sobers and Holford saw West Indies safely through to the close, and a slim lead. When Holford was finally out on the afternoon of the fifth day, West Indies were only 81 runs ahead, with four wickets remaining. The temptation for Sobers now to hit out must have been overpowering, but he refused to give into it, steadily picking off singles while first Murray and then Griffith held up an end. Most observers were to agree that, even by the very high standards of Garry Sobers, this was undoubtedly one of his finest innings.

Suddenly, shortly after the ninth wicket fell, Sobers declared at 391, leaving himself unbeaten on 113. Unable to believe it at first, the English players headed for the pavilion with the truth slowly dawning upon them. They needed to score 159 runs to win the game, but on this treacherous pitch that would be by no means easy, especially as there were only 155 minutes of playing time left, which meant they had to take chances to score at greater than a run a minute, and against Lance Gibbs, one of the greatest offspinners ever to play the game. Sobers was going for a win, gambling that he could skittle England out.

Despite the fact that he must have been desperately tired after his long spell at the wicket, Sobers decided to open the bowling himself. In the space of his opening over, the hunter became the hunted. He took the wickets of both Boycott and Cowdrey, each falling to the Sobers trademark of late swing into the right-handed batsman. England were two down without a single run on the board. Once Hall and Griffith had reduced England to 19-4, bad light mercifully came to England's rescue. Only two results were now possible, depending on whether England could survive the extra 75 minutes due on the sixth day. How richly ironic had become Cowdrey's decision to ask for the extra period of play. England would now have been happy for the match to end, while Sobers was planning to use the extra 75 minutes to take the remaining six English wickets.

The sixth morning was a fraught affair for England. Only D'Oliveira gave any impression of permanence, and even he was dropped without scoring. That proved to be the decisive event of the game, as D'Oliveira was to finish unbeaten on 13, with David Brown desperately propping up an end for the last 12 minutes of playing time to gain England the draw. It is only fair to point out, however, that the English batsmen wasted time shamelessly during this period of play, with frequent gardening and mid-pitch conferences, prompting a wry smile from a certain Yorkshireman in the press box.

Hardly had the English team's nerves stopped jangling than they suffered a desperate blow. Fred Titmus, after captaining the side against the Leeward Islands in the next tour match, suffered a terrible freak accident while swimming off the Sandy Lane beach in Barbados, getting his left foot caught in a boat's propeller, which horribly mangled it. With the help of two local lads on the beach, Hobbs and Cowdrey commandeered a car and bundled Titmus into it. Rushed to hospital and straight into emergency surgery, the bad news was that four of his toes could not be saved and had to be amputated. The slightly better news came from the surgeon who performed the operation. A visiting Canadian, who dashed in still wearing his beach shorts, he reassured Titmus that he had recently performed a similar operation on an ice hockey player, who had been able subsequently to resume his career.

So the pairing of Cowdrey and Titmus had been ruptured tragically after only a few weeks, and England now needed both a new vice-captain and a new front line spinner. The first vacancy was filled predictably by Tom Graveney, who had experience of captaining Worcestershire. The second, much more unexpectedly and romantically, was filled by none other than Tony Lock, who was located by telephone in Australia. He agreed to fly to the West Indies after Western Australia's final Sheffield Shield match. That meant that he would not be available for the third Test at Bridgetown, but should arrive in time for the fourth Test in Port of Spain.

Again springing a selection surprise, England chose the untried Pocock to replace Titmus for the third Test, rather than Hobbs. Perhaps the fact that they knew they could rely on the part-time but useful legspin of

Barrington was a factor. In the event, Pocock was to make little impact on the proceedings, taking just one wicket in each innings in what turned out to be a high-scoring draw on a good batting pitch. West Indies scored 349 and 284-6, the stalwart of each innings being Butcher, but with another big-hitting century from Clive Lloyd in their second innings. England batted only once, their total of 449 being set up by a first-wicket partnership of 172 between Edrich, who went on to score 146, and Boycott. Parks's disappointing run with the bat continued. When he fell for a duck, he had scored just 50 runs in the series to date, and only six in his last three innings.

Their batting practice in Bridgetown appeared to have put new heart into the West Indies, who were now looking more like the unofficial world champions that they claimed to be. The most significant thing to occur at Bridgetown for England was the arrival of Tony Lock, who appeared in the England dressing room on the third day.

One change in the England side, Lock for Pocock, had already been telegraphed. Another, Knott for Parks, had not, but was felt by the tour selectors to be sadly necessary. Knott was known to be the better wicketkeeper. Parks had been preferred for his batting, and his batting had failed him. Jim Parks would never play for England again.[28]

The one change made by West Indies at first seemed to be of a similar nature, with veteran fast bowler Wes Hall being dropped. Unlike the unfortunate Parks, however, this was not the end of Hall's Test career. Indeed, the move seemed to be an attempt to change the balance of the side, as an opening bowler, Hall, was replaced by an opening batsman, Joey Carew. A further change saw legspinner Willie Rodriguez replace David Holford.

Both moves seem difficult to justify on cricketing grounds. Neither Hall nor Holford had played badly. The West Indies batting line-up did not need strengthening and, even if it had, it would have seemed more sensible to blood either Geoff Greenidge or Fredericks. It was said that Carew had

[28] His son, Bobby, would later once keep wicket for England as a substitute for the injured Bruce French at Lord's in 1986, as a result of a sporting gesture by the New Zealand captain, Jeremy Coney.

been chosen because he could also bowl part-time offspin, but Fredericks bowled left-arm wrist spin while another contender, Maurice Foster, was reckoned at least as good a batsman as Carew and a much better offspinner.

It is difficult to avoid the conclusion that the changes were politically motivated. Both Carew and Rodriguez were Trinidadian; indeed, Carew was captain of Trinidad. In the volatile atmosphere in which Caribbean cricket is played, the selectors were pandering to the local crowd, hoping to avoid at Port of Spain any repetition of the shameful events at Kingston.

The match was to end in a surprise win for England who successfully chased down a target of 215 in 165 minutes following what can best be described as a quixotic declaration by Sobers.

According to Close, Sobers said immediately after the match: 'I could have played the game the England way, but that would only have led to another tame draw. We have had three of those already and that is no good for Test cricket.'[29]

What did he mean by 'the England way'? Well, there were many who thought that Cowdrey's approach had been unadventurous and unnecessarily defensive throughout the series, and that on occasions he had even stooped to time-wasting, as in this match where only 22 overs were bowled in the two hours before lunch (that's 11 overs an hour as opposed to the 16 an hour following which Close was censured for unfair play). Sobers was known to be a romantic character who sometimes took action simply to show up the other side, or even his own teammates.

He would later bowl bouncers at a startled and increasingly angry Dennis Lillee in protest at Lillee's own indiscriminate use of them. Most famously, he responded to his Nottinghamshire teammates' whingeing about how difficult it was to score quickly that day by hitting the unfortunate Malcolm Nash for six sixes in an over. (After the third one, Nash told his captain, Tony Lewis, 'don't panic, skipper, I've got it all in hand.')

Perhaps too he felt that, with England's scoring rate in the series to date almost as pedestrian as their over-rate, they would not try to go for the runs,

---

[29] MCC Tour of West Indies op. cit.

particularly if they lost a few quick wickets. Indeed, two of the England top four, Boycott and Barrington, had both been dropped in the past as disciplinary action for slow scoring, Boycott only the previous summer. (On that occasion Brian Close diplomatically suggested that such was the intensity of Boycott's concentration on his batting that he failed to notice his captain gesticulating repeatedly from the dressing room balcony.)

However, when one considers that Sobers's only specialist fast bowler, Charlie Griffith, had been injured early on in England's first innings, and bowled only three overs in the entire match, the decision seems even more bizarre, as does the fact that he gave part-time bowlers Carew and Butcher between them 12 of the 53 overs bowled in the final innings. Then again, Butcher had miraculously and unexpectedly taken five wickets in the first innings with his occasional legspin, and perhaps Sobers was hoping that he might be able to repeat the feat.

In fact, Sobers was very nearly right about England not going for the runs. In the dressing room Cowdrey dithered, finally coming down in favour of batting out time for a draw. The professionals, led by Ken Barrington and outraged at such timidity, forcefully disagreed and carried the day.

For England, the much-vaunted return of Tony Lock proved a disappointment; he took only one wicket in the match and conceded over 100 runs. Balancing this failure, however, was a marvellous performance by Alan Knott, who scored 69 not out and kept wicket immaculately, conceding only one bye in the entire match, compared with 25 by his opposite number, Murray.

The declaration sparked fresh civil unrest in the cricket-mad Caribbean. When the teams arrived in Guyana for the fifth and final Test, mobs roamed the streets, chanting and throwing stones at the West Indian party in the hopes of hitting Sobers.

England, going into the final match one up, toyed with the idea of dropping a bowler to play Milburn as a seventh batsman, but discarded it. Believing the wicket would take spin, they decided to play Pocock alongside Lock, Brown the unlucky seamer to make way for him. Back for the West Indies came Hall and Holford, while the relatively unknown Lester King, who had last played a Test match in 1962, replaced the injured Griffith.

The match, played over six days, turned out to be a classic, with England outplayed for much of the match. West Indies batted first and scored 414, built almost entirely around big centuries from Kanhai and Sobers. England lost Edrich early on, but Boycott and Cowdrey then saw them safely through to 185. Then disaster struck as they subsided from 185-2 to 259-8, even Boycott finally succumbing for a dogged 116. A near-miracle then ensued as Lock and Pocock, neither noted for their batting, put on 109 for the ninth wicket to pull England back within reach, finishing at 371 all out.

Now came John Snow's second great demolition job of the series, skittling the West Indies out for 264, taking 6-60 in the process. Only that man Sobers again prevented a total rout, with a fighting 95 not out. England now needed 308 to win, a tall challenge, but by no means impossible.

Sobers the batsman now became Sobers the wrist spinner, and with the score on 33 had Edrich caught by Gibbs at short leg. This sparked an amazing collapse which saw England lose five wickets in less than half an hour. When Knott joined Cowdrey at the crease at 41-5 there were only the bowlers still to bat, with four hours to go, and the match seemed lost. The Kent captain and wicketkeeper, however, stopped the rot, putting on 127 runs but, more importantly, batting out more than two and a half hours. Then, out of the blue, Sobers had Cowdrey out lbw. The West Indies were through to the tail, and there was still over an hour to go. In the dressing room, John Edrich hid behind the door, unable to watch. Jeff Jones stared fixedly at the wall, desperately hoping that his meagre skills with the bat would not be required. Snow batted out 45 minutes, Lock five and Pocock 12. When Pocock was out caught (a dubious decision by the umpire, with the crowd becoming very fractious) there were seven minutes left as the last man, Jeff Jones, came out to join Knott.

With the entire West Indian team clustered around the bat, Jones survived the last ball of Gibbs's over. Then Knott survived six from Sobers. One over to go, and one wicket to fall. With radio listeners back home in Britain hardly daring to breathe, Jones blocked the last over from Gibbs and the match was drawn. Sad to relate, at this point the Georgetown crowd now embarked an orgy of rioting even more disgraceful than that which Kingston had witnessed, invading the pitch and hurling bottles and stones at journalists and players alike. This prompted a charge by mounted police, which in turn led to prolonged fighting. The players were locked in the pavilion under police protection, and it was some time before the players could be evacuated from the ground. The police struggled to hold open a corridor, but this did not prevent the crowd throwing yet more stones, one of which hit Tony Lock on the head.

For England, the tragic loss of Fred Titmus apart, the tour had been a success, and several important questions had been answered. Edrich had established his position at the top of the order alongside Boycott. England had gained a star wicketkeeper in Alan Knott. John Snow had emerged as a fast bowler with genuine match-winning potential. Only in the spin bowling department was there still cause for concern, with neither Hobbs, Lock nor Pocock having been able to impose their authority on a game in the absence of Titmus.

As the England team flew home triumphantly, they could surely never have guessed that, of the original tour party, two of them would never play another Test match, while another six would play only a handful between them. Cowdrey's Five Tour Plan was already effectively in tatters. All that lay in the future, however, as they landed back in London, for the start of the English season was only a few days away, and in a matter of weeks England would face perhaps the toughest test of all – Australia.

CHAPTER 5

THE 1968 ASHES (PART I)

The summer of 1968 was plagued by bad weather. Every one of the five Test matches against Australia would suffer interference from rain to a greater or lesser extent, and three were largely spoiled as sporting contests as a result. Those Australians on their first visit to England must have thought they had come to a land of constant rainfall, as steady downpours effectively wiped out the first three weeks of their tour, leaving them woefully underprepared for the first Test at Old Trafford.

However, as players and journalists alike huddled in pavilions around the country, seeking shelter from the appalling conditions, one topic was becoming a recurrent source of discussion. For England were due to tour South Africa that winter, and one name was on everybody's lips: Basil D'Oliveira.

D'Oliveira was what the South African apartheid regime classified as a 'Cape Coloured' (as opposed to either black or white), and had been brought to England to play cricket and qualify for British citizenship largely through the efforts of the cricket commentator John Arlott, a prominent opponent of any form of racial discrimination. Arlott was a remarkable character who still arouses warm memories on the part of anyone who ever heard him on BBC Radio's Test Match Special. Previously the BBC's poetry correspondent, he had been largely responsible for discovering a young Dylan Thomas and presenting his words to a national radio audience, and his keen interest in poetry often flowed over into his description of events. Who else could describe a ball travelling to the boundary 'like a ripple of shot silk'?

Arlott finally managed to arrange a contract for D'Oliveira in the Central Lancashire League for the 1960 season. However, D'Oliveira knew that he would be unable to take up the offer, as he did not have the necessary money to travel to England and pay for his initial living expenses. What followed gave the lie to any suggestion that all white South Africans were slavish supporters of the Vorster government. Liberal white cricketers defied the race laws to play an exhibition match with D'Oliveira's 'coloured' team, and the players of both teams illegally took up a collection around the ground. So it was that he was able to move to England and embark upon his first-class cricket career, quickly moving from the leagues to county cricket with Worcestershire, where he would play alongside Tom Graveney. Following naturalisation he then progressed into international competition, winning his first Test cap against the West Indies in 1966.

Nobody could be in any doubt that the possibility of D'Oliveira being chosen as a member of the England touring party would raise massive political complications. Apart from anything else, under South African law it would be a criminal offence for him to stay in the same hotel as his white teammates, or to take part in any sporting contest with them. Nor were the precedents auspicious. In 1964 South Africa had been banned from the Olympic Games, and would again be banned for the 1968 Games in Mexico. In 1966 South Africa had asked the New Zealand Rugby Football Union for an assurance that their forthcoming 1967 touring party would contain only white players. The NZRFU refused to give any such assurance, and cancelled the tour. Interestingly, Billy Griffith, whose amateur status had caused the young Brian Close so much trouble, was managing England's tour of New Zealand at the time and was quoted as saying that if the MCC were ever faced with such a choice they would reach the same decision. This, then, was the problem. Would South Africa ask the MCC for a similar assurance and, if they did, would the MCC supply it? Alternatively, even if South Africa did not ask for such an assurance, would they accept any MCC touring side which included a non-white player?

For the moment, it was unclear whether the issue would even arise, as D'Oliveira was by no means a certain pick for the Manchester Test. His performances in the West Indies had failed to live up to the selectors' expectations; though playing in all five Tests he had scored only 137 runs at an average of 22.83, and taken just three wickets at nearly 100 runs apiece. D'Oliveira later admitted that he had not been a responsible tourist. In those less professional days before team curfews, he partied too often, too late, and too hard. Everyone in the West Indies wanted to extend an invitation to this great curiosity, a 'coloured' man playing for England, and D'Oliveira, who was known to be a little over-fond of a drink, had found himself being lavishly entertained just about every evening. Now his place in the side was under threat from at least two obvious competitors: Barry Knight of Essex and Tom Cartwright of Somerset.

Barry Knight was a brisk fast-medium bowler and a useful batsman, who had done the double four times, once by mid-July, and had shared a record stand of 240 for the sixth wicket in a Test match in 1963 with Peter Parfitt.[30] However, he had not played Test cricket since 1966 when he had disappointed with both bat and ball against the West Indies. Tom Cartwright was one of the best-loved figures in English cricket. A slow-medium bowler like D'Oliveira, he was much more of a like for like replacement. However, unlike D'Oliveira he had no pretensions as a serious batsman, he had not played for England since 1965, and had greatly disappointed when he had done so. He had a batting average of only 5, and had taken just 15 Test wickets, six of which had come in one match.

In the absence of Titmus, and with Barrington reporting himself injured, England's all-rounder cupboard was thus looking rather bare of quality candidates, though Ray Illingworth was being spoken of as a

---

[30] A record that would stand for 38 years, before being broken by Graham Thorpe and Andrew Flintoff in Christchurch.

logical replacement for Titmus; he had played in four Tests the previous summer, taking 23 wickets at an average of just 14, and many had been staggered when his name was not among those announced for the tour of West Indies.

The selectors were clearly hopelessly undecided on a number of key issues, not least the balance of the side, and in the end they took the unusual step of naming a squad of 14 players, declaring that they would delay their final selection until the day itself: Cowdrey, Boycott, Edrich, Graveney, Barber (returning to first-class cricket in 1968 and replacing Barrington), D'Oliveira, Amiss, Knott, Underwood, Higgs, Snow, Pocock, Cartwright and Brown.

Higgs came in to replace Jones, who was experiencing complications from a wrist injury picked up in the West Indies and which, though nobody could have known this at the time, would end his career prematurely. Even so, the chosen names raised a number of eyebrows. Why Cartwright alongside D'Oliveira, rather than Knight? Knight would give the variety of a different sort of bowling, as well as being much more likely to make runs. Why Pocock, who had achieved little in the West Indies, instead of the experience and greater batting potential of Illingworth? Why Barber, who was not even playing regularly for his county, when England already had an established opening pair anyway? Was this perhaps an attempt by the selectors to get one more 'gentleman' (Barber was an amateur) into the side? Barber himself was bemused by his own inclusion; he had played little cricket and was smarting from sunburn suffered while working on his farm.

The final selection caused even more raised eyebrows. England left out Underwood, Cartwright and Brown, thus deciding to go into the match with only three front line bowlers. This was surely carrying defensiveness too far. It was as if England had decided in advance to play for a draw.

This suspicion grew stronger when Australia won the toss and batted and, despite Snow taking two early wickets (Ian Redpath and Bob Cowper), Cowdrey began to set defensive fields, which resulted in at least one chance (what would have been an easy catch to the vacant third slip position) going begging. Later the youngsters Ian Chappell and Paul Sheahan proceeded to put together an impressive partnership for the fifth wicket, neither unduly troubled by the bowling. By close of play they had already put on 145 and Australia finished nicely positioned on 319-4.

During the final session of play, a run-out had seemed England's only hope of getting a wicket. After only a few minutes of Friday's play, this is exactly what happened, Chappell sacrificing himself after a dreadful mix-up with Sheahan. This unfortunate incident seemed to affect Sheahan badly; shortly afterwards he gave D'Oliveira an easy catch in the gully off Snow. Suddenly the Australian innings evaporated, with the wicketkeeper Barry Jarman the only remaining batsman to reach double figures, and Australia were all out for 357, far short of what they must have been contemplating overnight. Snow was the most successful of the English bowlers, with figures of 4-97.

When England batted, Boycott and Edrich began cautiously against the three Australian quicks: McKenzie, Hawke and Connolly. Very cautiously, in fact, taking 38 overs to bring up the first 50 of the innings. It seemed a merciful relief when bad light brought proceedings to a premature end just after 5pm. Heavy rain fell overnight, but thanks to the sterling efforts of the ground staff, play began only 20 minutes late on the Saturday morning.

It was more of the same from England. With Boycott at his dourest, content to survive at the crease without scoring runs, and Edrich struggling to find his touch, it was grim watching. Then, having taken three and a quarter hours to score 49, Edrich was run out by a fine throw by Doug Walters, while attempting a third run. Lawry had by this time turned to the offspin of Bob Cowper to supplement Johnnie Gleeson, the mystery bowler who delivered legspin, but spun off his fingers rather than with the wrist. With only one more run added, Cowper had Boycott caught behind by Jarman for 35, ground out remorselessly over more than three and a half hours. Clearly being dropped for slow scoring the previous summer had not proved the salutary experience for which the England selectors might have hoped.

As if to vindicate Boycott's ultra-cautious approach, however, the England batting line-up now simply collapsed, seven specialist batsmen notwithstanding. Only Barber and Snow reached double figures and the unfortunate Dennis Amiss was out for a duck on his Test recall. Cowper, who had been picked principally as a batsman, finished with the remarkable figures of 26-11-48-4. However, the last-wicket pair of Pocock and Snow had at least managed to steer England to 165, and so they were spared the indignity of being asked to follow on.

In Australia's second innings Pocock took wickets steadily, finishing with 6-79, but a final total of 220 left England the little matter of 413 to win.

This time Boycott began more positively, but departed with the score on 13, caught by Redpath up close off bat and pad. When the same bowler, McKenzie, had the England captain caught behind, England were 25-2 and the writing was on the wall. Edrich and Graveney then took England cautiously but safely through to tea on the fourth day at 70-2.

It was Cowper who got the breakthrough soon after tea, though all the credit belonged to Barry Jarman who pulled off a brilliant catch to dismiss Edrich. This brought Amiss to the crease, but, clearly hugely nervous, he lasted only nine deliveries, making a terrible hash of a delivery from Cowper and being clean bowled. Poor Amiss, of whom so much had been expected, had bagged a pair in this vital recall game, which might well prove his last chance to break into the side.

England scanned the Manchester sky for rain on the Tuesday morning, but there was to be no rescue from that quarter and they were all out for 253, D'Oliveira top-scoring with 87 not out. Australia had won by the comfortable margin of 159 runs.

John Snow later said that he felt the selection of a 14-man squad had unsettled the side. The former Australian captain Bobby Simpson, who was following the tour as a cricket writer, felt that Australia deserved to win because they played attacking cricket, whereas England went into the match with an unbalanced side and then adopted defensive tactics. As he pointed out, 'seven batsmen may save matches, but they very seldom win them';[31] it is difficult to take issue with this.

More worrying, here was a second former Test captain noting how unduly defensive and unenterprising Cowdrey's captaincy could be, and

---

[31] Bobby Simpson, *The Australians in England 1968*, Hutchinson, Sydney, 1968

Simpson was a much more dispassionate observer than Brian Close. Add Garry Sobers's views into the mix, and there is room for serious concern about Cowdrey's skills as a captain. Indecisive, content with slow scoring and slow over rates, setting overly defensive fields too soon in the day, being a party to the selection of a badly unbalanced side. Close says that in the West Indies Cowdrey had frequently phoned him in the evening to ask him what he should do the next day. Close says he was happy with this, as it meant his own morning predictions on the radio and in the press were usually uncannily accurate.[32]

Whatever part Cowdrey may himself have played in the tactical approach, any neutral observer would surely agree that England went into the Old Trafford match trying not to lose it, rather than trying to win it. Such an approach deserved to be punished, and it was.

England's selection approach at Lord's for the second match still seemed uncertain, but many cricket followers around the country found what happened next very difficult to believe.

On the day of the match, England omitted the only two real successes of Old Trafford: Pocock and D'Oliveira. This prompted the beginning of the flood of letters which would be sent to Cowdrey and the MCC during the summer accusing them of having left D'Oliveira out of the side for political motives, to make it easier for them not to pick him for the winter tour. Cowdrey, however, always remained adamant that the decision had been made for cricketing reasons, because he thought the brisk fast-medium of Barry Knight would be more effective at Lord's with rain forecast than the slow-medium of D'Oliveira.

The rain did indeed arrive as forecast, and very nearly robbed the match of any meaning whatsoever. So much time was lost that England were still pursuing their first innings at close of play on the third day, whereupon they declared overnight at 351-7, a solid performance built around steady contributions from four of the six specialist batsmen, only Edrich and Graveney missing out. Milburn, on his return to the side, made 83 in fine fashion, including two sixes.

---

[32] DBC, conversation with the author, 7 May 2011

Snow, Brown and Knight simply destroyed the Australian batting line-up on the Monday, English seamers enjoying classic English seamers' conditions. Once Bill Lawry had gone to a brilliant catch by Knott with only one run on the board, none of the remaining Australians seemed to have any answer to the swinging ball. Barry Jarman, who had chipped a finger while keeping wicket, bravely came in down the order, only to be hit almost immediately directly on the damaged digit and have to retire. Australia finished on just 78 and were promptly invited to follow on.

The Australians proved more resolute in their second innings and survived to be 50 without loss at the close. More heavy rain fell overnight and the next morning, and when play finally began in the afternoon, England had less than two and a half hours to take the nine Australian wickets they needed, or ten should Jarman choose to bat. In the event, it never looked like being enough. Underwood bowled beautifully – 15 of his 18 overs were maidens – but failed to run through the side. The only winner turned out to be the weather, as had always seemed likely.

Knight, incidentally, had justified Cowdrey's faith in him, taking 3-16 in Australia's first innings, and scoring 27 not out batting ahead of Alan Knott at number 7.

Lord's had been a definite moral victory for England, so they reconvened at Edgbaston just over two weeks later with a new sense of optimism. At Birmingham too, however, they were destined to be robbed of a victory by the weather. For Australia, Brian Taber replaced the injured Jarman, and Eric Freeman came in for Neil Hawke to gain his first Test cap. England this time limited themselves to 12 men in more conventional fashion. From the team at Lord's, Milburn dropped out with an injured wrist to be replaced by Keith Fletcher, and Ray Illingworth was called up to join the squad.

England also approached the selection of the final team in a fresh manner, this time leaving out a batsman (Fletcher) to play an extra bowler (Illingworth). However, for the whole of the first day the players could only sit in the pavilion and watch the rain fall; not a single ball was bowled.

On the Friday morning Cowdrey won the toss and, not without some hesitation, opted to bat. He need not have worried. The pitch proved sluggish, but the batting even more so. Once again Boycott and Edrich proceeded at a crawl; by lunch only 65 runs had come from a generous ration of 35 overs. Again, one must question Cowdrey's captaincy. England badly needed a win, and with a whole day already lost surely it was worth trying to score some quick runs, even at the risk of losing a few wickets? The crowd certainly thought so. Fortunately for the sake of the game as a spectacle, Cowdrey and Graveney later pushed the scoring rate along after Barrington had gone for a duck, Cowdrey scoring a century in his 100th Test match, though he pulled a muscle in his leg in the process and completed his innings with a runner. The next day England batted on to 409 all out.

This was not to prove a happy match for captains. Now it was Lawry's turn to be injured, not once but twice, before the first over of Australia's reply had even been completed. First he pulled a muscle. Despite being hardly able to move, he decided to battle on. This was to prove a bad decision, since two balls later John Snow got a ball to kick from only just short of a length, in a way that was to make him one of the world's great fast bowlers, breaking one of Lawry's fingers in the process. Lawry would take no further part in the match. Nor, after tea that day, did Cowdrey, handing over command on the field to Tom Graveney.

Despite good contributions from Cowper, Chappell and Doug Walters, wickets fell steadily the next day to England's new spin pairing of Illingworth and Underwood, each of whom took three wickets. Once Australia saved the follow-on, any excitement seemed to be drifting out of the game, but suddenly Australia's last five wickets fell cheaply and England were in with a chance again.

This time England did go for the runs, though even now they scored at less than three and a half an over, and Geoff Boycott took nearly an hour and a half to score 31. That he subsequently played 36 (or indeed any) limited overs matches for England must surely rank as just about the unlikeliest fact in what Fred Trueman always described as 'a very funny game'.

At 142-3 Cowdrey declared, setting Australia 330 to win, and at the close they had made nine without loss. After only an hour the next morning the rain returned, though, and there was no further play in the match.

The fourth Test at Headingley remains a pub quiz question setter's delight in that both teams were led by stand-in captains, neither Lawry nor Cowdrey having recovered from their injuries. Tom Graveney captained England (the only time he would do so), while Barry Jarman, himself coming back from injury, stepped up to captain Australia (likewise the only time he would do so). Australia brought in John Inverarity, a tall, correct-looking right-handed batsman and very useful slow left-arm bowler, for his first cap, to open the innings, and promoted Cowper above Redpath to open with him. England's selection difficulties were less easily, and thus less tidily, settled.

CHAPTER 6

THE 1968 ASHES (PART II)

In the period between the Edgbaston and Headingley Tests, England already knew they would be without Milburn, who had failed to recover from a wrist injury, and Boycott, who had hurt his back during the third Test, though surely not through over-aggressive stroke-play. It seemed highly likely that they would also be without Cowdrey, and as a further added complication Graveney cut his hand badly and was in doubt until the very day of the Test.

England decided that Roger Prideaux of Sussex would come into the side as an opening batsman, winning his first cap. Then the selectors' gaze, in their quest for further batting replacements, came to rest on an unlikely but highly romantic candidate: Ted Dexter. Dexter, known to many as 'Lord Edward' because of his imperious manner, was one of the most brilliantly talented batsmen ever to play the game and, to the delight of spectators, he mostly only knew one way to play, which was all-out blazing attack. He was also a useful medium pacer, good enough to have bowled first change for England and take more than a wicket every Test. Yet he could be moody, quixotic and unpredictable, 'a T.E. Lawrence of the cricket field', 'apt to practise golf shots in the outfield',[33] and a county captain who arranged drinks breaks to coincide with horse races, with a transistor radio smuggled onto the drinks tray for him to listen to the commentary.

As well as an exceptional international cricketer, Dexter was talented enough to be a scratch golfer, a private aircraft pilot, and a monster motorbike rider, elegant and handsome enough to be an international male model, and intelligent and commercial enough to run his own successful business. A man who ran for parliament and owned racehorses, he moved easily among royalty, nobility and film stars. There was only one Ted Dexter. As Christopher Martin-Jenkins summed him up: 'there are few things that he would not do better than the average mortal'.

Of course there were those who objected, albeit timidly, that he had not played any form of first-class cricket for the past three seasons, and suggested that this might prove something of a disadvantage when pitched into a Test match fresh from the gallops, the golf course or the cocktail circuit. Since Dexter was an amateur he could not be ordered about, but he graciously condescended to play in a County Championship match for Sussex against Kent, then just about the strongest side in the country. Looking slightly bemused at having been put to this totally unnecessary effort, he blasted a majestically murderous double century. The doubters crept quietly away, and when his name was announced a few days later, the overriding emotion expressed was surprise that he had been away for so long.

As England's list of injured and doubtful batsmen lengthened, the selectors again called up Keith Fletcher of Essex, thus confirming that he had leapfrogged ahead of the wretchedly unlucky Dennis Amiss; Trevor Bailey, an Essex man and now a summariser on Test Match Special, was pleased. Finally they also called up Phil Sharpe, a fine batsman and by common consent the best slip catcher in the country. A Yorkshireman, Headingley was his home ground.

On the day, though, England sprung something of a surprise by leaving out Knight, including the new boy, Fletcher, and ignoring Sharpe. The highly partisan Yorkshire crowd voiced their displeasure. As it was, Headingley was

---

[33] Christopher Martin-Jenkins, *Who's Who of Test Cricketers*, Orbis, 1980

not to prove a lucky ground for poor Keith Fletcher over the years as a slip catcher, and every time he dropped a catch which the Yorkshire folk felt Phil Sharpe could have caught with a tea strainer, they howled their derision.

Certain Yorkshire folk also still bore grudges over the Close affair. Peter West, who had been booed by the entire crowd the previous year after criticising Close on television, was forced to have a police bodyguard for the entire match after anonymous threatening letters were received at the ground.[34]

Once again, the make-up of the team seemed a defensive move by England (Cowdrey presumably still having the final say in selection matters; though present only as a non-playing captain, he pointedly remained dressed in his blazer and whites). England needed to win this match to have any chance of regaining the Ashes. If they lost or drew, then Australia, who already held the urn, would retain it. Yet they were going into the match with only four specialist bowlers plus Dexter or Barrington to back them up.

Jarman won his only Test toss, and decided to bat.

Though Snow bowled the debutant Inverarity early on with a fast yorker, Australia progressed steadily. Some noted that various of the England bowling changes seemed to be made by remote control, coming immediately after an appearance on the boundary by Cowdrey to have a word with third man or long leg; Graveney would later confide, 'Colin was a dreadful back-seat driver'.[35] Australia closed the day on 258-5 with Chappell and Jarman at the crease, and the game seemed nicely poised.

The next morning Australia subsided rather tamely just before lunch, with Underwood taking the last three wickets to fall. Poor Keith Fletcher had dropped three catches during the innings on his Test debut, none of them easy, but each one roundly booed by the Yorkshire crowd.

Edrich and England's second debutant, Prideaux, now made batting look easy in taking England to 123 in just under three hours. However, they were both out during the evening session and at the end of the second day England were 163-3, Dexter having come and gone cheaply.

---

34 *This Sporting Life* op. cit.
35 TWG in conversation with the author

Next day, Graveney and Barrington steadied the ship with a stand of 68, but thereafter wickets fell steadily, Fletcher's nightmare debut continuing with a seventh ball duck. However, a spirited 45 not out by last man Derek Underwood saw England finish only 13 runs behind on the first innings. This was still a close match, and at close of play Australia were 92-2.

Heavy rain fell the next morning and, though it only delayed the start by about 20 minutes, was to have a significant effect on the day's play, since for a long time the spinners could not grip the ball properly, while the fast bowlers struggled with their run-ups and footholds. Graveney opted for containment, and Australia went slowly to lunch, having lost Redpath, who gifted a wicket to John Snow when he smacked him down the throat of deep square leg.

By the afternoon the conditions had improved for England's bowlers, but the outfield was now quicker too. Had Australia been behind in the series rather than in front they might now have pressed on more aggressively, but as it was they were content to graft, and finished the day on 283-6, probably already safe from defeat.

They batted on the next morning. Finally all out for 312 (Illingworth taking 6-87), they set England an improbable 326 to win at more than a run a minute on a pitch which was by now taking considerable turn, as Illingworth's performance testifies.

To their credit, England did their best to go for the runs and, briefly, it seemed as though they might be in with a chance as Edrich and Dexter put on a quick spurt of runs after Prideaux was bowled by McKenzie for 2. After lunch, however, England struggled against tight bowling. Dexter was strangled, frustrated and then bowled. Edrich was caught behind off Alan Connolly, who bowled well throughout the series and would be offered a contract by Middlesex. After that it was simply a case of whether Australia could take the remaining wickets they needed for victory, but Barrington and Fletcher brought England safely through to the close, Fletcher batting for over an hour.

With the draw, Australia retained the Ashes; the best that England could hope for now was to win the final Test at the Oval to square the series, so Australia would keep the urn whatever happened. It would be for England to try to win them back in 1970–71, which Cowdrey had already designated as the last of his five tours. On a sadder note, this match marked the last appearance of Ken Barrington, truly one of the all-time greats, and one of England's staunchest servants, chest pains which would later be diagnosed as cardiac problems bringing a premature end to his career. Tragically, a further heart attack would kill him at the age of only 50, while acting as manager to Ian Botham's tour of the West Indies in 1981. The abrupt loss of the ever-chuckling man they had dubbed 'the colonel', who had been bowling his treasured legspin to them in the nets only a few days previously, shattered the team.

Yet the real drama of the summer was still to unfold.

As England readied themselves for the final Test at the Oval they called Ken Higgs back into the squad, along with Colin Milburn, who had now recovered from injury. Boycott, however, had not, and was still unavailable. This was all fairly straightforward. What followed was not.

On the eve of the Test, Prideaux reported sick with a virus. Cowdrey suspected, correctly as it turned out, that his fellow amateur was not nearly as ill as he made out, and was happy to miss the game, feeling that he had already done enough at Headingley to secure his place for South Africa and not wanting to risk jeopardising it by a failure at the Oval. It is widely believed that Basil D'Oliveira was the man chosen to replace him in the side, but this is not strictly true, as he had already been summoned to join the squad. However, it is true that when Prideaux reported sick, D'Oliveira played in his place. These facts are common ground. As the next chapter reveals, everything else about D'Oliveira's reappearance in the England side is conjecture and hearsay.

For the record, Cowdrey, writing some years after the events had become deeply controversial,[36] claims that he had become aware, while playing for Kent against Surrey the previous week, that the Oval wicket was likely to be helpful to medium-pace bowlers, and that he had asked the selectors for discretion to call up a medium pacer to play instead of Higgs. They agreed, he says, naming Cartwright, Knight and D'Oliveira in that order. He

---

[36] *M.C.C.* op. cit.

checked first with Cartwright and then with Knight, both of whom felt themselves not fit for the rigours of a five-day Test match.

He then rang Worcestershire and left a message for D'Oliveira to report to the Oval. D'Oliveira had forced himself back into contention as a bowler, not a batsman, he insists, by taking 11 wickets in a County Championship match against Hampshire. However, he continues, when Prideaux reported sick there appeared to be a simple solution. Milburn, already in the side, would move up to open, and D'Oliveira 'came into the side mainly as a batsman, though his bowling could be useful'.[37]

If Cowdrey did indeed feel that the pitch suited medium pace, Australia did not. They left out the fast-medium Freeman and brought their specialist offspinner, Ashley Mallett, into the side for his Test debut. Lawry was fit to play, but since Cowper had broken his thumb in a tour match, Inverarity kept his place at the top of the order. England won the toss and batted.

They lost Milburn, Dexter and Cowdrey on the way to a rather nervous 113-3, but then Graveney and Edrich embarked on a stand of 125 for the fourth wicket. When Graveney was caught by Redpath off McKenzie for 63, this brought D'Oliveira to the wicket.

It is difficult to overstate the drama of the situation. The coming winter would be the only opportunity Basil D'Oliveira would have in his playing career to return to the country of his birth as a member of an international touring party. This was the one objective which he had set himself above all others when he had come to England back in 1960. He had on his own admission underperformed in the West Indies the previous winter. He had been dropped, many felt unfairly, after the first Test of the current summer. This match now represented his one and only remaining chance to achieve that ambition.

Yet it was an ambition which, if achieved, had the potential to cause a major international incident. It was an ambition which, if achieved, would force men to confront fundamental ethical issues of right and wrong. Would force them to set their conscience against their personal interests,

---

[37] M.C.C. op. cit.

and try to balance these in turn against the good of the game. Would raise, directly and unequivocally, the awkward question which somehow the establishment had always until now managed to avoid: was it acceptable to treat one man differently from another just because of the colour of his skin? The players on both sides knew it, and realised that for the duration of this game they had become bit players on the stage of history. The politicians and administrators knew it, and squirmed in that knowledge. Cricketers around the country in every club and county knew it, and willed D'Oliveira to succeed. The cricketing world watched, and held its breath.

The record books show that D'Oliveira ended the first day on 24 not out, with John Edrich already on 130, and that D'Oliveira went on to make 158, a famous innings which is remembered by all who saw it, or heard it described on the radio while, unfairly, Edrich's 164 has been largely overshadowed. These figures alone do not suggest any hint of the tension which gripped not just the Oval, but the whole country, as D'Oliveira progressed steadily towards his century. He was dropped by Jarman on 31, a difficult chance. This was later seized upon by some cricket writers as evidence that his innings at the Oval had in fact been a massive fluke, which could equally well have ended there and then. John Edrich came down the wicket and told D'Oliveira not to throw away the century that was waiting for him.

When he played a loose shot or two along the way, umpire Charlie Elliott would tell him at the non-striker's end the next over to get his head down. When he reached 50, Elliott congratulated him. When he came to his century, watchers and listeners alike breathed a sigh of relief. Johnnie Gleeson said quietly: 'well done, Bas'. His selection for the South African tour party now seemed to be certain. Shortly afterwards, Gleeson dropped an easy return catch, which seemed to some to be no more than a sign that destiny was riding on his shoulder that day.

When he came to his 150, selection had surely been rendered a formality. When he was out, the whole crowd rose to give him a roaring ovation that carried on for some time, even when he was back in the dressing room. They were leaving the selectors in no doubt as to their views.

He was the ninth wicket to fall, and England were all out shortly afterwards for 494. It was still a decent pitch for batting, however, and Australia would bat into the fourth day in scoring 324, built around a trademark Bill Lawry century which took nearly eight hours, and a fighting 43 not out by the new boy, Ashley Mallett, which helped save the follow-on. England had a first innings lead of 170, but the match appeared to be heading for a draw.

England had no choice now but to go for quick runs, and Milburn rose to the challenge, hitting two fours and a six. Sadly for England and the crowd, he then mis-hit Connolly to Lawry at mid-on. His replacement, Dexter, was the ideal man to continue the assault, but Lawry replaced McKenzie with Mallett, and he and Connolly bowled steadily. Mallett was rewarded with the wicket of Edrich, another catch for Lawry, this time at mid-off, and Connolly with that of Dexter, who was deceived and bowled by a clever slower ball. Thus ended the all too brief Dexter revival; though he was only 33 he would never play in a Test match again.

England pressed on, with wickets falling steadily as the batsmen tried to force the pace, with Cowdrey resorting to uncharacteristic slogging to leg. Graveney and Knott were both run out, Cowdrey and D'Oliveira both out attempting big shots. Eventually England were all out for 181 with about 40 minutes still to play plus the whole of the final day, setting Australia an improbable 352 to win. Cowdrey did, however, draw criticism for not having declared half an hour or so earlier, when Illingworth was out with the score on 149.

The remaining time was enough, however, for England to take two vital wickets that evening: Lawry departed to a diving catch by Milburn off Brown, and Redpath became one of the many batsmen to fall lbw to Underwood's arm ball. So Australia ended the day at 13-2, with an England win suddenly looking much the most likely result.

The next morning, though, Cowdrey heard that thunderstorms were likely for later in the day. It was vital, therefore, for England to make rapid progress through the Australian batting line-up.

First Chappell and then Walters fell to Underwood. Australia were now 29-4 and on the ropes, but Sheahan and Inverarity dug in to resist England. Shortly before lunch, Illingworth had Sheahan caught by Snow at midwicket, in two minds whether to block or hit. Jarman came in and was immediately in all sorts of trouble against the English spinners, though Inverarity was playing beautifully at the other end.

However, the first session was not even quite complete when the threatened thunderstorm arrived, a late summer cloudburst that literally flooded the Oval, which by the time the rain stopped about three quarters of an hour later, resembled a number of medium-sized boating lakes. Cowdrey gloomily took off his boots and socks, rolled up his trousers, and waded out to inspect the damage. It seemed inevitable that the match would now be abandoned.

Yet the final drama of this most dramatic of Test matches was still to be played out. Hordes of volunteers from the crowd helped the ground staff to mop up the water. The umpires came and went, amidst the flood relief operations. Finally, with no surface water visible, but the outfield still sopping wet, they announced that play could recommence at 4.45. This gave England precisely 75 minutes to take the last five Australian wickets.

This remarkable Test match would later be remembered for all sorts of reasons, but an often overlooked point is that it was almost certainly the last Test match (perhaps even the last first-class match) which would be played on a legendary 'sticky wicket', a pitch which had been soaked by rain but was now drying out. In the days of covered pitches, such a thing is no longer possible,[38] but back when the playing surface was left uncovered during the day, it was precisely this possibility which prompted teams to have someone like Underwood or Lock in the side, someone who could turn the ball sharply at medium pace on such a surface.

The theory was, however, that while the pitch was really wet it would be completely dead, giving help neither to quick nor slow bowlers. It was only as it started to dry that someone like Underwood might become unplayable. Indeed, so dead did it prove initially that Underwood twice suffered the indignity of being pulled for four. Finally, after nearly three quarters of an hour, it was that man again, D'Oliveira, who got the vital wicket, bowling

---

[38] Though it would occur accidentally at Lord's a few years later, with Underwood again the beneficiary.

Jarman off his pads. Soon afterwards, Underwood began finding turn, and with every single England player crowding around the bat, it became a simple matter of whether the last four Australian wickets could hold out for half an hour. It looked unlikely when Underwood took the next two wickets in quick succession. This brought Gleeson to the wicket to join Inverarity, and a game of cat and mouse ensued, with Inverarity trying to farm the strike, and England trying to stop him. Underwood switched from round the wicket to over, and the change of angle fooled Gleeson, who was bowled. However, there were now only six minutes to go – probably no more than two overs.

Perhaps the pressure finally told on Inverarity, or perhaps his front foot got stuck in the mud a little, but for whatever reason he now offered no stroke to Underwood, was given out lbw and England had won the match and squared the series. Underwood ended with 7-50, having taken the last four wickets in just 27 deliveries. From this time onwards he became the Australians' bogeyman, the one bowler they least wanted to face.

Oddly, for a man who later claimed to have selected D'Oliveira primarily as a medium-pace bowler, and in the expectation that this would be the most effective type of bowler on the Oval surface, Cowdrey gave him just nine of the 247 overs which England bowled during the game.

After the gripping Oval Test match, Cowdrey gave the customary television interview, during which he assured the nation that the tour party would be selected on purely cricketing grounds, and headed off in a taxi to the selection meeting. The players departed to their next matches, Graveney, Snow and D'Oliveira all travelling separately to Worcester, for the Sussex match the following day.

When the team was announced on the radio by Brian Johnston in alphabetical order, there was a gasp in the Worcester dressing room when John Edrich's name was reached. That meant D'Oliveira had been left out. Tom Graveney started swearing. D'Oliveira, the nervous strain of the summer suddenly reaching unbearable proportions, collapsed in tears and, proving inconsolable, was sent home by Graveney in a taxi to be with his wife.

These are the facts. The reasons behind them have been deliberately ignored thus far. Though they unfolded in parallel with the cricketing events of 1968, they form a story of their own, and it is now time to delve into them. In doing so, it is only fair to point out that many of these matters remain disputed to this day. Most of the participants have since passed away, and reasonable conjecture has occasionally to fill in where empirical evidence is lacking. However, modern readers are indebted to various writers and academics who have between them unearthed a great many facts during the intervening years which were not publicly known at the time, but can now be put together. Their invaluable contribution should be noted and acknowledged.

In particular, an academic paper by Bruce Murray, of Witwatersrand University,[39] based on access to South African government archives, is a magisterial and authoritative guide to the events in question, admirable both as a piece of academic scholarship and as an exciting piece of detective work. Much of what follows draws upon his work. Peter Oborne's *Basil D'Oliveira: Cricket and Controversy*,[40] (which in turn also draws on Murray's article) has been an invaluable source, as has an unpublished university research paper by Alexandra Edmonds, daughter of former England cricketer Phil and broadcaster and journalist Frances.

Writing at the time about what would rapidly become known as the D'Oliveira affair, Ted Dexter described it in the *Sun* as 'honest bungling by honest men'. As will shortly become apparent, only the 'bungling' part of this description was in fact true.

---

[39] Bruce K. Murray, Politics and Cricket: The D'Oliveira Affair of 1968, *Journal of South African Studies*, Vol.27 No.4, December 2001
[40] Peter Oborne, *Basil D'Oliveira: Cricket and Controversy*, Little, Brown, London, 2004

CHAPTER 7

SOUTH AFRICA'S INTERVENTION (PART I)

It is now known that the South African government, headed by Balthazar Johannes Vorster, was deeply concerned about the possibility of D'Oliveira being picked by England, or rather by the MCC, as a member of the 1968–69 touring party from the very first moment that he played for England in 1966. A security file was opened on him, and Vorster personally received regular reports on his form and performances, for example during Cowdrey's tour of the West Indies in early 1968.

The reference to the MCC in the last paragraph is a very deliberate one. The selection process was twofold. First the England selectors picked the squad as a sub-committee of the MCC, but then the full MCC committee had the right to veto individual players, as had of course happened with Brian Close. (The system would change in 1969, with selection responsibility passing to the TCCB, but the change was only nominal, since the TCCB was in effect an MCC shadow organisation. Even then, for some years England would continue to be called 'MCC' when touring overseas.)

The reason this is important is that, since the South African (and Rhodesian, to give it its official title) Cricket Association (SACA) was largely under the control of the South African government, Vorster assumed the same to be the case of the MCC. Given that the Labour government of Harold Wilson had resisted UDI in Rhodesia, and was known to be deeply unsympathetic to apartheid, Vorster, despite having been named after one of the Three Wise Men, therefore seems to have been deeply suspicious of the MCC as a bunch of left-wing potential trouble-makers. Had this been known to the rank and file of MCC members they would doubtless have found it highly amusing. It has, however, an important bearing on what follows, and should be borne in mind.

As early as the beginning of 1967, Billy Griffith, the secretary of the MCC, had flown to South Africa in an attempt to get some guidance on whether a 'coloured' cricketer would be accepted as a member of an MCC touring party. These talks were inconclusive, though they did prompt a South African minister to say to the press that mixed-race teams were not allowed in South Africa, and that this was well known overseas; hardly a coded message. Vorster was embarrassed and got the minister to try to deny having made the statement, but the damage was done. Back in Britain, a motion was put forward in the House of Commons calling for the 1968–69 tour to be cancelled. This doubtless fuelled Vorster's paranoia about a political nexus between the MCC and the UK government; in reality, the MCC was hugely displeased at politicians attempting to muscle in on what they (the MCC) saw as a purely sporting matter.

In January 1968 the MCC decided to force the issue, and wrote SACA a letter which, while couched in guarded and polite language, clearly sought an assurance that they could pick anyone they liked for the forthcoming tour, regardless of colour.

At about the same time, the South African government considered and arrived at a multi-pronged strategy to deal with the situation. Their ideal option was that D'Oliveira would not perform sufficiently well to justify selection for the tour. Failing this, plan A was to try to ensure that D'Oliveira would not be available for the tour, and so could not be selected. Plan B was to try to persuade the MCC (whom, remember, the South Africans saw as controlling selection) not to pick him, regardless of his performance.

Plan A was eventually attempted, but before moving on, it should be noted that there was something of a catch-22 quality about plan B. In order for it to work, the MCC would have to be made to realise that if D'Oliveira was selected then the tour would be cancelled by South Africa; only this knowledge could possibly deter them. Yet, if this fact was made known publicly, then the tour would almost certainly be cancelled anyway by the dreaded MCC–Wilson government cabal.

For the sake of clarity, let us abandon any attempt at a chronological narrative, and instead pursue each of these plans separately to their conclusions.

Plan A itself took two forms; let us call them A1 and A2.

A1 consisted effectively of a bribe. D'Oliveira would be approached and offered a very large amount of money to accept a coaching contract in South Africa that winter. This approach was duly made by a business executive called Tienie Oosthuizen, who worked for the wealthy South African businessman Anton Rupert's Rembrandt Group. The offer was put to D'Oliveira in an office in Baker Street. As the summer worked its way towards its dramatic climax at the Oval, he was put under extreme pressure to accept it before the England selectors met. One telephone conversation was recorded by D'Oliveira and his agent. The transcript[41] shows an increasingly desperate Oosthuizen offering to pay money immediately into a bank account if D'Oliveira will accept, and hinting darkly at possible unpleasant outcomes should he not.

D'Oliveira successfully evaded giving a firm answer. Oosthuizen persisted, saying he would call again at 8.30 the next morning. That evening, D'Oliveira was called by Cowdrey to the Oval. The planned call was cancelled and never took place. The first leg of plan A had failed.

If A1 had seemed remarkable, the second variant of plan A is almost so bizarre as to be totally unbelievable, yet it happened.

In June 1968 D'Oliveira reported to Lord's for the second Test against Australia. He was in good spirits, having been England's top scorer and only really successful batsman at Old Trafford. During the evening before

---

[41] Given in full in Peter Oborne, *Basil D'Oliveira*, Little, Brown, London, 2004

the match, when the England side traditionally met for dinner to discuss tactics, D'Oliveira was buttonholed by Billy Griffith, who put to him the amazing suggestion that he should announce himself unavailable for England that winter, but ask to play instead for South Africa.

The sky had fallen in. D'Oliveira was staggered. Why did Griffith think that he had spent so many years qualifying for England? Did Griffith really imagine that he would want to represent the hated apartheid regime? Or that they would consider picking him even if he did? And why was Griffith, an official of the MCC, making an approach which can only possibly have been instigated by the South African government? From what is now known, this suspicion was indeed correct. It seems almost certain from a letter written to Vorster in May (before the Lord's Test) that the plan originated with SACA.

It is sad indeed that Griffith, who had won the DFC flying gliders during the war, should have sunk to such unimaginable depths of shabbiness. Yet the fact that he did so is a mark of the desperate manoeuvres into which certain officials felt forced by plan B, the unfolding of which will be explored later.

As if to convince D'Oliveira that he had not imagined the whole thing, exactly the same proposal was put to him the next morning by *The Daily Telegraph*'s cricket correspondent, E.W. 'Jim' Swanton. Swanton was deeply embedded within the cricket establishment. He was particularly friendly with Gubby Allen, the MCC treasurer; indeed, he was writing his biography at the time. Swanton would later admit that the idea was the brainchild of SACA.[42] Again D'Oliveira angrily swept the suggestion aside.

A short while later Cowdrey came up to D'Oliveira in the nets looking very embarrassed and told him that he would not be playing in the match after all. So, the second limb of plan A was stillborn, but D'Oliveira was out of the side, and it looked as if plan B was working instead.

So, let us take a look at plan B, which had been unfolding in parallel.

Remember that the MCC had written a letter to SACA at the beginning

---

[42] *Basil D'Oliveira* op. cit.

of 1968 asking them for an assurance that they could pick whomsoever they liked for the winter tour. At first, SACA, in consultation with the South African government, dealt with this by ignoring it. MCC's reaction was to dispatch a special plenipotentiary to discuss the matter in person, a former prime minister no less. Sir Alec Douglas-Home, immediate past president of the MCC, was travelling to South Africa anyway, and was asked if he might drop in on Vorster while he was there and see if he could feel things out. Douglas-Home agreed.

However, for reasons best known to himself, though he saw Vorster he never asked the one direct question to which the MCC back in London were desperate to have the answer. Yet when he reported back, he gave it as his opinion that if D'Oliveira was chosen he was likely to be accepted by South Africa, and that the MCC would be better advised not to try to force the issue for the time being, and just let matters take their natural course. It remains unclear on what basis he formulated this view, but it was one which was gratefully accepted by the MCC. While Douglas-Home's motives remain obscure, it is clear that he muddied the waters dreadfully. By allowing the MCC to believe they could continue happily fudging the issue, and by misleading them as to Vorster's true intentions, he delivered the worst of both worlds. They duly decided that, in the light of his advice, they would not press for any reply to their letter.

By this time, however, a response had actually been drafted. Taking advantage of the fact that the MCC's own letter had been expressed in such diplomatically bland language, the response was equally anodyne. In fact, it was a response in name only, not giving any clear assurance one way or the other. Jack Cheetham, a former South African captain, was tasked with delivering the letter personally to Gubby Allen and Billy Griffith at Lord's. A response was by now, however, the last thing they wanted, and when Cheetham proffered it, they persuaded him to return it to his pocket forthwith. Thus their official line became that no response to their letter was ever received. If it is true, then it is so only on the merest of technicalities. A response was prepared and delivered to them, but they chose not to accept it.

Their motives are not hard to guess. If they had formally accepted receipt of the letter it would have had to go before the MCC committee, who would recognise at once that it did not in fact answer their concerns, and press for clarification. In the light of Douglas-Home's advice, that was the last thing that Griffith or Allen wanted. In effect, the two MCC officials deliberately suppressed the letter when their official duty clearly demanded that they should have relayed it to the committee.

Back in South Africa, SACA were surprised and happy that the issue had been successfully avoided, yet Arthur Coy of SACA warned Vorster that, according to Cheetham, the MCC were sufficiently 'compromised' with the Wilson government that they were likely to pick D'Oliveira whatever his form, purely for political reasons and with the intention of embarrassing South Africa. It was apparently on receipt of this advice that plan A was conceived, the result of which has already been described.

Vorster's other response to Coy's warning was to ask to meet with Lord Cobham, who had extensive family and business connections with South Africa and was currently in the country. He needed Cobham to carry back to the MCC as discreetly as possible the true state of affairs: that if D'Oliveira was selected the tour could not go ahead. Cobham, who met with Vorster in March, was subsequently said by Coy to have been deeply upset by this news, and to be desperate for the tour to go ahead. From the way subsequent events unfolded, it is clear that Cobham's bombshell about Vorster's true intentions was passed on to Allen, who then apparently brought both Griffith and MCC president Arthur Gilligan, brother of Harold Gilligan (both brothers were former England captains), in on the secret.

Yet again one must question the conduct of Allen and Griffith. As paid officials of the MCC, it was their clear duty to pass this explosive new information on to the committee, yet they failed to do so. They were in fact perpetrating both a cover-up and a serious deception of their own organisation.

This was the position when D'Oliveira was unexpectedly left out of the Lord's Test, a Test match that was attended by various South African dignitaries, including Arthur Coy, who was a guest in Cobham's box and had been sent with specific instructions from Vorster to have further private conversations with influential establishment figures. It is not known exactly to whom he spoke (though it would have been strange if the official representative of a Test nation's cricket board was not granted audiences with key MCC officials), or what was said, but his mission was clear: to spread the word that D'Oliveira would not be allowed in.

There is no way of knowing what further private communications may have taken place between the Test matches at Lord's and the Oval, but one final desperate throw of the dice took place after D'Oliveira had actually scored his hundred. Oosthuizen phoned the Oval and left a message with the Surrey secretary, Geoffrey Howard. It was, Oosthuizen said, a personal message from the South African Prime Minister for Billy Griffith. He was to tell the selectors that 'if today's centurion is picked, the tour will be off'.[43]

So much for plan B. The message had been conveyed, and so far as Vorster was concerned it was now up to the selectors to decide whether they wanted the tour to go ahead or not. He doubtless assumed that Allen & Co. would have apprised the selectors of the true situation just as they themselves had been informed of it separately by both Cobham and Coy. Before turning to the selectors, however, two further matters should be noted, of which D'Oliveira only became aware when he reported for duty at the Oval.

First his agent discovered that a certain highly placed official was spreading the rumour that he had been offered a bribe to make himself unavailable for the tour. The identity of the official has never been established, but there are two obvious candidates. This was to be the final ironic twist of plan A. What is significant is that certain key people within the English game were clearly aware of its existence, and knew enough about the details to be able to peddle this warped version of the facts. D'Oliveira was sufficiently concerned to speak privately to Cowdrey and assure him that it was untrue.

Second, he became aware that earlier in the summer letters had been

43 From Howard's memoirs, as told to Stephen Chalke. Howard is an independent and unimpeachable source, and anyway would have had no reason at all to invent such an extraordinary story. Stephen Chalke, *At the Heart of English Cricket*, Fairfield Books, Bath, 2001

sent to 30 touring party candidates asking them to confirm their availability for South Africa, but that he was not among them.[44] It is obviously ludicrous that D'Oliveira, who had until recently been a regular member of the Test side, should not have been recognised as one of the 30 best players in the country, and seems to offer clear evidence that even well before the event, various important figures had already taken the decision that he would not feature as a member of the touring party, no matter what. If the letters had been sent by the selectors, rather than the MCC, then this would also be clear evidence that at least one of the selectors had been let in on the nasty secret that Allen, Griffith and Gilligan were nursing in their bosoms.

Which brings us neatly to the question of whether the selectors, or any of them, knew the true position and, if so, when.

The four selectors were Doug Insole (the chairman), Peter May, Alec Bedser and Don Kenyon. To these four would be added the captain, Cowdrey, who by tradition would have the final word; if the captain insisted on a particular player then it was felt right to give him the team he wanted, since it was on the success of that team that he would ultimately be judged. Cowdrey is therefore clearly a key figure, but let us look first at the others.

The chairman, Doug Insole, was close to Gubby Allen. We do not know who signed those 30 letters, but if Insole had done so it would seem likely that he would have known the truth. Even if they were signed by Allen, one would expect that Insole, as chairman of selectors, would have had some input into the list of recipients. We don't know, but if this were the case it might help to explain D'Oliveira's surprise exclusion at Lord's.

There exists one other argument in favour of Insole and at least one other selector (May?) having been in on the secret for some time. Everyone who has ever known him describes Doug Insole as an honourable man. If, when Geoffrey Howard delivered Oosthuizen's message, it had come as a bolt from the blue, then one might suppose that the honourable course for Insole to take would have been to excuse

---

[44] Interestingly, neither was Barry Knight, for reasons which may become clear.

himself from the proceedings, leaving the other selectors to continue, insulated from the truth? The fact that he did not do so suggests either that no such message was received or, alternatively, that at least some of the selectors had known the truth for some time. The only person who could settle this question is of course Insole himself, but sadly he declined to be interviewed for this book.[45]

Peter May was married to Arthur Gilligan's niece and was extremely well connected in the cosy, gentlemen's club world that was the cricket establishment in the 1960s. There is no direct evidence that May knew about the intervention of the South African government, though it would have been easy for Gilligan to pass the word, while if either Allen or Griffith had told Insole, then there would have been no reason not also to confide in the tight-lipped May, who was after all a former England captain, and could surely be trusted. The evidence here is entirely circumstantial, but the supposition that May did indeed know, at least by the time of the Oval Test, is the most likely explanation for Cowdrey's apparent change of heart, of which more in a moment.

With regard to both Bedser and Kenyon there must remain considerable doubt. Both were professional cricketers (Kenyon was still playing) and it is quite possible that Allen and Griffith did not consider them sufficiently 'chaps like us' to trust them with their terrible secret, though Bedser and May were former Surrey and England teammates, so anything is possible. Kenyon was D'Oliveira's county captain (Graveney deputised whenever Kenyon was not available), a fact which has been frequently overlooked.

History has placed Colin Cowdrey in a horrible position, and his own convoluted attempts to extricate himself in his autobiography make things worse, rather than better. It is common ground that he had a long discussion with D'Oliveira after his century about the practical difficulties that might be encountered in taking him to South Africa; Cowdrey himself admits that he was impressed and persuaded by D'Oliveira's responses. D'Oliveira has always maintained that Cowdrey went further, giving him to

---

[45] He did, however, say: 'There seems to be an assumption that there is something sinister yet to be revealed. Well, there isn't.' Letter to the author 22 February 2011.

understand that he wanted him in the party ('you're on the boat, Basil'),[46] and would argue for him at the selection meeting.

In the taxi on his way across London to the meeting he said to Jack Bailey, assistant secretary of the MCC, 'it looks as though we shall have problems with South Africa … They can't leave Basil out of the team. Not now.'[47]

The first part of the statement might be seen as evidence that Cowdrey was already in on the secret, but this is fanciful. It was reasonable to anticipate problems with South Africa in any event. The second part of the statement reads very strangely, however, and may actually be unexpected evidence of Cowdrey's good faith, at least initially. Why would he say 'they' when he, as captain, would surely have the final say? Is this perhaps a sign that Cowdrey, a non-confrontational man who hated being the bearer of bad news and always wanted to be on good terms with everyone, a man who was known to suffer from periodic losses of self-confidence, simply lacked the strength of character to stand up to his fellow selectors? Evidence suggests that on various occasions he exhibited signs of indecision as a captain, and allowed himself to be swayed by the views of others, particularly when strongly expressed. Knowing all this, does it not seem reasonable that he would strive to be part of a consensus, rather than a member of the awkward squad sticking up for his own opinion?

Cowdrey left the Oval at the very least strongly inclined to include D'Oliveira; although he tries to cast doubt on this in his book, the evidence of both D'Oliveira and Bailey is compelling. He was probably the one key figure who could sway the final decision one way or the other if he chose to. A few hours later the meeting ended with D'Oliveira not having been picked. Thus, one can only conclude that somewhere along the way he changed his mind, or at least that he no longer felt strongly enough about it to influence the decision.

One possible explanation has already been proffered; that Cowdrey was too weak to stand up to his fellow selectors, despite having apparently

---

46 Subsequent TV interview
47 Quoted in *Basil D'Oliveira* op. cit. but original reference Jack Bailey, *Conflicts in Cricket*, Heinemann, London, 1989

promised D'Oliveira that he would do so. Ray Illingworth would say: 'He never seemed able to make a decision about anything, he never had the courage of his convictions, and he had to be talked into things'.[48] Illingworth also suggested that on various occasions Cowdrey promised people things which then never happened.[49]

There is, however, another possible explanation.

Geoffrey Howard says in his memoir *At the Heart of English Cricket* that he gave Oosthuizen's message to Insole personally. If this is the case then Insole would have been in on the secret by the time the selection meeting took place. If Insole knew, it would have been natural for him to tell May, even if he had not in fact already done so, or even if May had not already heard the news from Gilligan. If May knew, what could have been more natural than for him to take Cowdrey aside as he arrived for the meeting and tell him too? May was Cowdrey's closest friend. He had been best man at Cowdrey's wedding, and was godfather to his oldest son, whom he would later elevate entirely undeservedly, but mercifully briefly, to the English captaincy.

If Cowdrey was suddenly let in on the secret before the meeting began, he must have been aghast, not just at the prospect of one of his beloved Five Tours not taking place, but at the impossible position in which he had (quite innocently) placed himself. Far from being the villain of the piece, Cowdrey may simply have been an honourable man pushed beyond the limits of his character and overwhelmed by events.

---

[48] *Yorkshire and Back* op. cit.
[49] *Basil D'Oliveira* op. cit.

CHAPTER 8

SOUTH AFRICA'S INTERVENTION (PART II)

What happened in the selection room that evening remains shrouded in mystery, as the minutes cannot be located in the archives. This may not be as sinister a fact as many writers have implied, since the missing book also contains the minutes of many other committee meetings.

In addition to the captain and four selectors, two MCC officials, Billy Griffith and Donald Carr, were in attendance, as well as Allen and Gilligan representing the MCC's own selection committee, to give guidance on any players whom the MCC might find unacceptable. There is no suggestion that any such indication was given in respect of D'Oliveira, though interestingly they did make it clear they would veto Barry Knight, owing to unspecified irregularities in his private life. There have been rumours over the years that various other people were present who had no real right to be there, including at least one unspecified senior establishment figure holding some sort of sinister watching brief. With the minutes unavailable, perhaps such speculation is inevitable, but it remains just that – speculation. It is known, however, that there was at least one South African 'mole' in the room reporting back to Coy, and from the fact that Coy was later able to offer

Vorster a verbatim account of two separate MCC meetings, it seems it must have been one of the MCC representatives.

Doug Insole began by suggesting that they should pick a side as though for Australia, and on purely cricketing grounds. Then, early on, it was apparently agreed that D'Oliveira would be considered purely as a batsman. This was a key moment, and smacks strongly of a political 'fix'. Cowdrey himself admits that his interest in bringing D'Oliveira back into the side for the Oval was largely because of his medium-pace bowling, though strangely he then made little use of it (is it at all possible that by the time the match started the selectors' approach had already been agreed, and Cowdrey was asked not to bowl him?). In every Test match in which he had captained D'Oliveira, he had treated him as an all-rounder, albeit a batsman who could bowl. He admits that it was his bowling form which attracted him before the Oval, not his batting form (which had in fact been dreadful since Lord's). Why, then, should the selectors suddenly agree to treat him as a specialist batsman?

As an all-rounder, D'Oliveira had been seen as a direct rival to Knight. Cowdrey had given a preference for Knight as the reason for omitting D'Oliveira at Lord's (yet more evidence that Cowdrey regarded him as an all-rounder). With Knight now vetoed by the MCC, D'Oliveira would be the obvious like for like replacement, albeit with a rather different bowling style. Though Cowdrey seems genuinely to have believed Tom Cartwright to be a better bowler than D'Oliveira (as indeed the figures say he was, at least at county level), he had been ineffective when picked for England in the past, and certainly had scant claim to be considered as a Test all-rounder, with a batting average of just 5.2, though in fairness he had scored a first-class double century back in 1962, when he did the double. At the very least, D'Oliveira would have merited serious consideration against him, and on current form would have been difficult to overlook.

As a specialist batsman, it was a different story.

There were only seven places available, and three of them were reserved for openers. Boycott and Edrich were natural picks, and Prideaux was preferred to Milburn for the third spot, though Milburn was apparently also considered again when the middle order was discussed.

Of the remaining four places, two were spoken for by the captain and vice-captain, Cowdrey and Graveney. That left two.

It was felt that, as a matter of policy, a young batsman should be taken to help build the team for the future. It is difficult to quarrel with such a move. Keith Fletcher was chosen ahead of Dennis Amiss.

That left only one place, and Ken Barrington, having expressed his readiness to tour, was chosen despite concerns about his health (he would in fact pull out of a Scarborough festival game shortly afterwards with chest pains, and then later a double-wicket competition in Australia for the same reason). Again, it is difficult to criticise this decision, at least pending clarification of Barrington's state of health. He was one of England's heaviest-scoring batsmen ever, and it would have been unthinkable to leave him out, although to their credit the selectors do seem to have considered doing so in favour of D'Oliveira, with Milburn also being discussed.

Crucially, in an unguarded moment in his memoirs, Cowdrey describes Cartwright as 'the man who had taken D'Oliveira's place'.[50] From this it is clear that, at least in Cowdrey's mind, the selectors had in fact faced a straight choice between D'Oliveira and Cartwright, *not* between D'Oliveira and Barrington, whatever they might subsequently say to the contrary. As will become clear, this later deception would ultimately unravel in a way which would comprehensively hoist the selectors with their own petard.

Thus it was that there was no place for D'Oliveira when the squad was announced on 28 August 1968. He was, however, named as a possible replacement should anyone drop out through sickness or injury – presumably the selectors had their concerns about Barrington, though Cartwright and Jeff Jones were also currently injured.

Cowdrey says that the selectors appreciated that D'Oliveira's omission might spark an explosion. Interestingly, he continues, revealingly: 'we also knew quite well that few people would believe us that this was the selectors' best England team to win in South Africa'.[51]

In the event this was to prove something of an understatement. A

---

[50] *M.C.C.* op. cit.
[51] *M.C.C.* op. cit.

positive cyclone of fury broke over the heads of the selectors from public and press alike. In fairness, some voices, notably John Thicknesse (*Evening Standard*), E.M. Wellings (*Evening News*) and John Woodcock (*The Times*), supported the selectors, but Woodcock would later admit that he had got the D'Oliveira affair badly wrong. What none of these journalists knew, of course, was that key players in the process had been manipulated by the South Africans, and hopelessly compromised by keeping important information to themselves.

The decision was attacked by the likes of John Arlott (in what reads as a deliberately objective article, given his known support for D'Oliveira and opposition to apartheid) and Richie Benaud, who pointed out that at that time D'Oliveira had a higher Test batting average than anyone in the squad except Barrington. He might also have mentioned that D'Oliveira was lying fourth in the national bowling averages that season, well ahead of Cartwright. Perhaps surprisingly in view of his complicity at Lord's, E.W. Swanton also attacked the decision. Thousands of letters of support poured in to D'Oliveira and his wife, so many in fact that their local sorting office had to lay on special deliveries. Almost as many letters came to the captain and selectors, denouncing their actions, some enclosing white feathers. One wag sent Doug Insole a telegram of congratulations signed 'Adolf Hitler'.

Griffith told the press that 'never at any time was any pressure put on the selectors by anyone in South Africa.' This was of course entirely untrue and with it, Billy Griffith DFC jeopardised his personal reputation.

Barry Knight, speaking many years later, claimed that by the time of the Oval Test it was common knowledge in dressing rooms around the country that Vorster would cancel the tour if D'Oliveira was picked.

We thought the MCC didn't have the guts to pick him. When the party was first announced, I thought 'They're as weak as gnat's piss. They're kow-towing to Vorster.' The pros were revulsed (sic). It was always them and us.[52]

---

[52] 'A Cricketing Odyssey' op. cit.

If this really was the case, then it seems impossible to believe that the selectors were not in full possession of the facts.

Former England captain the Reverend David Sheppard, a future bishop who had in 1960 refused on grounds of conscience to captain the Duke of Norfolk's XI against the touring South Africans, led a protest movement to convene a special meeting of the MCC to cancel the tour. The vote, seconded by a young Mike Brearley, was lost, though by that time it had become academic except as effectively a vote of no confidence in the selectors. Had the MCC's members been in full possession of the facts (see below) it would surely have carried unanimously.

Cowdrey, who in his youth had considered entering holy orders himself, was made distinctly uncomfortable by his former teammate's opposition. The autocratic Peter May, who was not accustomed to having his decisions questioned, was distinctly unamused by the proceedings, and responded to Sheppard's subsequent letter of reconciliation with a frosty rejection, thus ending a long friendship which had begun when they were undergraduates at Cambridge.

Prior to the meeting, Sheppard had been faced by a gathering of the full committee of the MCC, led by Sir Alec Douglas-Home, which pressed him to withdraw his call for a meeting. During the course of this meeting Gubby Allen lied directly about whether any reply had ever been received from South Africa, and Douglas-Home did not contradict him. Sheppard, who had been told in confidence by Cobham that there had indeed been a reply, felt placed in an impossible position as he could not expose the lie either now or at the subsequent protest meeting without betraying Cobham's trust.[53]

With Cartwright's fitness still in doubt, the selectors now faced a catch-22 of their own making. In explaining D'Oliveira's omission to the press, Insole had revealed that he had been considered purely as a batsman, as his bowling was likely to prove ineffective on South African pitches. Should Cartwright, who had been picked primarily as a bowler, have to pull out, with whom could they replace him, having already ruled out Barry Knight? Public

---

[53] *This Sporting Life* op. cit.

opinion would demand D'Oliveira, whereas their own logic would seem to rule that out. All they could do was to pray fervently that Cartwright would not pull out.

Tom Cartwright was known to be understandably upset by the controversy surrounding his selection. What was not so well appreciated at the time was that, as a devout Christian and a committed socialist, he was also deeply troubled by the prospect of touring South Africa. He and his wife had been disgusted by apartheid while living there one winter as Tom fulfilled a coaching contract, and on a previous tour he had been introduced by Mike Brearley to liberal opponents of the regime, some of whom had been imprisoned for their beliefs. In fact, as his biographer makes clear,[54] he was considering declaring himself unavailable on grounds of conscience, as Sheppard had done in 1960, and as the English flanker John Taylor would do in respect of a subsequent British Lions tour. Had the selectors known this, they might have been seriously alarmed.

According to Cowdrey, on Saturday 14 September he found himself playing against Cartwright at Edgbaston in an exhibition match (Cartwright bowled him). That evening, Cartwright, who had bowled during the day without any sign of discomfort, was due to visit a specialist for his final fitness test. Cowdrey accompanied him, and was relieved to hear Cartwright being given the all-clear. On the Monday, Cartwright reported himself unfit to tour, citing a 'terrible reaction' after his bowling on Saturday.[55] It then took the selectors only ten minutes to select D'Oliveira in his place.

If this all sounds a little strange, it is because it is not true. Cowdrey goes to great lengths in his book to convince the reader that he thought Cartwright was fit, that his decision came out of the blue, and that once it was made D'Oliveira was the natural and instant choice as his replacement. Unfortunately Cartwright's story flatly contradicts Cowdrey's version of events.

It was Donald Carr, then assistant secretary of the MCC, not Cowdrey,

---

[54] *Tom Cartwright: The Flame Still Burns* op. cit.

[55] Tom Cartwright never played for England again. One of the best-loved figures in the game, he is today chiefly remembered as the mentor of the young Ian Botham. He played his last game of cricket at the age of 70, and died of a heart attack a year later in 2007.

who accompanied Cartwright to the specialist. In fact he took him twice, and a medical report had already been submitted after the first occasion which cast doubt on Cartwright's fitness to tour, hence the second appointment. He then attended a meeting at Lord's with Carr, Allen and Insole. They all tried hard to persuade him to tour, but sensed that he had moral misgivings and that his decision (he said 'no') was not based solely on concerns for his long-term fitness.

Far from accepting the decision stoically, as he maintains, Cowdrey, on hearing the news, rang Cartwright at home in Birmingham that evening and tried to persuade him to change his mind. He told him that if he started the tour and then pulled out, the selectors could call up Don Wilson, who would already be out in South Africa on a coaching assignment, as an emergency replacement. Thus even at this late stage, Cowdrey was still desperately trying to avoid having D'Oliveira in the squad. 'Desperately' because Wilson was a left-arm spinner rather than a right-arm seamer, and thus this would have been a substitution which would have been impossible to explain in cricketing terms.

When Cartwright again demurred, the game was up, and the selectors were now forced to accept the inevitable consequences of a problem entirely of their own making. Announcing the change, Griffith claimed that 'the selectors have been desperately honest all along the line'. This assertion was treated with understandable scepticism.

Vorster, having out-manoeuvred Allen & Co. throughout, now put the final touch to their discomfiture. With the selectors having chosen a batsman to replace a bowler, this substitution could not be accepted as having been reached on cricketing grounds. Rather, it was a political move, prompted by political motives to embarrass South Africa. Regretfully, the tour could not be allowed to proceed. (England and South Africa would not play their next Test match until 1994, 29 years after their last.)

Over four decades later, a few facts can be discerned amongst all the mess created by half-truths, downright falsehoods and increasingly desperate manoeuvrings, and should be clearly stated.

The first is that the MCC as an organisation emerges entirely blameless from the D'Oliveira affair, at least for a short while. Its committee had sought an assurance from South Africa and so far as they were aware, no reply had been received. In addition, many of the MCC's members were genuinely outraged by D'Oliveira's omission – witness the Sheppard–Brearley protest movement. What went wrong was that certain officials, who were under a clear duty to pass on information, chose not to do so, and in the process grossly misled their own organisation, as well as placing the selectors in an invidious position.

The second is that the participants seem to have acted for what they thought were the best of motives, namely what they saw as the good of the game. What they failed to recognise was that in so doing, their own moral compasses got hopelessly scrambled.

There is no suggestion that any of them were racist, or even supporters of apartheid, though Gilligan had been an active British fascist, and Bedser was a member of the far-right Freedom Association. However, there were many apologists for the Vorster regime within the British establishment at the time, several of whom had close links of family, friendship or business with South Africa. For example, Peter May's own father-in-law Harold Gilligan, brother of Arthur, was at the time South Africa's representative on the International Cricket Council.

In addition, there was a strong feeling that sport and politics should be kept separate. The British Lions would subsequently tour South Africa, for example, and the British Olympic squad go to Moscow, both against the direct wishes of the British government. These two undercurrents undoubtedly worked together to support the belief that the tour going ahead was all that really mattered.

Finally, lest this be thought a simple tale of right and wrong, it should be revealed that D'Oliveira lied about his age when he started playing cricket in England. Though one can understand why he did so, it was nonetheless a lie, and prompts an interesting question. Had the selectors known that he was already 35 in 1966, rather than 31 as they thought, would he ever have been picked for England at all?

For the record, things started to unravel fairly quickly at Lord's. Even by the spring of 1969 it had become obvious to an increasingly alarmed MCC committee that Lord Cobham, described by David Sheppard as 'wildly indiscreet',[56] was a loose cannon, and that his indiscretions posed a serious threat. By April 1969 both the non-disclosure of Cobham's message, and the 'plan A2' approach to D'Oliveira had become public knowledge. The MCC issued a statement admitting the former, 'setting in perspective the facts connected with Lord Cobham's interview and the reasons for the action that had been taken', but denying the latter.[57] Incidentally, this was highly risky, for the loose-talking Cobham had also been sounded out by Vorster in March 1968 about making a similar approach to D'Oliveira and had agreed to do so, though there is no evidence that this ever actually happened.

In the April 1969 committee minutes there is a section headed explicitly 'The Cobham Affair' which confirms that the full story was now known:

> Some criticism has been expressed that the Lord Cobham's interview with the Secretary [Griffith] had not been reported to the Committee ... after considerable discussion a resolution was passed ... stating that the President [Gilligan], Treasurer [Allen], and Secretary had acted in a manner which had the full approval of the Committee.

Remarkably, not only did the committee ratify retrospectively what had happened, but went on to authorise in advance Allen and Griffith, together with the president of the day, to use their discretion to hide further communications from the committee in the future if they felt it appropriate to do so. In fact, the minutes read throughout as though they should be dated 1 April 1969, rather than 16 April.

Thus, amazingly, having been initially totally innocent, within a few months the MCC had in effect become an accessory after the event.

Billy Griffith then offered to resign, though strikingly neither Allen nor Gilligan did likewise. Clearly Griffith has been selected as the fall guy, if indeed there is to be one. By this stage in the proceedings, however, it was already clear how this was going to play out. The committee

---

[56] David Sheppard, *Steps Along Hope Street. My Life in Cricket, the Church and the Inner City*, Hodder & Stoughton, London, 2001
[57] Diana Rait Kerr and Ian Peebles, *Lord's 1946-1970*, , Harrap, London, 1971

unanimously rejected his suggestion and '… he was asked to give the matter no further thought.'

At the same time, frantic efforts were clearly underway to try to rein in Cobham and agree a party line:

It was agreed that Lord Cobham should be consulted as to what steps should be taken if the question of his interview with the South African Prime Minister in March 1968 was raised at the [forthcoming] AGM.

By the time of the next meeting on 7 May, the morning before the AGM, the party line had clearly been agreed, and every procedural eventuality had been considered:

The President indicated to the Committee what he proposed to say should there be any questions regarding Lord Cobham when the [re]appointment of the Treasurer [Allen] was announced. He also reported his prepared statement should the matter of Lord Cobham be raised as a result of the notes in the Annual Report regarding the Special General Meeting held in December 1968 [the Sheppard / Brearley protest meeting].

There was also worried discussion about the position of David Sheppard, presumably because he might have felt released from his own previous vow of silence on the subject of Cobham's disclosures. It was agreed that Griffith should meet with him 'in a purely private capacity', find out his 'plans for the future', and ask him to report these to an emergency committee.

Frustratingly, Sheppard, who died in 2005, does not mention any of this in his books, ending the story with the meeting in December 1968 at which he was subjected to considerable personal attacks, some of which he felt had been orchestrated on behalf of the committee by Dennis Silk,[58] the

---

[58] *Steps Along Hope Street* op. cit.

newly appointed Warden of Radley College, and future chairman of the TCCB and president of the MCC. Being a bishop, and an all-round good egg, Sheppard forgave him. Peter May, 'who found it difficult to forgive people who crossed him',[59] proved uncooperative.

It is strange that there was no massive re-eruption of the D'Oliveira affair in the media in consequence of whatever leak occurred in early 1969, but perhaps editors did not realise the enormity of the 'Lordsgate' cover-up they had discovered, or fell into the usual trap of believing that readers have only a limited attention span for any one story. There is perhaps also another explanation.

It is clear from the archives that the MCC did from time to time use the threat of disciplinary proceedings to try to control what got written by cricket journalists who were themselves members of the MCC. There is for example a disciplinary file on E.W. Swanton arising out of an article he wrote in 1965. There is even one on Ted Dexter. In some cases, for instance that incorrigible repeat offender F.S. Trueman, undertakings as to future conduct are demanded and given. If these examples got to an advanced enough stage to warrant warning letters, it seems only logical to assume that there were others, perhaps many more, that did not reach this stage, being dealt with informally.

It is tempting, though almost certainly fanciful, to think of some precursor of Alistair Campbell stalking the Long Room, having a quiet word with this or that editor or correspondent over tea and fruitcake, giving them a firm steer in the direction of what was 'in the best interests of the game', and hinting darkly at references to the committee, should they try anything subversive. Yet it does seem plausible to believe that the MCC could and did attempt to prevent anything detrimental to themselves from being published; 'for the good of the game', naturally.

Gubby Allen would subsequently be knighted and Billy Griffith receive the CBE, both 'for services to cricket', *after* the full extent of their duplicity during the summer of 1968 had been known for some time – clearly a case of the establishment looking after its own, though rarely can this have been done so cynically.

---

[59] *Steps Along Hope Street* op. cit.

Basil D'Oliveira also received the CBE, in 2005, having already been made an OBE in 1969. When freedom finally came to South Africa he was welcomed back by Nelson Mandela, and the cricket trophy now contested by England and South Africa bears his name. Sadly at the time of writing he is confined to a nursing home suffering from severe dementia, the result of Alzheimer's disease.

In the event, only four MCC members resigned in protest in 1968. After much discussion, the committee decided to allow their reinstatement the following year in return for apologies for their conduct, which were duly forthcoming. One, a clergyman, politely declined.

Perhaps the D'Oliveira affair may be said to have been finally laid to rest in 2008, when Archbishop Desmond Tutu, a close friend of Nelson Mandela and a consistent advocate over the years of peaceful change within South Africa, gave a lecture at Lord's commemorating the spirit of cricket in the name of (perhaps ironically in the light of what is now known) Colin Cowdrey. In it he paid tribute to David Sheppard and Basil D'Oliveira. He also diplomatically praised the England selectors for choosing D'Oliveira, though he did wryly add 'after initially shying at the hurdle'.

CHAPTER 9

ENGLAND'S ALTERNATIVE 1968—69 TOUR AND A SUMMER AT HOME

Struggling to find an alternative host after the abrupt cancellation of the South African tour, the MCC hit upon what was then Ceylon (which was not then a Test-playing nation) and Pakistan. One cannot imagine that Pakistan was a popular choice among the players. Ian Botham would later famously remark that Pakistan was somewhere you tried to send your mother-in-law. In the event, no matter how bad they thought it might be, it turned out to be much, much worse.

By the time they arrived in Pakistan a sad prelude had already occurred. Jeff Jones, who had appeared to have recovered full fitness during the summer, suffered a recurrence of his elbow injury during the Ceylon leg of the tour and left the squad in tears to fly home. It was clear to all that his career was over. Occurring just as Ken Barrington's career was obviously also drawing to a close as a result of heart problems, this must have cast a dampener on the team's spirits.

The first Test in Lahore was marked by another incident in John Snow's occasionally turbulent relationship with England captains. Asked to prove his fitness by bowling flat out in the nets off a long run, Snow ignored the request. Apparently at the insistence of Graveney, the vice-captain, who was traditionally in charge of organising nets, he was left out of the side for disciplinary reasons, though Cowdrey was characteristically too embarrassed ever to make this clear to him.

So Bob Cottam came in for his first Test alongside David Brown and D'Oliveira, the 'specialist batsman' playing as the third seamer, with Pocock and Underwood as the spinners. England scored 306 in the first innings, built around a century from Cowdrey and fifties from Edrich and Knott. Pakistan were a strong side, though, with Hanif Mohammad still playing alongside his underrated brother, Mushtaq, and some exciting emerging players such as Majid Khan, and the match was well balanced, ending in a draw.

The second Test was scheduled for Dhaka, capital of what was then East Pakistan, but in the grip of serious civil unrest which would eventually develop into a full-blown war, and see the birth of a new country: Bangladesh. Both the Pakistani authorities and the British diplomats on the spot wanted the game to go ahead, but on arrival there was general agreement that the cricketers were effectively abandoned both by the army, who were supposed to be keeping order but in fact were afraid to venture into the city centre, and by their own consular staff, who, despite having been urging the England team to carry on as normal, were found to have been busy at the same time arranging for the emergency evacuation of all British residents.

The centre of Dhaka and the cricket ground were both under the control of rioting students. Gunfire could be heard regularly during the night. In the morning, gagged and bound bodies would be found floating in the Buriganga River, a branch of the Ganges which was now estimated to contain 20 per cent water and 80 per cent sewage. In short, the England players had flown straight into a state of anarchy, in which it seemed clear that the possibility of even greater violence was ever present, and being barely contained by the young students who seemed to be at the head of a mass uprising. When they asked to fly straight out again they were told quite seriously by the student leaders that if they did so then their safety could not be guaranteed. Cowdrey and the tour manager, Les Ames, asked what that meant. The students told them they would not reach the airport alive. Cowdrey and Ames believed them.

The match itself was a surreal experience, played in a stadium controlled by patrolling student militants, the dressing room a blank, windowless cell with only one dim light bulb. It ended in a draw, with the players of both sides only too glad to get away to safety.

On arriving in Karachi for the third Test, the England players were somewhat shaken to see marksmen stationed around the pavilion. Karachi too was in the grip of serious civil unrest. Several anti-government protesters were on hunger strike and one had just succeeded in starving himself to death. To complicate matters further, the cricket fans of Karachi were upset that Saeed Ahmed was leading their national side instead of local boy Hanif Mohammad.

After repeated interruptions to play on the first two days, both Milburn and Graveney had made centuries and England were 412-6; Milburn had been summoned from England as a batting replacement, and was unfortunate enough to join the team in Dhaka. Cowdrey, having started the match, learned of the death of his father-in-law and left to return to England, handing over to Graveney.

It was on the third day, with Alan Knott four runs away from a Test century, that the real trouble, which had been threatening for some time, finally arrived. A body of demonstrators several thousand strong marched through Karachi, overwhelmed the security forces at the gates, and simply swarmed all over the ground, destroying the stands, and using seats and rubble as missiles. Knott, hoping against hope that order could be restored for him to complete his century, stayed in the middle longer than was wise, and had to scamper back to the pavilion through a barrage of projectiles.

The England players were finally allowed out of the ground only after promising the leaders of this particular demonstration that they would return the following day and complete the match. They lied. Instead Ames managed to get them booked on a flight that night, and they travelled to the airport in great secrecy to make good their escape. The tour was abandoned.

The Karachi Test was abandoned on 8 March 1969. England faced a split summer featuring two three-Test tours by West Indies and New Zealand respectively, the first Test due to start at Old Trafford on 12 June. During these intervening three months something completely unexpected was to occur which would profoundly alter the course of this narrative. On 24 May, while batting in a Sunday League match, Colin Cowdrey heard a sharp noise from behind him. Thinking that something had struck the stumps, he started to turn around to look. Suddenly he collapsed in terrible pain. He had broken his Achilles tendon. He was carried from the ground in agony and his worst fears were rapidly confirmed: he was out for the season.

By coincidence, England had lost another batsman less than 24 hours previously. Colin Milburn, who had been in fine form during the early part of the season, and could reasonably have expected to keep his place in the side after his performance in Pakistan, was involved in a car accident. Tragically, he was blinded in his left eye. The right eye was also damaged. As many immediately suspected, this was to prove effectively the end of his career, though he did make an unsuccessful attempt to return to county cricket in 1973. He was to die of a heart attack in 1990 at the age of just 48. His accident affected many people very deeply: as an outstandingly popular figure and a larger than life (literally) character, it was universally felt that his loss would seriously diminish the game.

He played in only nine Test matches, though it should have been more, but changed the course of four of them. His 126 against the West Indies in 1966, and his 83 against the Australians in 1968, both at Lord's and both in very difficult circumstances, will live in the memory. His 139 at Karachi would remain his last innings for England. In good form, with Barrington having retired, and Cowdrey out of the picture, he would surely have played in all six Test matches that summer.

Ray Illingworth, who had left Yorkshire at the end of the 1968 season to captain Leicestershire, went to see 'Ollie' in hospital in June with his county teammate Graham McKenzie, one of the Australian bowlers whom Milburn had plundered at Lord's the previous year. After visiting a resolutely cheerful Milburn, they continued on their way to Leicestershire's next match, against Sussex. As they arrived at their hotel in Brighton they were puzzled to see a crowd of journalists and photographers waiting outside. Wondering which celebrity was expected, they got out of the car, only to be engulfed. During the day, it had been announced that Illingworth would be the new England captain.

As with Close before him, this was a significant decision. Len Hutton had captained England as a professional in the 1950s, but this had been a highly controversial move. Some suggested that a way should be found for him to become a 'shamateur'. Others petitioned to have David Sheppard appointed in his place for a tour of Australia. As an added complication, the rules of the MCC did not allow a professional cricketer to become a member (which is why Hedley Verity is not listed on the war memorial board at Lord's). Close had been the only other professional to be selected as captain – only to lose the captaincy in questionable circumstances. It seems likely that had M.J.K. Smith been playing first-class cricket in 1969, he would have been offered the job back. As it was, the selectors had no choice but to turn to a professional.

The announcement surprised many, not least Cowdrey, who had publicly tipped Graveney as his successor. It had been widely assumed that Graveney, who was after all the serving vice-captain, had twice taken over the captaincy from Cowdrey, and once captained England in his own right, would be appointed on a stand-in basis for the rest of the summer. Instead Illingworth was appointed – but only for one Test match.

Indeed, Illingworth, undoubtedly one of England's best captains and a man who would lead England to regain the Ashes in Australia, would later ruefully reflect that he was never actually appointed for a full home Test series, unlike Mike Brearley, who had played under the old regime as a 'gentleman' but whose batting record in Tests was modest (though Illingworth was too polite to say this). Was this simply another manifestation of different attitudes towards a northern working-class professional who left school at 14, as opposed to a southern middle-class public-school-educated gentleman with a postgraduate degree from Cambridge? Brearley, the last amateur to captain England and an establishment figure despite his role of genteel protest during the D'Oliveira affair, would in due course be invited to become president of the

MCC, as indeed would Graveney. Illingworth never was, though in his first six official series as captain (including an away series in Australia) England lost only a single Test match.

Illingworth, then, was a professional cricketer through and through, having come up the hard way. Though he had only limited experience as a county captain in early 1969, he was to prove one of the most successful ever at Test level. His field placings and bowling changes were shrewd and considered. He was decisive and determined on selection matters. In the field, he believed in putting batsmen under pressure if his attacking bowlers failed to make a breakthrough, waiting for them to get frustrated and make mistakes. For this reason he was to see D'Oliveira, with his career economy rate of less than two runs an over, as an important part of the England bowling line-up. This aspect of D'Oliveira's game is often overlooked. Not only did he seem to have the uncanny knack of taking a key wicket just when it was most needed, but he created pressure for the bowlers at the other end as a result of the containment which he was able to exert at his own.

Two aspects of Illingworth as captain deserve mention. First, he was often criticised for underbowling himself; this was in fact almost certainly the case. Leicestershire during his captaincy actually played two offspinners, the other being former Yorkshire teammate Jackie Birkenshaw. Birkenshaw was in the team very much on merit, and was a good enough bowler to play Test cricket himself, but the fact that he was a regular fixture in the team is highly suggestive that Illingworth did not bowl nearly as much as captain as he had done previously as a player. At Test level, he took significantly fewer wickets as captain than he did in an almost identical number of Tests previously, again a sign that other captains were more likely to bowl him than he was himself.

Yet a bowler captain always has a difficult balance to strike, and in fairness to Illingworth, there were others, such as Botham and Flintoff, who surely erred in the opposite direction.

The second point of note, however, is that even if indeed Illingworth did make less contribution with the ball as captain, the opposite was true of his batting. Again, captaincy can affect batting form. Botham, for example, had a significantly lower average as captain. However, for some, like Graham Gooch, the added responsibility of captaincy seemed to act as a spur. Illingworth was certainly in the latter camp.

Illingworth in his 35 matches as captain averaged 32.75 against international opposition[60] with two centuries, and once enjoyed an extraordinary run of six successive fifties, which had previously only ever been achieved for England by Denis Compton. In his 31 previous games, he had averaged 16.11 and only once reached 50. More importantly, his big scores always seemed to come when England were in trouble and most needed them. Add in well over a hundred Test wickets, his reliable catching and ground fielding, and he must be reckoned to have made as great an all-round impact as anyone ever to captain England (Tony Greig would have been a good point of comparison, had his career as captain not been cut short).

So Illingworth went to Old Trafford in June 1969 for what might be his one and only match as captain determined to win it, and be confirmed for the rest of the summer. Win it he duly did, though even now the selectors only grudgingly gave him the next two matches.

The 1969 West Indies attracted great excitement, as West Indian touring sides always do, but was to prove a pale shadow of the great 1966 side, or indeed of the subsequent West Indies teams that would achieve a whole new period of dominance. Without the great Hall and Griffith, their seam attack often looked ineffective, with John Shepherd of Kent, who bowled military-medium, proving the unexpected potential match-winner. Sobers was carrying a shoulder injury which supposedly affected his bowling, though it was with the bat that he had (for him) a strangely subdued series. He would later admit to being exhausted after playing too much cricket over the last eighteen months or so; given his unprecedented all-round contributions to the side, this is hardly surprising. With Gibbs too having a quiet series, West Indies sometimes seemed to be struggling to see where the next wicket was coming from.

In the batting department there was still no call-up for the young Geoff Greenidge, but Roy Fredericks would give a brief glimpse of his immense

---

[60] This includes five matches against the Rest of the World.

talent, and Steve Camacho would prove a steady opener alongside him. Another new sight for English fans was Charlie Davis, a batsman who seemed to have little of the natural talent of his teammates, but made up for it with an intensity of concentration and determination which they alas often seemed to lack.

For England, Geoff Boycott, newly restored to health, reclaimed his opening spot alongside John Edrich, effectively coming in for the tragic Colin Milburn. Phil Sharpe was a surprise choice to many to replace Cowdrey, but as well as being a phenomenal slip catcher he had batted steadily for Yorkshire and deserved his chance.

England made 413 in their first-innings, built around a five and a half hour 128 from Geoff Boycott on his return to the international scene. An increasingly desperate Sobers used no less than seven bowlers, including the occasional offspin of 'Joey' Carew. It was John Shepherd, plugging away steadily for 5-104, who looked by far the most impressive.

At the end of the second day West Indies, who had lost both their openers to Snow and Brown with only five runs on the board, were already in terrible trouble at 104-6, with Lloyd and Shepherd at the crease and still needing over a hundred to save the follow-on. Anyone expecting heroics was to be disappointed. Snow took both their wickets on the third morning, and West Indies were all out for 147. Illingworth duly invited them to follow on.

As if determined to atone for their first-innings performance, Fredericks and Carew put on 92 for the first wicket, and the remaining West Indian batsmen defended stoutly, including an uncharacteristically dour 13 from Clive Lloyd which took nearly an hour and a half. Though they stretched their second innings well into the last day, their final total of 275 left England just ten runs to win, which Boycott and Edrich accomplished at two an over, slightly above their usual rate of scoring.

So Illingworth had won his first Test, and was duly appointed for the rest of the series: the two matches at Lord's and Headingley.

A sad incident took place during the Old Trafford Test, which brought a glorious Test career to an unfortunate end. On the Sunday, which was of course a rest day in those days, Tom Graveney had played in a one day match as part of his benefit season, thus earning himself a thousand pounds, which was over six times his Test match fee. He was promptly dropped, and never played for England again.

Peter Parfitt came into the side in his place at his home ground, Lord's. Perhaps this was in part because England had decided to play an extra batsman (Jackie Hampshire of Yorkshire, making his Test debut) in place of Underwood, and it was felt that Parfitt's offspin might come in useful. In the event, however, Parfitt bowled only one over in the match.

Again Fredericks looked impressive, putting on over 100 for the first wicket with Steve Camacho. West Indies batted well, and England were fortunate to have Sobers run out. With Hampshire and Sharpe both taking good slip catches, and John Snow taking 5-114, West Indies were all out for 380, built around a patient first Test century for Charlie Davis, who batted for over six hours.

By the close on the second day England were in desperate trouble at 46-4, Sobers, despite his injured shoulder, opening the bowling and taking two quick wickets. As the crowd made its way home on the Friday evening, West Indies looked favourites to square the series. Yet against all the odds, England were still batting on Saturday evening, thanks to a century on debut by Hampshire, a gritty 50 from Knott, and a patient 97 not out from the captain. Illingworth would go on to convert this into his first Test century on the Monday morning as England gloated over their unexpected riches of 344.

West Indies declared at 295-9 in their second innings, Camacho and Fredericks again having started well, and a tired-looking Sobers reminding everyone of his class with an accomplished 50 not out. This set England 332 to win, and when they lost John Edrich with one run on the board, things looked ominous. However, Boycott steadied the ship with a characteristic century, sharing a good fourth-wicket partnership with Sharpe, who, in contrasting style, scored a thumping 86 at nearly a run a minute. When both were out in quick succession, followed by Hampshire (who was run out) England were suddenly in danger at 272-6. Illingworth, Knott and Knight batted out the remaining tense half an hour for a draw.

So England went to Headingley with their lead in the three-match series still intact, Underwood regaining his place, with the unlucky Parfitt (who had batted for two hours in England's second innings at Lord's) dropping out.

Vanburn Holder, who played for Worcestershire as an overseas player alongside D'Oliveira and Graveney, had taken over from Wes Hall as the West Indies' senior opening bowler. Hall, one of the great fast bowlers, was always going to be a tough act to follow, and the comparison was in any case unfair, since Holder was a totally different sort of bowler. Bowling at a steady fast-medium, he was in fact a typical English seamer, and at Headingley in 1969 he found typical Leeds conditions which suited him down to the ground. His 4-48, with the other 'English seamer' Shepherd bowling tightly for 3-43, had England struggling for runs throughout, and losing wickets steadily. Despite long, defensive knocks from Edrich, D'Oliveira and Knott, they could manage only 223 in their first innings, which ended early on the second day.

They could hardly have expected to find themselves batting again that same evening, but that is in fact what happened. The same conditions which had suited the 'English seamers' Holder and Shepherd (Worcestershire and Kent respectively), also proved ideal for Barry Knight, who took the first four wickets to fall, including Sobers. West Indies, not helped by Shepherd being injured and unable to bat, were dismissed in 65 overs for 161. Yet, in what was to prove a see-saw match, it was they who would ultimately find themselves chasing victory.

England struggled again in their second innings. Sobers, whom some had thought at the beginning of the series might not be able to bowl at all, returned the amazing figures of 40-18-42-5. England at one stage were 147-7 when Illingworth was dismissed by Holder, so were indebted to their bowlers, Knight, Underwood, Brown and Snow, for seeing them through to 240, leaving West Indies 303 to win.

With two-thirds of the required runs knocked off, only three wickets down, and plenty of time left, West Indies looked to be cruising to an easy win. Had a gentleman amateur been captaining England he might at this stage have been thinking about bringing on his 'picnic' bowlers and conceding the match. Illingworth, however, was a Yorkshireman who, like Close, believed in fighting to the end, and this match was to prove perhaps his finest hour as a captain.

Underwood had taken two of the three wickets to fall, and suddenly took another, dismissing Butcher with the score at 219-4. Less than a hundred was needed, with Sobers the new man in.

Instantly, Illingworth took Underwood off. In the stands and the commentary box, people scratched their heads. Underwood had looked the only English bowler capable of taking wickets. Why not give him a chance against Sobers before the great man was set? Illingworth, however, had a plan.

He brought Knight on, and asked him to bowl Sobers a wide half-volley. Illingworth reasoned that Sobers would be unable to resist trying to crack it through the covers and, if there was any movement at all, might edge it to first slip where Phil Sharpe, probably the best slip catcher in the world, was ready and waiting. Perhaps sensing at the last moment what was going on, Sobers swung wide, to avoid giving the outside edge which England were seeking. Instead he got an inside edge, and played on.

The doubters in the crowd now nodded knowledgeably. Surely Illingworth would now reintroduce Underwood? Yet no; instead he brought himself on.

Again, there was method in his apparent madness. His reasoning was that Underwood was much less effective against left-handed batsmen (he found bowling to Sobers a particularly challenging experience),[61] and felt that he himself had a better chance of dismissing the batsman at the other end, the left-handed Lloyd. Four runs later he had Lloyd caught at the wicket, the ball turning away from him, whereas Underwood's delivery would have been turning into him. He promptly brought back Underwood to dismiss the injured Shepherd, and then took the new ball, with which Knight and Brown (not Snow, and therein lies a story) polished off Mike Findlay, Holder and Gibbs to leave the West Indies 30 runs short.

It had been a thrilling Test match, and a great victory for England and

---

[61] Derek Underwood, *Beating the Bat*, Stanley Paul, London, 1975

Illingworth. An Australian cricket writer[62] would later write a detailed account of the day, and hold it up as a model of captaincy.

The victory came with a bitter aftertaste for one member of the England team, however. In yet another brush with authority, John Snow had ignored Illingworth's request to bowl flat out in the closing stages of the game, believing that he knew best, and that he was more likely to take a wicket with medium-pace seamers, as Holder, Shepherd and Knight had done earlier in the game. Illingworth insisted that he be dropped for the next Test for disciplinary reasons.

This time it was Alec Bedser, having succeeded Insole as chairman of selectors, who was too embarrassed to break the news to Snow; instead, he was officially being rested because the selectors wanted to have a look at the promising young Alan Ward, reputedly the quickest bowler in England. Illingworth, on hearing the news, rang Snow to tell him personally exactly why he had been omitted, and at whose insistence. Clearly he was a very different sort of captain from Cowdrey.

So it was that when Lord's hosted its second Test match of the summer, against New Zealand, Alan Ward was given his first cap in Snow's place, the only other change being a recall for Keith Fletcher at the expense of Hampshire. Jackie Hampshire remains one of the unluckiest of English Test batsmen. He was never given the sort of extended run in the side that his natural ability, and his debut century seemed to justify, and he would later be brought back to face Dennis Lillee at Adelaide in 1971.

Graham Dowling's New Zealanders were an ordinary side, including some players who were only part-time cricketers. The team did, however, include two genuinely world-class performers in Glenn Turner and Hedley Howarth. Turner was a 22-year-old who would prove himself one of the best batsmen ever to play the game, once scoring four double centuries in a single tour of the West Indies, and ending his career with a Test average of 44.86, and a first-class average of just under 50. He would subsequently play many dominant innings for Worcestershire in county cricket.

Turner had been on fire in the tour matches leading up to the first

---

[62] Ray Robinson

Test, and great things were expected of him. In the event, however, he was to prove strangely muted, and this would be one of his very rare series failures.

Hedley Howarth was a fine slow left-arm bowler. Phenomenally accurate, he was very difficult to score against, and thus frequently found himself bowling in defensive rather than attacking mode. His Test bowling average of nearly 37 does not do justice to his ability. His economy rate of only just over two runs an over does.

The Lord's Test match turned out to be an easy victory for England, though it would have been hard to predict when England were all out for 190 in the first innings. Steady bowling by the New Zealand seamers in helpful conditions saw England collapse to 63-5, to be rescued by D'Oliveira, Knight and Illingworth, who top-scored with 53. The trio of fast-medium bowlers included Dayle Hadlee, whose unusual run-up was memorably described by John Arlott as resembling Groucho Marx in pursuit of a waitress. He was one of five sons of Walter Hadlee, who played Test cricket for New Zealand between 1937 and 1951. Walter would die aged 91 in 2006 having seen another of his sons, Richard, become one of the greatest bowlers ever to play the game, and New Zealand's first cricketing knight.

When New Zealand batted it was the spinners who did the damage, Illingworth and Underwood each taking four wickets as New Zealand subsided for 169, losing their last seven wickets for just 77 runs.

England's batsmen proved more solid in the second innings, with an opening partnership of 125 between Boycott and Edrich, who went on to make a century. Their total of 340 set New Zealand 362 to win, but in the event they were skittled out for just 131, Derek Underwood taking 7-32.

Snow had served his sentence, so was brought back for the Trent Bridge Test in place of David Brown, who had failed to take a wicket in either innings at Lord's. This match was badly affected by rain, with almost two whole days being lost, and ended in a draw. New Zealand batted into the second day for 269, built around a long partnership between Bev Congdon and Brian Hastings.

England's massive 451-8 declared in reply took the match into its fourth day and, with rain then intervening again, New Zealand were left on 66-1. For England, the in-form Edrich scored 155, and Phil Sharpe contributed a century as well.

The third and final match of the series at the Oval proved something of a non-contest, England winning by eight wickets thanks to another match-winning performance by Derek Underwood, who took six wickets in each innings. England recalled Geoff Arnold of Surrey, who had been on the fringe of selection for the last few years, in place of Barry Knight. More significantly, this match marked the debut of Mike Denness of Kent. This was a slightly puzzling move. While Denness was an effective batsman in county cricket, there were many others who might have been picked ahead of him, including Parfitt, Hampshire, Amiss, Alan Jones of Glamorgan, Roy Virgin of Somerset, John Jameson of Warwickshire, or even his own Kent teammate, Brian Luckhurst.

Even at the time, the selection seemed strange. With the benefit of hindsight it seems slightly sinister. There was no winter tour planned, but a South African series due the following summer. Were the selectors even now, with Illingworth having led the side only six times, and very successfully at that, casting around for his successor?

Colin Cowdrey was of course lurking in the wings, though as yet still unfit, and Denness was very much his protégé at Kent. Should Cowdrey prove for any reason unable to return, Denness might be just the sort of amiable establishment figure to step into his shoes. The selectors may well have been blooding him against relatively weak opposition in the hope that he could establish himself in the side as a batsman ahead of his more obvious rivals. If so, they were partially successful. Denness was all at sea in the first innings, taking 47 minutes to score two runs, but grafted doggedly for over two hours in the second innings to finish with 55 not out.

Arnold, on his home ground, looked promising but misdirected. He bowled steady outswing, but his line tended to start too wide, so that his deliveries passed harmlessly to Knott in front of the slips. He failed to take a wicket in either innings, but gave away less than two runs an over, both figures reflecting the fact that the batsmen were rarely forced to play a shot. However, one felt that if he could learn to start the ball on off stump, or develop an inswinger or an offcutter, then he could yet prove very effective, particularly in English conditions.

This summer was to mark the end of another England Test career in addition to that of Tom Graveney. Barry Knight's colourful private life saw him declared bankrupt, after which he emigrated to Australia to pursue a coaching career. One of his charges, a young batsman called Allan Border, would later make his own considerable mark on the game.

CHAPTER 10

AN END TO THE SOUTH AFRICAN TOUR AND ENGLAND V THE REST OF THE WORLD

More surprisingly, Phil Sharpe would only ever play one more game for England – an unfair fate for a man who averaged over 46 in Test matches as well as being one of the great all-time slip fielders. His batting average was better than that of several England captains, including Denness, Lewis, Close, Smith, Greig, or even Cowdrey, who is spoken of as one of England's greatest batsmen. It was also higher than Edrich's or Graveney's, and only marginally lower than Boycott's.

Perhaps if Sharpe had played for Middlesex, Kent or Surrey, rather than Yorkshire, he might have been given more chances to show his ability at the highest level. Fred Trueman said: '... there was no doubt in my mind that the MCC would opt for a southern player if possible, a northerner when pushed, and a Yorkshire pro when they couldn't avoid it.'[63] Certainly Yorkshire folk thought southern bias resulted in Fletcher (career average 39.9) getting into the side ahead of him, but the Headingley crowd is noted neither for its neutrality nor its objectivity.

---

[63] *As It Was*, op. cit.

So the 1969 season drew to a close, and once again South Africa were the two words on everybody's lips. They were due to tour England in the summer of 1970, but would the tour go ahead?

Cricket enthusiasts fervently hoped so, particularly when Bill Lawry's Australians were comprehensively thrashed in South Africa over the winter. It rapidly become clear in those games that Ali Bacher's South African team was not just the strongest team in the world, but perhaps one of the great all-time sides. Still featuring the evergreen all-rounder Trevor Goddard, who had opened both the batting and the bowling, they now had the best new-ball attack in the world, in Peter Pollock and Mike Procter, together with some very special batsmen such as Barry Richards, Eddie Barlow, Graeme Pollock and Lee Irvine. The side brimmed with all-rounders: Barlow, Goddard, 'Tiger' Lance, and of course Procter, who would subsequently enjoy a long and distinguished career in England with Gloucestershire. Barry Richards, by the way, was a good enough batsman to be chosen by no less an authority than Don Bradman to open the batting for his notional all-time Test eleven.

Yet, as in 1968, administrators had to juggle what they felt to be the best interests of the game with political considerations. With some misgivings, their instincts were that politics should be kept out of sport, and that the tour should go ahead. They had for over a year been urging SACA 'to give some indication in public that definite progress was being made to further interests of non-white cricketers in South Africa'. This was, it transpired, for purely political motives: 'It was felt that, quite apart from all other circumstances, this was an essential factor if the Tour was not to become the subject of a continual public demonstration.'[64]

Needless to say, no such statement was forthcoming, to the MCC's mounting frustration. Regardless, in January 1970, they issued a formal invitation to South Africa, believing it to be in the best interests of cricket to do so. While such an attitude is to some extent understandable even

---

[64] Minutes of MCC main committee, 15 January 1969

today, it is difficult not to level a charge of political naivety, at the very least. South Africa had recently refused a visa to the black tennis player Arthur Ashe, leading to their expulsion from the Davis Cup, and consequent isolation in yet another sport. They had also banned the International Cavaliers cricket team in the absence of an assurance that this would be all-white, and had engaged in public debate about whether a Japanese jockey who wanted a visa to ride in a race in South Africa could be treated as a 'courtesy white'.

Above all, it was only just over a year after the D'Oliveira affair, a major controversy that left some very fresh wounds; indeed, the ripples are still felt over 40 years later. Peter Hain's anti-apartheid movement, which had been active during the D'Oliveira affair, now went into overdrive: their 'Stop The Seventy Tour' campaign became a national protest movement.

In sociological terms it was grammar school pupils, newly educated at university, who formed the core of the protest marches, much as their predecessors had done a decade earlier with the CND's 'Ban The Bomb' campaign. The movement crossed political boundaries and social divisions, though. John Arlott went public, saying that he would decline to commentate for Test Match Special, and received a condemnatory letter from Peter May for his pains. Cricket administrators and MCC members became the butt of jokes, sketches and songs on satirical radio and television shows.

The MCC committee, advised by the newly formed Test and County Cricket Board, held out, however, fortified by letters of support from the likes of the Monday Club (a right-wing 'ginger group' within the Conservative Party). It should be mentioned in passing that the TCCB and the MCC seemed to be different largely in name only, reminding the writer of a part of his career spent as a young lawyer, when he received a letter from another lawyer saying 'apart from the fact that they have same directors, the same shareholders and the same registered office, there is no connection between these companies at all'. The secretary of the TCCB, for example, was one Billy Griffith, who of course just happened also to be secretary of the MCC. In fact, it is apparent from the MCC archives[65] that their committee only ceded control to the council of the TCCB in the first place because it was a requirement of obtaining funding from the Sports Council (just as later women would only be allowed into the pavilion at Lord's after it became a requirement of Lottery funding).

So it was that schoolboys attending the traditional Easter coaching course at Lord's (including the thrill of being able to change in the England dressing room) were treated to the sight of the ground being patrolled by security guards with dogs, the playing area ringed by floodlights, and the square protected by several layers of barbed wire. Inevitable comparisons were drawn with *The Colditz Story*. Why these extreme precautions? Well, the anti-apartheid movement was talking of taking direct action. While it is probable that they simply envisaged mass sit-down protests, flashing mirrors in the batsmen's eyes, or trying to shoot the bails off the stumps during play with air rifles, Lord's was taking no chances. Protestors did in fact attempt to break into Lord's to play an impromptu multiracial game of cricket and, when thwarted, played in the road outside instead, bringing traffic to a standstill.

The situation was complicated by the forthcoming Commonwealth Games scheduled to take place in Edinburgh that July. Although South Africa had already been banned from the Games, many African nations were threatening to boycott the Games if the South African cricket tour went ahead.

Nonetheless the TCCB and the MCC decided in mid-May that the tour would go ahead, stating that this would be the last time that a white South African team would tour Britain. Lord's had presumably become aware that the International Cricket Council were likely shortly to vote to exclude South Africa from all international competition, but this was apparently being presented as a reason why the tour should go ahead rather than, as many people believed, a strong argument to the contrary. Home Secretary Jim Callaghan was not alone in questioning this reasoning.

---

[65] Minutes of main committee, 2 August 1967

Just four days later, following a direct request from Callaghan on public order grounds, the TCCB was forced to back down and cancel the tour. However, the fact that they took 90 minutes to come to a decision suggests that its committee members were far from unanimous.

For South African cricket, the cancellation of the tour spelt disaster. Following their exclusion by the ICC in 1970, they entered a cricketing wilderness, from which they would not be released until 1991. That winter tour by Lawry's Australians in 1969–70 would be their last Test series until 1992 – 23 long years later. Thus, with the exception of Trevor Goddard, who was coming to the end of his career, Ali Bacher's South Africans were denied the place in history which would otherwise undoubtedly have been theirs. So frustrated did various players become by this prospect that they organised a walk-off protest against government policy during a match at Cape Town in April 1971.

Incidentally, let us remind ourselves that not all white South Africans supported apartheid. When mixed-race sport was finally and grudgingly allowed, Ali Bacher came out of retirement to play pointedly for a black cricket club.

So it was that instead of the visiting South Africans, England found themselves playing a hastily assembled Rest of the World XI, captained by the incomparable Garry Sobers. Despite the fact that four of the planned South African touring side were named in the team (Barlow, Richards, Procter and Graeme Pollock), this was accepted as a victory for the anti-apartheid movement.

The resulting games might most accurately be described as 'the series that never was', as they would subsequently have their Test status withdrawn, and be expunged from the record books. It seems difficult to justify this decision on anything other than blatantly political grounds, particularly as a largely uncompetitive exhibition match staged in Australia in 2005 has been allowed to keep its status, an unfairness which has never been explained or justified. First, as the great scorer and statistician Bill Frindall maintained to his dying day, once a match had been officially designated a Test match, and played as one, then its existence in the record books could not, and should not, be eliminated. Second, this was certainly amongst the strongest opposition that

England have ever faced in international competition – strong enough to make a mockery of describing recent matches against Zimbabwe or Bangladesh as Tests.

Pity in particular poor Alan Jones of Glamorgan, who played a single match for England, only to have his solitary Test cap taken away when it was subsequently decided that facing McKenzie, Procter and Sobers was not a sufficient challenge to have warranted its award in the first place. Even that loyal establishment figure, Mike Denness, would later describe this as a 'Mickey Mouse' decision.[66]

Ray Illingworth was under no illusions as to the scale of the task at hand. 'They were good', he would later say simply. 'There'd never been a side like it. They had everything.'[67] Even so, he thought the two sides were evenly matched in the fast-bowling department. The main difference, he acknowledged, was in the depth of the Rest of the World's batting, with Procter, a genuine all-rounder, coming in at nine. He might have mentioned the quality of their batting as well, with a top six guaranteed to strike fear into the hearts of many bowlers: Barlow, Richards, Kanhai, Pollock, Lloyd and Sobers! Against this stellar array, England chose to go into the first match with only five specialist batsmen: Brian Luckhurst and Alan Jones (both receiving, as they then believed, their first Test caps), Denness, Sharpe and D'Oliveira. There was also an experimental look to the bowling with Ward and Shuttleworth alongside Snow, and spinners Underwood and Illingworth completing a five-man bowling attack (six counting D'Oliveira). Shuttleworth was another phantom first cap, bearing a passing resemblance to a young Fred Trueman, both physically and in his bowling action. Some felt that he was lucky to be making the team ahead of his Lancashire teammate, Peter Lever.

The series was to be a personal triumph for Ray Illingworth, but he began by winning the toss and batting, and it turned out to have been a bad toss to win. With the ball swinging around in seamer-friendly conditions, Sobers was close to unplayable; McKenzie, who had learned by now how to

---

[66] *Wisden Cricketer*, 2005
[67] *Wisden Cricketer*, 2005

use English conditions to his advantage, was only slightly less so. England's new look batting line-up was simply 'annihilated', as Illingworth would later candidly admit.[68] When Knott and Snow were also quickly dismissed by Sobers, 29-5 became 44-7. Only Illingworth dug in, scoring 63, and some dogged defence at the other end by first Underwood and then Ward saw England limp to 127 all out, having survived just 55 overs. Not for nothing would one cricket writer later ruefully observe that England lost the series because their bowlers did not make enough runs. Sobers finished with the amazing figures of 20-11-21-6.

When the Rest of the World batted, they scored 546 in an awesome portent of what England might have to face for the rest of the summer. Sobers the batsman made a swashbuckling 183, and Eddie Barlow a more restrained 119. Even Underwood was unable to stem the flow, most unusually conceding more than three runs an over. When England came to bat again, it was simply a question of whether they could salvage any honour from the game by scoring the little matter of 419 to make the Rest of the World bat again (they didn't).

Luckhurst had shown evidence of the ability for which he had been picked by making 67 at the top of the order. D'Oliveira, Illingworth and Knott all played long knocks, Illingworth falling six short of what would have been a well-deserved century. However, it was apparent that, with Knight no longer available, the side appeared unbalanced, seeming to have one too many bowlers and one too few batsmen. The batting line-up had a distinctly fragile feel about it: both Jones and Denness had failed twice.

England addressed both problems when the teams reassembled at Trent Bridge. They brought in an all-rounder, Tony Greig, yet another phantom first cap, in place of a specialist bowler. David Brown returned to partner John Snow as the new-ball attack. Wholesale batting changes were also made, with Jones, Denness, and Sharpe all dropped, and Edrich, Cowdrey and Fletcher coming back into the side. Cowdrey's return was significant, as once again Illingworth had not been selected as captain for the entire series, and everyone knew that the selectors would

---

[68] *Wisden Cricketer*, 2005

Colin Cowdrey (in sweater) leads the MCC to the West Indies in 1967. Fred Titmus the professional is trim in blazer and tie.

The MCC selectors in 1965 – note M.J.K. Smith, the absent-minded professor, reading the newspaper.

Garry Sobers, as captain of the Rest of the World, receiving a trophy at Lord's.

Colin Cowdrey (left) after the 200th Test between England and Australia, Lord's, June 1968.

A crowd watching a Test match at Lord's, sometime after the construction of the new tavern stand. Note the spectators sitting on the ground, a practice that was discontinued after the West Indian pitch invasions of 1976.

Brian Close in typically pugnacious mood.

Floodlights and barbed wire at Lord's, Easter 1970.

The end of the road for the 1970 South African tour.

Basil D'Oliveira cover drives during his historic innings at the Oval in 1968.

Tony Greig batting against Australia at Old Trafford, June 1972.

Illingworth is chaired off the field in Sydney by his devoted team of professionals on 17 February 1971. Underwood has just taken the last wicket and England have won the Ashes. From right to left: Knott, Underwood, Luckhurst (face obscured), Illingworth, Edrich, Shuttleworth (looking like a young Fred Trueman and fielding as substitute for Snow), Lever (fair hair), Fletcher (cap), D'Oliveira.

Colin Cowdrey is caught and bowled by Gleeson at Melbourne during his tour from hell in 1971. After dropping two vital catches and failing with the bat he did not play again in the series.

Tony Lewis enjoys a moment with Mrs Indira Gandhi in 1972 after being picked to captain England, despite never having played in a Test match.

John Snow, one of England's greatest fast bowlers, playing in his last Test against the West Indies at Headingley in 1976. His action seems to have lost little of its power.

Geoff Boycott playing an uncharacteristic attacking shot at Trent Bridge in 1977, returning from his three-year self-imposed exile: 187 runs, dismissed once, over 12 hours at the wicket.

shortly need to choose a captain for the winter tour of Australia, which Cowdrey had nominated back in 1967 as the fifth series of his Five Tours plan. Was this a sign that Illingworth the professional stand-in would now be shunted aside, and asked by the selectors to return quietly to the ranks, allowing Cowdrey the gentleman captain to play himself in with a few games in charge before the touring party was selected?

If so, they must have experienced mixed feelings about the second match of the series.

When the Rest of the World batted first they lost wickets steadily, the medium pacers D'Oliveira and Greig taking four apiece. It was only thanks to a fighting century by Clive Lloyd and a rumbustious 43 by Mike Procter that they reached 276. However, the Rest of the World had a medium pacer of their own in Eddie Barlow, who, after Edrich and Luckhurst had given England a solid start, took all of the first five wickets to fall, reducing England, who had reached 78 without loss, to 109-5. Once again it was Illingworth who had to play a captain's innings, and play it superbly, though he fell tantalisingly close to a century once more, this time on 97. First, solid support was proffered by Knott. Then John Snow batted brightly to share in another of his trademark last-wicket stands, this one worth 84 invaluable runs. England were all out at the close of the second day for 279. It could hardly be closer.

Now it was Eddie Barlow's turn to dominate with the bat, scoring 142 out of 286, D'Oliveira and Greig this time taking three wickets each. This left England 284 to win and square the series.

Edrich was out with the score on 44, but Luckhurst then added 120 with Cowdrey, his county captain, in what would turn out to be a decisive second-wicket stand. Fletcher and Luckhurst saw England through to the end of the fourth day with the score at 184-2 – exactly one hundred more runs required to win. On the last day Fletcher and Luckhurst simply hit off the remaining runs with few signs of nerves, Luckhurst finishing on 113 not out, an innings which Derek Underwood would later say was worth a double century against any other bowling attack.[69] Against all the odds,

---

[69] *Wisden Cricketer*, 2005

England had won a match against the strongest opposition the world had to offer, despite a heroic all-round effort from Barlow.

It was a double triumph for Illingworth, both as captain and player. His scores so far in the series were 63, 94 and 97, and he had top-scored in every innings in which he had batted. Not bad for someone who had been picked originally primarily as a bowler, and also had the added strain of captaining the side.

Even now, Illingworth was only appointed as captain for one game, the next match, at Edgbaston. It was rumoured that the selectors wanted to pick the captain for Australia during or after the Edgbaston game, so they were at best (from Illingworth's point of view) undecided and, at worst, still looking to give Cowdrey two games back in charge that summer, but feeling unable to do so because of Illingworth's recent performances.

Illingworth says that he was reasonably confident of getting the job, even before the start of the 1970 season.[70] So, from the sound of his autobiography, was Cowdrey, who says that for him the captaincy remained a daily issue in the lead up to Edgbaston. He says that it had been automatic to confirm Illingworth as captain for Trent Bridge while 'I was brought into the side', as if implying that the selectors had not thought it right to give him the captaincy for his first game back. He also says that Alec Bedser had telephoned him and explained the selectors had not thought it fair to consider him for the match at Lord's as he first had to prove his match fitness after his long layoff.

Interestingly, bad feeling from the 'gentlemen versus players' divide raises its head here once again. There was not a single player in the side apart from Cowdrey himself who would have qualified as an amateur under the old system, and Illingworth says candidly: 'The thing about Cowdrey was that the pros didn't trust him. He was a funny bloke. He'd promise you the moon and then nothing would happen.'

In the event, the captaincy issue fizzled out as something of a damp squib, the selectors choosing Illingworth even before the Edgbaston match finished, ironically while Cowdrey was actually batting in the middle.

---

[70] *Yorkshire and Back* op. cit.

Perhaps prophetically, Cowdrey made a duck when England batted first. It was that man again, Sobers, who did much of the damage, but Mike Procter also came to the party with 5-46. Only a steady century by D'Oliveira and a 50 from Tony Greig enabled England to reach 294 all out. When the Rest of the World batted, it was a different story, with Sobers yet again to the fore, this time in a fifth-wicket partnership of 175 with Clive Lloyd, who scored 101. The Rest declared, nine wickets down, at 563.

England batted better in their second innings, Cowdrey contributing a measured 71 before being caught behind off Peter Pollock. By the time he came off the field, his fate had already been sealed. For the record, England were bowled out for 409 after good contributions from D'Oliveira, Illingworth and Knott, leaving their opponents 141 to win. This they duly accomplished, though not without losing five wickets to Underwood and Illingworth, who found the sort of turn and bounce that none of the Rest's bowlers had except, yes, you've guessed it, Sobers, who had switched from seam to spin with predictably successful results, taking 4-89.

While Illingworth was still unbuckling his pads after yet another stout captain's innings, Alec Bedser told him that the selectors would like him to captain the side in Australia, but with Cowdrey as vice-captain. Tired and distracted, Illingworth promptly agreed.

It is clear that Cowdrey was both deeply disappointed and deeply hurt by the decision. He had set the leadership of England on this particular tour as his goal for the pinnacle of his career, the culmination of his Five Tours Plan. Finally and irrefutably, the dream was over. By the time Illingworth's reign came to an end, whenever that might be, he would now almost certainly be too old to be considered. The baton would pass instead to a younger man: perhaps Boycott, who was rapidly assuming the mantle of the senior professional in the side, though he had not yet had any captaincy experience, or maybe one of the coming men such as Fletcher (who was clearly being groomed by Brian 'Tonker' Taylor to succeed him as captain of Essex) or Greig (who was already being talked of as a future captain of Sussex).

It is easy to see the pain in Cowdrey's autobiography if one is prepared to read between the lines. One of the very few photographs to be included is an innocuous one of Cowdrey and Illingworth standing next to each other at catching practice; innocuous, that is, until you read the caption and discover that it was taken at Edgbaston 'on the day Ray Illingworth was chosen to lead MCC to Australia in 1970' (there are none at all from the Australian tour itself, which most who went on it would look back on as the supreme highlight of their career). Elsewhere he confesses mournfully that 'there were moments in that summer of 1970 when life would have been infinitely preferable on the moon'.

Most tellingly of all, he devotes just *half a page* (out of 244) to the six Test matches of the historic Australian tour; thereafter the book becomes mostly a mistily nostalgic account of his career with Kent. It reads as if written by a Byzantine emperor who has chosen to relinquish the purple, and live out his days as a benevolent provincial governor, abandoning war and statesmanship in favour of drainage and irrigation schemes.

The selectors had announced their decision to the press, and had not anticipated Cowdrey proving uncooperative. They were accordingly nonplussed when he asked for time to reflect on his response. When days stretched into weeks, they grew increasingly desperate for an answer, persuading Illingworth to write a personal letter pressing Cowdrey to accept. Illingworth did so, as follows:

> I agreed and wrote the letter, but with the proviso that the selectors retained a copy of it. So obviously I had reservations and misgivings about the appointment, and clearly Colin had too when he waited yet another week before accepting. Having taken so long to decide, I think his misgivings were such that he should have said 'no'. Quite obviously he didn't like the idea of serving under me, and it might have been better for both of us if he had declined to do so.
>
> However, with his acceptance … it is quite possible that the whole course of cricket history was changed. If Cowdrey had declined the job, or if the selectors had consulted me … I would have gone for Geoff Boycott. To my mind he was the best man technically for the job …

The implications of what might have resulted are immense ... if he had done a good job, he might well have been the automatic successor to me ...

But Cowdrey accepted, and the outcome was a highly unsatisfactory relationship between captain and vice-captain, during what turned out to be a difficult and controversy-riddled tour.[71]

Cowdrey by contrast deals with this period of delay in a few lines, suggesting unconvincingly that his main concern was whether he was too old for the job, but that 'eventually I fell in with their wishes'.[72]

The final words of Illingworth's account will whet the reader's appetite to know all about the 'difficult and controversy-riddled tour' in question, but first, the finale of the series that never was.

Having lost at Edgbaston, the England selectors started to experiment with new players, particularly bowlers, with the coming Ashes series obviously very much in mind.

The fourth match at Headingley saw two local boys introduced: the quick bowler Chris Old, and the left-arm spinner Don Wilson. Old, whose brother played rugby for England, was one of those frustrating players who, it is felt, never quite fulfilled his potential, either as a bowler, for he seemed rarely to be free from some niggling injury or other, or as an all-rounder; a lusty striker of boundaries in Sunday League matches, he would average less than 15 in Tests.

Wilson was never to establish himself at international level, but his selection was significant. Since that magic summer evening at the Oval back in 1968, Derek Underwood had been building himself a huge reputation as a potential match-winner on a helpful surface, hence his nickname 'Deadly'. The key words here are 'on a helpful surface'. Illingworth, while acknowledging this, felt him to be much less effective on a good pitch. Thus began the period when Underwood's place in the side was no longer assured, and England began their flirtation

---

[71] *Yorkshire and Back* op. cit.
[72] *M.C.C.* op. cit.

with other left-arm spinners, such as Don Wilson and, later, Norman 'Granny' Gifford.

In retrospect, the figures were to prove Illingworth wrong. Across all playing conditions Underwood was demonstrably a more successful bowler than any of his rivals.[73] Yet Illingworth did not have the benefit of modern-day hindsight, and his belief was honestly held. It is possible that he underestimated Underwood's virtues as a parsimonious stock bowler on good wickets. It is highly probable that he also underestimated the psychological sway that he exercised over Australian batsmen in particular; they were always happy to hear on the eve of a Test that Underwood would not be playing, and it is generally regarded as a good thing to do what the enemy don't want you to do, rather than vice versa.

England lost the match at Headingley, which featured yet another brilliant bowling display from the medium pacer Eddie Barlow (7-64 in England's first innings), and yet another century from Sobers when the Rest of the World batted, plus a 50 in their second innings for good measure. It may have been thought by some to be a tragedy for cricket when South Africa's tour was cancelled, but few who saw any of these phantom Tests will ever forget them. Never before or since has such a widespread display of talent been compressed into one side. Nor can any series ever have been played in such resolute and cheerful good spirit. It was almost as if one had been granted a brief glimpse of some cricketing nirvana to which the game can normally only vainly aspire. Looking back, it has almost the quality of one of those legendary Edwardian summers which preceded the First World War, an era of long balmy evenings, croquet on the lawn, brilliant intellectual conversation, and dazzling creative energy, all of which would be swept viciously aside by the violence and brutality that was to follow.

Neither Old nor Wilson made any pressing case at Headingley for a trip to Australia that winter; they took only three wickets between them in the entire match, England's most successful bowlers being Snow, Greig and

---

[73] There is lengthy statistical analysis in *Beating the Bat* op. cit., compiled by no less an authority than Bill Frindall.

Illingworth. Yet both were retained for the final match at the Oval. Alongside them, there was a recall for Dennis Amiss, and a first call-up for Peter Lever of Lancashire, who had been impressing all summer on the county circuit, and many thought unlucky not to have been chosen already, perhaps ahead of his teammate Shuttleworth.

England batted solidly all the way down the order in the first innings, eventually bowled out for 294. The only batsman to miss out was Brian Luckhurst, who was bowled by Procter before a run had been scored. Procter would in fact inflict a pair on him in this game, but most felt that his place in Australia was probably already secure.

The Rest's first innings quickly turned into an exhibition match as Pollock and Sobers came together at 96-4 and, disdaining defence, carried the fight to the English bowlers. As the two batsmen competed against each other, shot for shot, Mushtaq Mohammad remembers someone on the balcony – somebody who was himself one of the greatest cricketers in the world – saying in awe that they would never see anything like it again. Sobers was wearing his trademark grin and calling jokes down the wicket to Pollock and bowlers alike in between hitting the ball all round the Oval. Just for once, Underwood might have been relieved not to be playing.

Once these two were out, Procter continued the entertainment with some big hitting in a quick 50, and the Rest finished on 355 all out. So quickly had they scored, that it was still only the third morning. The only consolation for England was that somehow amongst the mayhem their debutant Peter Lever had picked up seven wickets. These included knocking out Garry Sobers's off stump, though to be fair Sobers was advancing down the pitch towards him at the time, well wide of the off stump while attempting to flick him through midwicket, which may have been slightly over-adventurous even by his standards. Old by contrast was again disappointing, and would finish the match wicketless. It seemed clear that, if there was any justice in the world, Lever had leapfrogged his Roses rival in the fast-bowling stakes.

England built a competitive total of 344, of which Geoff Boycott scored nearly half himself, finishing on 157. Again, there were solid but unspectacular results down the order. Amiss added 35 to his first innings

24. Fletcher made 63, but seemed to be establishing a trend of getting a good start but failing to go on and convert it into a really big score. Sobers, perhaps trying sportingly to make a real game of it, gave Clive Lloyd a lengthy bowl, but Lloyd, as if to prove that this really was a whole side of all-rounders, refused to follow the script and took three wickets, including the vital one of Boycott.

The Rest were set 284 to win which, for this batting line-up, was never going to be enough. This time it was Rohan Kanhai's turn to dazzle with a buccaneering hundred, including several of his trademark back-foot slashes through cover point, one or two of which seemed to be played with *both* feet off the ground.

It was Sobers, appropriately, who hit the winning run, and as spectators swarmed onto the field and spontaneously formed an honour guard leading to the pavilion, Procter hung back with the England players and waved him on. He knew the crowd had only one real hero: Garry Sobers. The police were there but they weren't needed. Anyone who has ever been present when Sobers came out to bat, and felt the electric thrill of anticipation that ran around the ground, no matter how grey the day, how sparse the crowd, nor how dead the match, will understand.

He was the greatest all-rounder ever to play cricket and probably will remain so, particularly given the punishing demands of today's gruelling international schedule. This series was one of his greatest achievements. Even though he treated the games as the enjoyable exhibition matches they were intended to be, and gave others lengthy bowls in preference to himself, it was impossible to keep him out of the game for long, whether as batsman, fast bowler or spinner. As a batsman, perhaps nobody other than Bradman has ever timed the ball better. As a fast bowler, he was the one whom many very good batsmen least liked to face. As a slow bowler, he was good enough to play first for the West Indies as a specialist spinner, albeit one who would go on to score 365 not out at the age of just 21. He was above all an entertainer; when he was on the field in any capacity you could be certain that, whatever transpired, the cricket was not going to be dull.

CHAPTER 11

THE 1970–71 ASHES (PART I)

As the euphoria of this remarkable series faded, the selectors faced the problem of selecting the squad for Australia, and one familiar name was again causing problems: that of Basil D'Oliveira.

It seems clear that there was a substantial anti-D'Oliveira clique within the selectors and that, left to their own devices, they would not have picked him. He had actually been left out of the team for the Oval, and though it seemed clear that this was to allow the selectors to have a look at Dennis Amiss, it had never been publicly confirmed.

It seems fanciful to think that he may have suffered from lingering resentment at his role as the innocent agent of the selectors' largely self-inflicted embarrassment two years earlier. However, the reason that was officially advanced – that he had been a bad tourist under Cowdrey in the West Indies – seems rather thin. He *had* been a bad tourist in 1968; he acknowledged that himself. Yet he had toured Pakistan the following winter in much more trying circumstances, and had been both a good tourist and a good performer.

Perhaps there was a temptation to prefer the tall, blond Tony Greig, but the grounds for such a preference were far from overwhelming. It was clear that Greig had great natural talent, but it seemed to be a raw talent, as yet unformed. His bowling could be very effective, yet at other times could be embarrassingly wayward. His batting could be destructive, yet he lacked shot selection – the knack of when to attack and when to defend. Only in fielding skills, which were truly brilliant in any position, could he be said to be undeniably superior.

In the end, the reason that D'Oliveira was chosen in 1970 but not in 1968, was that in 1970 his captain insisted on having him in the squad, whereas in 1968 his captain did not. Illingworth told the selectors that when D'Oliveira had been left out of the team for the Oval, the captain had given his word that he would be chosen for Australia. Either Basil goes, he told them bluntly, or I don't. Faced with uncompromising Yorkshire determination plainly expressed, the selectors backed down.

Illingworth and Cowdrey had already been chosen as captain and vice-captain. The three opening batsmen effectively chose themselves: Boycott, Luckhurst and Edrich. So did the wicketkeeper, Alan Knott, while Bob Taylor was universally acknowledged to be his obvious substitute.

In the spin bowling department Underwood could not be denied a place, but Illingworth wanted, and got, Wilson too to keep his options open on good wickets.

In the fast bowling department, England ignored the likes of Brown and Arnold, and gambled on three young talents allied with the experience of Snow. A young Bob Willis was discussed but discarded, as was Chris Old. Instead, the selectors chose the Lancashire fast-medium pairing of Lever and Shuttleworth together with the undeniably quick but undeniably injury-prone Alan Ward. For 'Big Dave' Brown, it brought to an end his Test career of 26 matches. Having taken his wickets at an average of only just over 28, he was surely unfortunate never to represent England again.

That left the middle-order batting; here there were concerns, and no clear choices. With Cowdrey and D'Oliveira now pencilled in, there were two specialist middle-order places up for grabs. Fletcher and Amiss were the two men most recently in possession, but there were doubts over both.

Fletcher had done just enough against the Rest of the World to retain his place, but Amiss was felt to have done not quite enough to regain his. John 'Jackie' Hampshire of Yorkshire was his slightly surprising replacement, having been ignored by England all summer. Certainly both Phil Sharpe and Peter Parfitt must have felt they had equally strong cases for selection. In the event, England might certainly have benefited from Sharpe's slip catching, but it was not to be.

David Clark had already been announced as manager of the touring party, even before any decision had been made on the identity of the captain; this was to prove an unfortunately premature move. Of Clark's courage there could be no doubt – he had fought and been taken prisoner as a paratrooper officer at Arnhem – but his character was not to prove adequate to the demands of the coming tour. Where flexibility, pragmatism, tact and the common touch were required, he seems to have had only stubbornness, authoritarianism, and an affable hauteur to offer, particularly when he felt his authority to be challenged. Certainly in maintaining good relations with captain and players he was to fail dismally, and end the tour largely ignored by them.

Clark had been one of those amateurs brought in to captain a side in which he would not have been able to command a place as a player. In his case, a first-class career average of 15.8 for a specialist batsman tells its own story. That the county in question was Kent will perhaps go a long way towards explaining why his relationship with Illingworth, who would later describe him as 'amiable but somewhat ineffectual',[74] was to break down so quickly and completely.

For if Denness was Cowdrey's protégé at Kent, Cowdrey had been Clark's. Clark had first selected him for Kent, and was the man who had awarded him his county cap. It is clear from the warm language in Cowdrey's autobiography that he had a very deep and genuine regard for Clark, and is anxious to show him in the best possible light, even trying to gloss over his limitations as a player. Clark had previously managed the MCC tour of India in the winter of 1963, a tour which Cowdrey had

---

[74] *Yorkshire and Back* op. cit.

originally been asked to captain before he broke his arm in that famous match at Lord's. Mike Smith led the team in his place, but Cowdrey did in fact fly out later as a batting replacement when illness claimed all but five of Smith's squad, leading to the celebrated episode of journalist and future TMS commentator Henry Blofeld being asked to be ready to take the field and earn his first Test cap (with characteristic Etonian modesty, he asked if he would be allowed to hold his place in the side notwithstanding Cowdrey's arrival).

Clark enjoyed an excellent relationship with both Smith and Cowdrey, all of them of course being public school gentlemen amateurs. For a tour captained by Illingworth, however, he was to prove a disastrous choice.

For one thing, he had been brought up in the era of amateur captains who were called 'sir' by the professionals, and who were accustomed to having their directions accepted without question by the 'players'. The idea of a professional captain who answered back, and bluntly at that, and who saw the manager as someone who was simply in charge of administration, must have been something that was simply beyond his ken. With the benefit of hindsight, it seems incredible that this likely outcome was not obvious to those in charge at Lord's, and that the appointment was not changed. Surely a former professional like Alec Bedser or Ken Barrington would have been a more appropriate choice.

Perhaps, however, it would have been simply unthinkable for the manager of the England cricket team to be anyone other than an officer and a gentleman (though Les Ames had played as a professional, he had served as a Squadron Leader in the RAF during the war, thus earning honorary 'gentleman' status). It was only a few years since the Duke of Norfolk had been appointed manager of an Ashes tour.[75] As a concession to informality he had asked the players (for the duration of the tour only, mind) to call him 'sir' rather than 'your Grace'.

For another thing, Clark was both a Kent man through and through, and a personal friend of Cowdrey. With the best will in the world, it is

[75] 'He was a true gentleman and a real cricket enthusiast, but he had no track record or qualifications suited to the job to which he had been appointed' – Fred Trueman, *As It Was*, Pan Books, London, 2004

impossible to imagine that he had not been rooting for Cowdrey as captain, and been almost as disappointed as Cowdrey himself when he had been denied the job. This was hardly likely to be conducive to a warm and friendly relationship with the man who had been given the post instead.

While Illingworth states the facts of what was to occur in his autobiography (Cowdrey does not, perhaps realising that his own brand of bland amiability would be unequal to the task), and leaves the reader to judge for himself, John Snow is quite explicit. He says 'the management of the tour was split', and that 'nobody wanted the parting of the ways between management and ourselves, but it was inevitable as a result of the manager's attitude'.[76]

For the social historians among cricket fans, Illingworth's Ashes tour clearly marks a very real break with the past. For the first time, an almost entirely 'professional' team ran its own affairs, at least in cricketing terms, and refused to be cowed by establishment figures. That they were able to do so is a mark not only of Illingworth's strength of character, but of his track record of success which made it all but impossible for the establishment to move him aside – at least, for a while.

For the establishment did not give up without a fight, and the ongoing tension between 'gentlemen' and 'players' would rattle on down the decades, with the appointment of former amateurs such as Lewis and Brearley, and with public schoolboys such as Mark 'Jardine' Nicholas (Bradfield) and Peter Roebuck (Millfield and Cambridge) being spoken of at different times as possible England captains. It was Marx, of course, who said that history repeats itself, first as tragedy and then as farce. A final Marxist twist to this particular plot would see Christopher Cowdrey (Tonbridge) actually appointed to the job by his godfather and father's best friend, Peter May. Cowdrey *fils* would play just six Test matches, scoring 101 runs and taking four wickets. His averages of 14 and 77 respectively 'remain a low point in the history of nepotism'.[77]

---

[76] *Cricket Rebel* op. cit.
[77] Lawrence Booth, *Cricket Lovely Cricket*, Yellow Jersey, London, 2009

If for Illingworth the tour was a stressful experience but one with a hugely successful outcome, for Colin Cowdrey it must have been a personal hell. Deserted first by the selectors, then by his batting form, and finally even by his slip-catching ability, he ended the series a sad echo of the man who had laid out his Five Tours Plan just three years earlier. Let the fast-bowling poet John Snow have the last word:

> The one sadness among the players concerned Colin Cowdrey, who never really came to terms with the trip after his hesitation in accepting the invitation to tour under Ray's leadership. Not getting the captaincy was a terrible disappointment to him. Ray and he didn't hit it off, and he didn't agree with the attitudes of the majority of us regarding the manager … so that by the end of the tour he was a self-created exile. The waste of his great ability was a big loss to the side …[78]

Those remembering Bill Lawry's tour of England in 1968 were expecting another well-matched Ashes series in 1970–71. While this seemed a reasonable assessment, it ignored the fact that the 1968 series had been ruined by the weather, and that England might reasonably have expected to win four of the five matches had rain not intervened. Since that time, Australia had of course been very badly beaten in South Africa, though there was no disgrace in that, since the claim of that side to all-time greatness has already been explored.

For Australia, the hugely talented Rodney Marsh had superseded Barry Jarman and Brian Taber, the first of an almost unbroken sequence of great Australian wicketkeeper–batsmen which would subsequently include the likes of Ian Healy and Adam Gilchrist. Their batting line-up from 1968 was largely intact. Bob Cowper was gone, and his occasional but effective offspin would be missed, but replacing him at the top of the order was the highly rated Keith Stackpole, who would become a major figure in the series, sadly partly as the focus of poor umpiring decisions.

---

[78] *Cricket Rebel* op. cit.

A young legspinner, Terry Jenner, had emerged as a competitor to the mystery man Johnnie Gleeson, and with the likes of Ashley Mallett also available, the spin bowling department seemed to be in capable hands.

Only with respect to fast bowling did the cupboard seem rather bare. Neil Hawke had played his last Test in 1968. Alan Connolly had played as an overseas player for Middlesex but without achieving any great success. Dave Renneberg, who was also on the 1968 tour, had dropped out of the reckoning. Laurie Mayne had been in and out of the side without ever really establishing himself. A young unknown called Bob Massie played against England in their Western Australia game, and finished wicketless. There was, therefore, a very real question mark over who would open the bowling alongside that evergreen stalwart, Graham 'Garth' McKenzie, and, with Eric Freeman not providing the answer to Australia's prayers as an all-rounder, there was even talk of the military-medium pace of Doug Walters being used as first change.

When England were badly beaten by Victoria, the English media lined up alongside their Australian counterparts to dismiss England's performance as pathetic. In fact, such criticism was largely unjustified. England got caught on a green, rain-affected wicket in their first innings, but recovered to score 341 in the second. Most of the damage was done by a strange young fast bowler called Alan Thomson, known as 'Froggy' to his teammates, as he bowled off the wrong foot.

Illingworth remained unruffled. He had a strategy for the series. He was confident that Boycott, Edrich and Luckhurst could make enough runs at the top of the order for England usually to have runs in the bank when they came to bowl, and he intended to use the pace of Ward and the hostility of Snow as the cutting edge of the English attack, using the likes of D'Oliveira and Underwood to create pressure by containment when the wickets were not coming. Incidentally, an experimental lbw law was in force which made it impossible to be out to a ball pitching outside the off stump, even if the batsman was struck in line, so Illingworth was not expecting much success against right-handers from his own offspin. Hence his preference for bowlers who could make the ball leave the right-hander, such as Underwood (with turn), and D'Oliveira (with swing).[79] In the event, England were to win not a single lbw decision *in the whole series*, which surely raises questions about the quality of the umpiring, of which more in due course.

Knowing that England's best chance of wickets would lie with their faster bowlers, Illingworth had already decided that it was important to come away from the first two matches undefeated. Brisbane and Perth were unlikely to prove friendly pitches to quick bowlers (both wickets have obviously changed somewhat over the years), so he was happy to take a draw in each case. He was confident that if England could be level after the first two matches, they would go on to win the series on surfaces such as Sydney and Melbourne.

He had also worked out his team for the first two matches and broke the bad news early to the likes of Hampshire and Wilson. Then disaster struck. Alan Ward, an integral part of Illingworth's plans, was injured even before the first Test, and would play no further part in the series. The gamble of picking someone who was fast but frail had not paid off. Nothing daunted, England rolled the dice again, calling for the uncapped Bob Willis to fly out as a replacement, rather than the experienced David Brown.

In the meantime, one of the Lancashire pair of Lever and Shuttleworth would have to be chosen to replace Ward for the first Test. Shuttleworth got the nod, though Lever was surely unlucky to be overlooked after his fine performance at the Oval.

England packed their side with batting, playing only three specialist bowlers in Snow, Underwood and Shuttleworth. Australia chose Terry Jenner and John Gleeson as a legspinning duo, and called up the inelegant but in-form Froggy Thomson to open the bowling with McKenzie. Given the later downgrading of the series that never was, this match would retrospectively mark the official debuts of no less than five players: Shuttleworth and Luckhurst for England; Thomson, Marsh and Jenner for Australia.

Bill Lawry won the toss and chose to bat. Almost at once, he was on his way back to the pavilion, attempting to hook John Snow, but getting a thin top

---

[79] *Yorkshire and Back* op. cit.

edge to Alan Knott: a rare mistake from the veteran opener,[80] and England saw a chink of light. Then came a crucial moment, the first of a multitude of bad umpiring decisions which were to mire the series in controversy.

As a result of some smart work in the field by Geoff Boycott, who had characteristically by hours of dedicated practice turned himself from an ordinary fielder into a very good one, and some quick thinking by Derek Underwood, who ran to the unattended bowler's stumps to take the return, Keith Stackpole was clearly run out. In fact an Australian newspaper was to feature a photo the next morning which showed his bat both in the air and well short of the crease even *after* Underwood had whipped off the bails. Umpire Lou Rowan, who was destined to become a major figure in the series for all the wrong reasons, gave Stackpole not out.

In the days before TV replays, umpires were required to make snap decisions based on their perceptions at the time, so it is difficult to be too severe on any umpire who makes an honest guess, but gets it wrong in the heat of the moment. However, it must be stated that this was a particularly obvious mistake, with many players on the field quite openly showing their disbelief at the time, and the first of a number of miraculous reprieves which Keith Stackpole was to experience during the series.

At the time, Stackpole had scored 18. He would go on to score 207, so the mistake certainly cost England dearly. At close of play, Australia were 308-2 and looking ominously well set, with Stackpole on 175 and Doug Walters 55.

In the morning, Stackpole went to his double century before being caught behind off Snow, and Walters to his century before being bowled by Underwood. However, these two bowling in tandem now sparked an amazing collapse during which Australia lost their last seven wickets for just fifteen runs, to finish all out for 433. England, who had been steeling themselves for the possibility of chasing 350 just to save the follow-on, could thank principally Snow, who took 6-114 and dismissed the last three batsmen without a single run being scored.

---

[80] Apparently at one time, a bottle-opener and a tin-opener were known universally as a 'Bill' in Australian homes.

Boycott and Luckhurst took England safely to 92 before Boycott was caught behind, getting an edge to Gleeson. To the surprise of the crowd, Alan Knott then emerged from the pavilion; perhaps Illingworth had taken note of the fact that Knott had made many big scores going in occasionally first wicket down for Kent. Whatever the reason, the move was to pay off.

England progressed steadily but slowly the next day. Luckhurst was run out for 74 with the score on 136, but the rest of the English batsmen sold their wickets dearly. With long seventies by Luckhurst, Knott and Edrich, and a Boycott-like 57 in nearly three and a half hours by D'Oliveira, England were still batting at the end of the third day at 365-6.

After the rest day, England picked up where they had left off, and batted long into the fourth day, putting themselves comfortably beyond defeat. Though Illingworth went cheaply for once, Snow stepped into the breach, batting for well over two hours to put on 78 for the eight wicket with D'Oliveira. They were finally bowled out late on the fourth day for 464, a first innings lead of 31.

With so little time left in the match, it looked like the only chance for a positive result would be for England to take a few quick wickets, which they did manage, Shuttleworth having Stackpole caught behind for 8, and Knott smartly stumping Chappell off Illingworth for 10. Australia finished the day on 56-2, and when Snow had Walters caught by Luckhurst early the next morning, the danger lights started flashing for Australia. However, long defensive knocks by Redpath, who would enjoy a good series, and Sheahan, coupled with a five and a half hour stay at the crease by Lawry, saw Australia to safety. The fact that three of the English bowlers conceded less than a run an over (and that Australia was using eight-ball overs at the time) tells its own story. The cricket was initially gripping but dour, but as the day progressed became merely dour. A moment of light relief was provided by Keith Fletcher who, brought on with Cowdrey as a picnic bowler once the game was dead, succeeded in dismissing Lawry with his very occasional legspin when the Australian captain, tiring of his long vigil, hit him straight to John Snow, who held the catch.

England could derive considerable comfort from the draw. They had fought back to achieve a first-innings lead, after Australia had been threatening at the end of the first day to run away with the game. They had put Australia under pressure in the second innings and, after Walters was out, might only have been one breakthrough away from a win. Only in the form of their two specialist middle-order batsmen, Cowdrey and Fletcher, might there be grounds for slight concern.

CHAPTER 12

THE 1970–71 ASHES (PART II)

When the sides reconvened at Perth two weeks later, Australia made a small but significant change. They decided to copy England's tactic of playing only three specialist bowlers, dropping Jenner to hand a first call-up to the exciting Greg Chappell, younger brother of Ian, who was already acquiring the Italianate nickname 'Chappelli', as in 'Chappell (I)' as opposed to 'Chappell (G)'.

England continued their approach of batting long and playing only three specialist bowlers, except in Perth, where Illingworth did not anticipate the wicket taking turn. There, like Australia, England omitted a spinner, Underwood, replacing him with another quick bowler, Peter 'Plank' Lever.

England batted first, but before their innings could even begin, another incident took place involving umpire Lou Rowan. Normally the groundsman (called a curator in Australia) approaches the batting captain and asks him if he would like a roller to be used before play and, if so, which one. Here this did not happen, so a slightly irritated England captain went in search of him. Once located, the curator proved unhelpful, claiming that no roller was allowed before play. Illingworth then headed off in search of the umpires, only to hear Rowan confirm the curator's view. Illingworth knew he was right, and showed Rowan the rules at lunchtime to prove his point, but it was by then too late to do anything about it.[81]

Such basic ignorance of the rules seems startling, even decades after the event, and does throw into question whether Lou Rowan should ever have been standing as a Test umpire in the first place. For the record, it should be pointed out that his decisions during this series were routinely attacked by the *Australian* press, and that most of the times he got himself into a confrontational situation his fellow umpires declined to support him. Interestingly, despite saying at the end of the series that because of his great love and respect for the game he would not be drawn into commenting on his controversial role in it, he did, in John Snow's words, 'rush into print in the most inventive way'[82] by writing a book about it shortly afterwards.[83]

The lack of a roller clearly did England no harm, however, as Boycott and Luckhurst put on 171 for the first wicket, and Luckhurst and Edrich then another 72 for the second. With Knott again putting in an appearance as nightwatchman when Luckhurst was bowled by McKenzie shortly before the close for 131, England ended the first day at 257-2, with Edrich looking well set on 39.

In the event, neither lasted long the next morning, as Knott was caught off Thomson for 24, and Edrich unluckily run out for 47. Fletcher and Cowdrey then continued to find the going difficult, though Cowdrey showed his class and experience by grafting for two and half hours for his 40, despite being clearly out of touch. Since the pitch appeared to be offering no turn, Lawry gave his two medium pacers, Walters and Greg Chappell, a significant number of overs: they picked up respectively Fletcher (bowled) and Cowdrey (caught and bowled). With McKenzie then polishing off the tail, only a resolute 34 from Illingworth saw England achieve the adequate but hardly compelling total of 397. On this pitch, 450 seemed more like a par score and, given the excellent start given them by their openers, they really should have reached it.

---

[81] *Yorkshire and Back*, op. cit.
[82] *Cricket Rebel*, op. cit.
[83] Lou Rowan, *The Umpire's Story*, Jack Pollard, Sydney, 1972

When Australia batted, they were soon grateful for their seven specialist batsmen. Unlike England, they got off to a dreadful start as Snow dismissed Stackpole and Lawry, and Lever got Walters, to leave them reeling at 17-3. Needing just under 200 to save the follow-on, it suddenly seemed a very long way away. From then on Australia resisted stoutly, saving only Sheahan, who lived up to his reputation for being regularly involved in run-outs, to reach 440 all out on the fourth day, chiefly built around a magnificent stand of 219 for the sixth wicket between Ian Redpath, who batted over eight hours for 171, and Greg Chappell, who scored a century on debut.

When England finished the day on 137-4, only 94 ahead, Australia briefly entertained dreams of snatching victory from what had seemed a dead match, but a gritty century from Edrich, and long defensive knocks from D'Oliveira, Illingworth and Knott steadied the ship, so that England were even able to afford the luxury of a declaration, leaving Australia 245 to win or, more realistically, two and a quarter hours to survive. Snow and Lever again took three quick wickets between them, but Lawry proved characteristically obdurate, and before play ended Fletcher and Cowdrey found themselves bowling in tandem again, though this time ending wicketless.

A slightly disharmonious note was struck on the final day when umpire Rowan warned Snow for bowling bouncers. In view of what was to occur to the game of cricket over the next couple of decades it is impossible to criticise such action; indeed, it should be applauded *provided it was justified*. In this case, it wasn't, as Rowan had simply got his facts wrong.

A bouncer is a delivery which is bowled deliberately short with the intention of arriving at the batsman chest or head high. Bowling a bouncer is rightly considered a dangerous act, which is why the rules had been changed after the infamous Bodyline tour of 1932–33 to outlaw intimidatory bowling. It was accepted that a bouncer could be bowled occasionally as a surprise tactic, either to deter a profoundly front-footed batsman from simply pushing forward routinely almost before the ball had left the bowler's hand, or in the hope of surprising someone into an ill-judged hook shot, resulting in a catch from a top edge. Even so, bowling them at non-specialist batsmen, who would be less able to judge the line and length in time to duck out of the way, was understandably frowned upon. At English county grounds in the 1960s a bouncer would routinely draw boos from the crowd.

When Charlie Griffith felled Derek Underwood with one at Lord's in 1966 it prompted an outcry. At a less genteel venue it might easily have sparked a riot. Griffith was felt to be a particular offender, not least because many claimed that he 'chucked' his bouncer with a straightening elbow, a claim which the primitive photographic evidence of the day seems to support. In 1962 he had nearly killed the Indian batsman Nari Contractor with a bouncer to the head, which caused a fractured skull, profuse bleeding and blood clots on the brain. Contractor lived, but never played cricket again. For many, this incident served as an awful warning of what dreadful tragedy might hover overhead whenever a bouncer was bowled. Most realised that, in retrospect, it had been little short of miraculous that no Australian batsman had been killed during the Bodyline tour.

What Rowan got wrong, however, was that Snow was not routinely bowling bouncers. Instead, he was demonstrating his ability to make the ball kick from only just short of a length, so that the batsman, shifting onto the back foot to play the ball at about waist height, suddenly found it coming to him at chest height instead. This is what batsmen mean when they say a ball has 'got big' on them. Instinctively, most batsmen, even good ones, will lift their hands and bat with the ball, and will end up playing it at chest height, without any real control on where the ball is going to travel. It takes a truly great player of fast bowling, such as Geoff Boycott, instead to have the presence of mind to push the hands *down*, and sway out of the line of the ball, particularly when significantly less than half a second is the only decision time available. Most great fast bowlers have shared this ability. Obvious examples include Michael Holding, Joel Garner and Dennis Lillee.

To make his point, Snow deliberately bounced the last ball of his last over *very* short, so that it sailed harmlessly well over the batsman's head, and then explained to Rowan that he had only done so for educational purposes so that the umpire would recognise a bouncer when he saw one in future (though he did not use those precise words).

Again, England could draw comfort from their performance. They had got a good start in the first innings, and had dug themselves out of what could have been a very unpleasant situation in their second. Doubts remained about the middle order, though. In the second innings Fletcher and Cowdrey had scored only one run between them.

Comfort and goodwill were, however, conspicuously absent from the England camp, for it was in the period containing the Perth Test match that the relationship between the team (or most of them) and management completely broke down.

Things had never been right. Cowdrey's angst was well known, and he made little attempt to hide it. Indeed, for most of the tour he lurked on the edge of proceedings, and the rest of the squad saw little of him as he went off visiting friends and attending social engagements. For someone who prided himself as the perfect cricketing gentleman, such behaviour is hard to explain and speaks to the deep despair which must have been tormenting him privately.

For example, one of the vice-captain's main responsibilities, as a sort of cricketing platoon sergeant, was to organise net practice; as discussed earlier, John Snow had once had a run-in with Tom Graveney in just such a situation. When the tour started, however, not only did Cowdrey make no attempt to do so, but he simply failed to turn up at all on the first day, without any explanation or apology. Realising the situation, Boycott and Edrich quietly stepped in and took over this task for the rest of the tour.

Whether Cowdrey was deliberately flouting Illingworth's authority, whether he was too depressed to be around his teammates, whether he could not stand the open acknowledgement of his own subsidiary status which organising nets would entail, or whether he simply didn't care, such behaviour is impossible to condone. Illingworth had asked Cowdrey to accept the post, Cowdrey had, at length, agreed, and Illingworth was entitled to expect his loyalty and support. In the event, he got neither.

Before the game with Western Australia which preceded the Perth Test match, Snow was having a gentle workout in the nets. He had bowled the equivalent of nearly 72 six-ball overs in the Brisbane Test, and was being rested for the state game, so he saw no reason to test himself flat out. David

Clark thought differently, and brusquely ordered him to 'bowl properly'. Snow treated such a command with the contempt which he felt it merited, and ignored him.

There then followed an angry harangue from Clark in the dressing room, whereupon Snow told him he could stuff his good conduct money for the tour, and went back to the nets to try and work off his anger by bowling at Hampshire and D'Oliveira. It is not known whether they felt he was now bowling flat out and, if so, whether they thanked David Clark for it.

When this failed to do the trick, Snow, on his own admission, went AWOL for 24 hours, and went to stay with a friend who lived locally. On his return, Illingworth was sympathetic, but firm. While he appreciated his efforts at Brisbane, as the senior bowler he must consider the effects of his conduct on the likes of Lever and Shuttleworth. Conform, or fly home, he was told. Snow took the point.[84]

As they boarded the plane to carry them away from Perth to Adelaide, the England team opened the morning newspapers and were staggered to see a report of an interview with David Clark in which he attacked the attritional cricket which had been played in the first two matches, and said that he would rather see a victory for Australia than another dull draw. Illingworth already knew about it, having been fielding calls from journalists in his hotel bedroom since the early hours.

At the first opportunity, Illingworth and Snow (whose bowling Clark had implicitly criticised in the interview, with comments about too many bouncers being bowled) sat down with their manager and confronted him, but he remained unrepentant and the meeting ended inconclusively after about an hour.

It remains unclear whether Clark was simply the victim of some unguarded remarks, perhaps which he thought were off the record, or was deliberately attacking his own captain, perhaps out of vindictiveness for Illingworth having failed to discipline Snow in Perth. However, if the former had been the case, he would surely have displayed regret and

---

[84] *Cricket Rebel* op. cit.

contrition in Adelaide, rather than defiance. What makes the situation all the harder to understand is that it had been England's agreed strategy to aim to draw the first two Tests. Clark would of course have been all too well aware of this.

Illingworth says:

I started off the tour with Mr Clark with a perfectly open mind. By the end of it I was forced to tell him that I honestly believed he was working more for the Australians than for us. He was, I told him, there as the team's manager, not as an ambassador of goodwill on behalf of MCC.[85]

Snow, perhaps unsurprisingly, is even blunter:

From the moment Ray took charge, and most of the party took one step sideways to line up behind him, the tour went smoothly enough. One only has to glance at the results from Perth onwards to see the dramatic change.[86]

This statement is significant in two respects. First it makes it clear that from this time onwards, as far as the team were concerned, Illingworth was in charge and Clark became a mere administrative adjunct – hardly a state of mind which Clark would happily accept.

Second, in his opposition to it, Clark was supported by Cowdrey, hence Snow's reference to 'most of the party'. From now onwards, the party would be hopelessly split, with Illingworth supported by 14 of the players on one side, and Clark and Cowdrey on the other. In such circumstances, the split could only deepen with each successive disagreement.

Again, one has to wonder why on earth the MCC appointed an autocratic amateur, used to orders being given and obeyed, to manage a professional captain who was totally self-confident in his cricketing knowledge, blunt,

---

[85] *Yorkshire and Back* op. cit.
[86] *Cricket Rebel* op. cit.

plain-speaking and determined to get his own way on all cricketing matters. The decision was all the more questionable given that the manager was a close personal friend of the man who had been, in his view probably unfairly, passed over for the captaincy. Surely that it was a recipe for disaster must have been plain at the time? Even the mild-mannered Derek Underwood would be moved to comment meaningfully 'it must be difficult for the Test and County Cricket Board to find a captain and manager who are compatible'.[87]

That it never occurred to them reveals the extent to which the 'gentlemen versus players' attitude still held sway in establishment circles. Professional cricketers had previously travelled to the ground by public transport, and did what they were told once they were there. In this 'upstairs, downstairs' world, the staff below stairs in the professionals' changing room had been expected to know their place, and not get ideas above their station. Ted Dexter, that ultimate gentleman, used literally to phone downstairs to the professionals' dressing room at Hove when captaining Sussex to give them instructions on who was to go in next,[88] possibly while replying to dinner party invitations.

On the Duke of Norfolk's tour of Australia in 1962–63, he had invited the amateurs to dine with him (black tie, naturally) in swish restaurants and swanky hotels, while the professionals were generally left to fend for themselves. On arriving at each new destination, each amateur was given his own separate car and driver, leaving the professionals to bring the luggage in whatever transport was left. One of those amateurs was Michael Colin Cowdrey, who would later marry one of the Duke's daughters.

The difference with Illingworth's team (and it may be telling that one instinctively thinks of it as that) could not have been greater. They were all, with the single exception of Cowdrey, old style professional cricketers. They admired and respected their captain, and gave him their unswerving support, knowing that they could expect the same from him in return. They came together and bonded in a way in which no England side had

---

[87] *Beating the Bat* op. cit.
[88] *Cricket Rebel*, op. cit.

ever done before. It was a team spirit that would carry them through the rest of a difficult tour victorious. It was a team spirit which they knew they were going to need, not just for the remainder of the tour, but when they returned home. For they had effectively mutinied, and it was unlikely that the powers that be were going to take this lying down.

Even Derek Underwood, who as a Kent man must have felt an instinctive loyalty to Cowdrey, was unstinting in his praise of Illingworth:

> Illingworth looked after his players' interests. He was always willing to tackle the authorities on their behalf … and insisted on the best for his team … he was not the ideal choice of captain in the eyes of many people, particularly when it came to handling the social duties … (but) his mission was to beat the Australians, not to perform as an after dinner speaker. If (he) had a fault, it was in being too honest …[89]

In the event, their trust in their captain would not prove misplaced. He would tell Lord's in uncompromising terms that there must be no question of any good conduct money being withheld, and he would get his way. In a final act of petty revenge, all Clark could succeed in doing was having Boycott and Snow summoned to Lord's after the tour for a dressing down by Gubby Allen for showing dissent to an umpire. They listened and then left.

After Clark had been metaphorically cast adrift in an open boat, England moved on to Melbourne for the Test match which was due to start on New Year's Eve. History records that not a single ball was bowled owing to rain. This would in turn lead to another spat with management, after Clark agreed to add an extra Test match to the tour schedule without consulting the players. They, not unreasonably, asked for confirmation that they would be paid a fee for the extra match, whereupon Clark refused. This led to a players' meeting held in Illingworth's hotel room, and an ultimatum to Clark, who phoned Billy Griffith in London. Griffith agreed, but only to £50, one third of the normal match fee, which the players

---

[89] *Beating the Bat* op. cit.

already viewed as little enough, given the total gate receipts of a Test match (in those days nobody even considered the media rights).

Understandably, this left a sour taste in the mouth. These were professional cricketers who theoretically risked a career-ending injury every time they played: it seems inconceivable that Clark should not have taken this into consideration before agreeing to the revised fixture list.

So, on everybody went to Sydney, knowing that this would now be officially a seven-Test series, with a punishing schedule. There would, for example, now be only two days between the Melbourne and Adelaide Tests, one of which would be needed for travelling.

England changed their tactics and their team at Sydney, as Illingworth had always intended, playing an extra bowler and leaving out a batsman to make way for him. Both decisions involved surprises. Alongside Snow and Lever, England gambled with the uncapped and untried Bob Willis, who had not even been in the original tour party. The batsman to make way for him was Colin Cowdrey.

In cricketing terms it was a straightforward decision. D'Oliveira was needed for his bowling, which meant a clear choice had to be made between Cowdrey and Fletcher, and Fletcher had been in marginally less indifferent form. For the distraught Cowdrey, his winter misery must have plumbed new lows. With Hampshire also in the party, there was now no guarantee that he would even be able to regain his place in the side.

CHAPTER 13

THE 1970–71 ASHES (PART III)

Australia also dropped a batsman for a bowler, bringing Ashley Mallett into the side in the place of the somewhat run-out-prone Paul Sheahan, while Alan Connolly returned to the side to replace the unconventional Froggy Thomson.

England won the toss and batted: once again their top three of Boycott, Luckhurst and Edrich gave them a solid start.

However, England suffered a batting collapse, losing four wickets for just 18 runs. Only a last-wicket stand of 41 between Peter Lever and the new boy, Bob Willis, spared their blushes, and they finished on 332 all out, a respectable total, but a disappointing one in view of having at one stage been 201–2. Nevertheless, the fact that eight of the wickets had been taken by the spinners, Gleeson and Mallett, showed that already the pitch was taking some turn, so there was some speculation that this could bring Underwood's skills into prominence in the fourth innings.

Australia reshuffled their batting order for this match, promoting Ian Chappell to open the innings. The experiment was not to prove a success, since he made only 12 runs in the entire match, all of them in the first innings. His was the first wicket to fall, caught off Snow with the score at 14. Shortly afterwards Bill Lawry joined him in the dressing room, caught in the gully by Edrich off Lever, and Australia were 38-2.

Walters and Redpath steadied Australian nerves with a partnership of 99, before Illingworth had Walters picked up at bat pad by Luckhurst. Shortly afterwards Underwood held one back to Greg Chappell and gratefully pocketed the return catch. Australia were 160-4. Again, though, it was Redpath who proved the obstacle in England's path, batting steadily through to the close with Stackpole, who had come in at number six.

Australia began the third day at 189-4 with the game nicely poised. Since the new ball was due shortly, Illingworth had an interesting decision to make. Should he continue bowling himself and Underwood, or should he give his fast bowlers a quick burst of one or two overs each? In the event, he did neither, electing to open the bowling with D'Oliveira. It was to prove an inspired move. D'Oliveira served up one of the accurate, slow-medium outswingers which he seemed to be able to conjure up ball after ball in just about any conditions, and Redpath, who had proved so obdurate the day before, followed it as if hypnotised, edging to Fletcher at slip. His four-hour stay was over, and Australia were 189-5.

Underwood now took the wickets of Stackpole, Marsh and Mallett in quick succession and suddenly Australia had been bowled out for 236. This short period of play on the third morning completely changed the complexion of the game. If Redpath and Stackpole could have put on another hundred runs between them, Australia might well have been in a potentially winning position, though they would still have had to bat last on a pitch that was already showing signs of wear. As it was, England were now firmly in the driving seat, with a first-innings lead of nearly a hundred, which might well be worth double that in view of what was obviously happening to the pitch.

Geoff Boycott was now to play perhaps the greatest innings of his life. On a pitch which troubled every other batsman, he batted for nearly seven hours to score 142 not out, and with D'Oliveira and the captain both scoring solid fifties in support after England had been 48-3, Illingworth was able to declare on the fourth afternoon at 319-5, leaving Australia a notional target of 416 to win. Given that Mallett had been obtaining considerable turn, and that Underwood was being widely tipped to run through the Australians, this was always going to be an impossible target.

Figures of 7-40 might have been predicted, but not the fact that it would be Snow, rather than Underwood, who would achieve them. Spotting that there was a particularly worn patch just short of a length on the line of off stump, he simply aimed every delivery at it. With some bouncing (Graham McKenzie was hit by one of these and had to retire hurt) and some not, some deviating and some carrying straight on, the Australians were simply routed. Bill Lawry did his best to emulate Boycott, carrying his bat through the disaster to finish with 60 not out, but only one other batsman (Stackpole) got into double figures as Australia were bowled out on the fifth morning for 116. England had won decisively by just under 300 runs, and were one up in the series.

Those who played in the match would later say that it was one of England's greatest victories. The batting of Boycott, who was only dismissed once in the match, and scored 219 runs on a very difficult pitch, and the bowling of Underwood and Snow were obviously the highlights, but everyone had contributed.

The magnitude of the win established a moral ascendancy for England which they were never to surrender. Though the rest of the tour would prove a long and punishing journey, it was at Sydney on 14 January (or, more accurately, on the morning of the third day when Australia's first innings abruptly subsided) that the turning point occurred. As Illingworth's team went on to Melbourne, they would have their problems over the next couple of months, but would never look back.

All were agreed that the pitch for the Melbourne Test was green, and would help fast bowlers with both bounce and seam movement. So it was to prove, though the bald statistics of the match do not reflect this.

Australia were forced into changes in the fast bowling department. Connolly had looked innocuous at Sydney, so back came Froggy Thomson. In place of McKenzie, who was still injured, Australia gave Ross Duncan his first Test cap. He was to finish wicketless in his only Test match, though he rather spoilt his clean sheet when he batted by scoring three runs.

Stackpole was restored as an opener, and Ian Chappell, whose place in the side was now under considerable threat after a string of poor scores, was listed to bat at three.

England made only one change, and again it was a slightly surprising one: Cowdrey for Fletcher. In truth England were probably simply shuffling the pack; they knew they had problems with their middle order, and Fletcher had failed to impress at Sydney, so they probably reckoned it only fair to give Cowdrey another chance. Yet with both him and Fletcher in such poor form, it seems strange that the tour selectors did not turn to Hampshire. Perhaps Cowdrey was preferred by virtue of his slip catching ability. If so, it was to prove a fateful decision.

Bill Lawry won the toss and decided to bat. Off the last ball of the first over, Stackpole gloved Snow very obviously to Knott. Umpire Max O'Connell, standing in his first Test match, called 'over' and strolled off to square leg ready for the next over.[90] Stackpole, who had started walking off the field, found himself recalled by O'Connell, who ruled him not out, though it was unclear whether he was doing so because he felt he had to because of calling 'over', or whether he had missed the ball rebounding gently off Stackpole's glove. Either way, it was another astonishing reprieve for Stackpole.

Despite Snow and Lever both finding some help from the pitch, Lawry and Stackpole then calmly weathered the rest of the opening period, and Australia went into lunch without loss, but shortly afterwards Stackpole mis-hit a forcing shot to Lever off D'Oliveira. Again, one must credit Illingworth's captaincy. Had Stackpole perhaps mentally prepared himself to be facing Snow and Lever again after the resumption, and found D'Oliveira's different pace unsettling, just as Redpath had in Sydney?

When Stackpole's wicket went down, Australia were 64-1, having taken over two hours to graft their way there. Then, with the score on 86, Lawry was injured and had to retire. This brought Ian Chappell to the crease, badly in need of a big score and with many Australian journalists calling for his head. Nervous and jumpy, he edged John Snow into the hands of

---

[90] *Cricket Rebel* op. cit.

Cowdrey at first slip before he had scored. It was a straightforward chance, but Cowdrey dropped it.

This was a new personal low for Cowdrey. Save only for Sharpe, he was reckoned the best slip catcher in England. He retains to this day England's joint highest career catching record for a non-wicketkeeper (alongside Ian Botham). Even when his batting had failed him on the tour so far, he had at least retained a safe pair of hands. Had all the miseries hovering over his head finally conspired to interfere with the razor-sharp reflexes that had made him one of the best international slip fielders in history? He did not have to wait long to find out.

Ian Chappell had scratched his way unconvincingly to 14 when he edged D'Oliveira to slip. Again it was a regulation catch and again Cowdrey dropped it. Illingworth would later have to take Cowdrey out of the slips, which raised fresh captaincy problems. This England side was short of slip fielders. So, problem number one, which was never satisfactorily resolved, was who should replace Cowdrey. Problem number two, which likewise was never satisfactorily resolved, was where to put the vice-captain. Cowdrey was slow, overweight, and a lumbering liability anywhere but at slip.

Given that Ian Chappell went on to make 111 (the 'Nelson' score so dreaded as a jinx by superstitious cricketers) and save his place in the side, these were significant misses with an influence beyond the match itself. For, if Chappell had been out for a duck, he would surely have been dropped from the side (subject to anything that might have happened in the second innings), which, for reasons which will become clear, may well have significantly altered the timeline of subsequent events.

From a combination of bizarre umpiring and dropped catches, England's chance had gone, and they knew it. As if to rub it in, Chappell and Redpath took Australia to 260-1 at the close of the first day. Had both Stackpole and Ian Chappell been dismissed for ducks, with Lawry forced to retire hurt shortly afterwards, things could have been very different.

The next morning, however, batting seemed more difficult and they were both out to Snow in quick succession, Chappell with the score on 266 and Redpath at 269. Lawry resumed his innings and steered Australia safely beyond the 300 mark, but now it was Willis's turn to take two quick wickets: Lawry and Greg Chappell, and from 260-1 overnight Australia were 314-5.

England now ran into stubborn opposition, however, in the shape of Walters, Marsh and the debutant Kerry O'Keeffe. Walters and Marsh put on 70 for the sixth wicket, and Marsh and O'Keeffe then put on a breezy 97 for the seventh wicket at a run a minute. Marsh ran out of partners in the evening session, leaving him stranded on 92 not out, a fine effort, which saw Australia advance their total to 493. The reliable Boycott and Luckhurst saw England safely through to the close.

England started the third day without any prospect of victory, and with the saving of the follow-on as their first objective. The good news was that in Geoff Boycott they had perhaps the one batsman in the world most suited to the task in hand. The bad news was that he was out fairly early on during the morning, caught in the slips off Froggy Thomson. Bad news then got worse, when Thomson had Edrich caught behind by Marsh. England were 66-2 when Cowdrey came out to join his Kent teammate Luckhurst, and the stage was set for one of the great battling comeback innings in history.

Sadly, it was not to be. Half an hour later Cowdrey was back in the dressing room having completely mistimed a shot against Gleeson and given him a return catch, which the bowler gratefully accepted. England were 88-3 and staring disaster in the face. Cowdrey, brought back into the side to revitalise the middle order, had scored just 13.

It seemed inconceivable that England should end the day close to having saved the follow-on and having lost only one more wicket, but that is exactly what happened. Luckhurst and D'Oliveira took England through to the evening session, occupying the crease and putting on 140 for the fourth wicket. So effectively had they drawn the sting of the Australian attack that Lawry was reduced to trying his part-time bowlers in the hope of making something happen – it was one of these, Doug Walters, who finally took the wicket of Luckhurst with his military-medium pace. This had been another great innings from Luckhurst, who batted nearly six hours for his 109.

When he was out, Illingworth took over, and he and D'Oliveira were batting at the close, with England 258-4. With two days still to play, and Australia still enjoying a first-innings lead of 235, England were not out of the woods yet, but they had recovered well from the loss of early wickets and were making a fight of it.

Again, it seemed unlikely that England would go on to bat out much of the fourth day, but that is in fact what happened. Illingworth was the next to go, caught by Redpath off Gleeson for 41, but by then he had batted for nearly two hours and seen England past the possibility of being asked to follow on. D'Oliveira came to a well-deserved century before being dismissed by Thomson; like Luckhurst, he had occupied the crease for nearly six hours.

Interestingly, bearing in mind what was to follow, the England innings was notable for many bouncers bowled by Froggy Thomson, who became increasingly frustrated as the day progressed, including no less than six in one eight-ball over against Ray Illingworth. No warning was issued by the umpires.

The cricket now became grim, attritional stuff, with Australia striving for wickets and England determined to hold them at bay for a long as possible. Alan Knott batted for over two hours for his 19. Snow and Lever each held on for nearly an hour, Snow batting with uncharacteristic restraint to score just one run before being bowled by the part-time legspin of Ian Chappell. It took a run-out to get rid of Lever. Underwood then took care of another half an hour or so.

England were finally dismissed for 392. Australia now had a lead of 101, but with only a day and a half left to play. Their only hope was to score runs quickly and then declare, setting England a target but leaving themselves with time to bowl them out again.

These plans were frustrated by a very tight spell of bowling of John Snow, who conceded less than two runs an over. While runs came more freely at the other end, Australia's first 50 took an hour and a half. Immediately afterwards, Willis had Stackpole caught behind, and Snow then dismissed Lawry and Redpath in quick succession. It was left to Greg Chappell and Doug Walters finally to supply some of the acceleration which Australia needed, but by now it was the fifth morning and time was running out. Incidentally, during this period Snow was warned for intimidatory bowling by umpire O'Connell, which the England players found perverse given his earlier indulgence towards Thomson.

England were left with precisely four hours in which to score 271 to win, but both D'Oliveira and Luckhurst had been injured in the field, and the latter, who had broken a finger, would definitely be unable to bat, while the former, with a badly bruised foot, would do so only if absolutely necessary. So, with only three fit specialist batsmen, and one of them in very poor from, Illingworth declined to chase a total which would have required a scoring rate of about four runs for every six balls. Boycott and Edrich, opening instead of Luckhurst, batted for exactly four hours, scoring 161 between them. England ended the match still one up in the series, and probably grateful for the draw after their awful position early in the first innings.

Snow had looked the pick of the England bowlers, particularly in the second innings, though Willis had bowled promisingly to justify his place in the side. Of the batsmen, Luckhurst and D'Oliveira had saved England with patient centuries, though Illingworth and Knott had both made valuable contributions in this game, when time had been as important as runs. The obvious problem area remained the middle order. Fletcher and Cowdrey had scored only 169 runs between them in the four matches so far, and now to add to Illingworth's problems, Cowdrey seemed to have become a liability rather than an asset in the field.

There was little time to reflect on these matters, however, as both teams needed to travel next day to Adelaide for the second of these back-to-back Test matches. There were other pressing matters for Illingworth to consider. His fast bowlers were tired after Melbourne: should he rest one of them by bringing Shuttleworth back into the side? Luckhurst's hand injury would not have healed in so short a time: who would bat in his place?

In the event Illingworth decided not to rotate his bowlers, a decision which would perhaps have a bearing on a controversial moment which arose during the match. As for the batting, it was a problem with only one possible solution. Cowdrey had to be dropped; he surely cannot have expected any less. With Luckhurst injured, the only two remaining batsmen, Fletcher and Hampshire, both had to play. Once again, it looked as though the sad final curtain had fallen on Cowdrey's illustrious Test career. Discarded after the second match, he had been offered one last chance, and he had made a mess of it.

In place of Ross Duncan, Australia awarded a first cap to a fiery young fast bowler called Dennis Lillee. He was in action straightaway, as Illingworth won the toss and batted. Boycott and Edrich continued England's record of good starts.

Their opening partnership stretched into the third hour of the day, and was just about to edge into the fourth when Boycott was run out. Though the decision was tight, it appeared to be correct – to everyone except Boycott, that is. He flung his bat down on the ground and stared at the umpire, showing clear dissent. Illingworth later asked him to apologise to the umpire, but Boycott rather petulantly refused, so Illingworth did so on his behalf.[91]

This brought a nervous Keith Fletcher to the crease with the score on 107-1. Having got set this time, though, he showed signs of going onto to that elusive big score. He and Edrich batted through the afternoon and the evening. There were only six minutes of playing time left when Lillee finally had Edrich caught by Stackpole for 130. This brought Alan Knott to the crease in his role as nightwatchman, and England ended the day on 276-2 with Fletcher 75 not out.

Both batsmen fell early the next morning with the score on 289, Knott to Lillee and Fletcher to Froggy Thomson. England were wobbling and Australia had two new batsmen to bowl at, one of whom was fighting to make a case for a permanent place in the side, and the other of whom was still in pain from his bruised foot. D'Oliveira and Hampshire did England proud, though, putting on nearly a hundred for the fifth wicket and reducing the Australian attack to frustration in the process. Bill Lawry tried no less than seven bowlers, including Keith Stackpole, an occasional legspinner. Both batsmen were eventually dismissed by the part-time medium pace of Greg Chappell, succeeding where the specialist bowlers had failed, D'Oliveira making 47 and Hampshire 55.

---

[91] *Yorkshire and Back* op. cit.

A good stand between Illingworth and Snow saw England through to a total of 470. By the close that evening, Australia had scored 50 without loss.

Lillee had taken five wickets in the England innings, but at this early stage of his career was nothing like the finished article that would come to be reckoned one of the great all-time fast bowlers. He was very quick, coming in off a very long run which on some grounds seemed to start just in front of the sight screen, but not terribly accurate, and as yet without the late swing that would make him so dangerous. He was fortunate that in Marsh Australia possessed a wicketkeeper who was only slightly less acrobatic than Knott; remarkably Australia only conceded one bye in the match, though there were a number of wides.

The next day only Stackpole really got on top of the English bowling attack, though Lawry, Ian Chappell and Redpath defended grimly, the latter taking over an hour and a half to score just nine runs. England chipped away, though, and suddenly there was a flurry of wickets, with both Chappell brothers, Redpath and Walters all falling in quick succession. Australia were 163-6 and still looking for over a hundred runs to save the follow-on.

Marsh, Mallett and Gleeson all sold their wickets dearly, however, and it was not until nearly the end of the day that Australia were finally all out for 235, well short of the total needed to avoid the follow-on. In what was to prove a highly controversial move, Illingworth now decided to bat again.

Since this decision was roundly criticised in the press, various armchair pundits declaring that Illingworth had thrown away England's best chance of winning the match, it is worth reviewing for the record Illingworth's reasoning, which he sets out in full in his autobiography.

First, the rest day had come and gone and his fast bowlers were very tired – indeed, Snow was not so much tired as exhausted. He had lost half a stone in weight since the beginning of the previous Test. In addition, Lever was carrying a shoulder injury.

Second, while England's bowling had been tight, he felt that Australia's middle-order collapse had been due principally to the batsmen making mistakes, a view reinforced by the apparent ease with which the likes of Mallett and Gleeson had been able to hang around later on.

Third, with his fast bowlers perhaps able to operate only in short bursts, this would throw the burden of taking wickets on himself and Underwood, and there was as yet no sign of the pitch taking any significant turn. However, it might start to turn on the last day, in which case England wanted to be bowling then, not batting.

While it is impossible to say what might have been had Illingworth decided differently, it is worth recording that subsequent events seem to have vindicated his approach.

England batted again and had reached 47 without loss by the close. There were now two days left for England to try to force a result.

CHAPTER 14

A CONCLUSION TO THE
1970–71 ASHES

The next day England recorded yet another fine opening partnership before Edrich departed at 103. Fletcher, D'Oliveira and Hampshire then nobly sacrificed their wickets going for quick runs, so it was left to the captain and his Yorkshire teammate Boycott, who made a fine 119 not out, to bring England to a position from which Illingworth thought, on what was still a good pitch, he could safely declare, setting Australia a target of 469 or, more realistically, having to bat out over four sessions to save the match.

There were now mutterings in the Australian press about Lawry's captaincy, but he ignored the pressure and got his head down. He fell finally to Bob Willis with the score on 65, but with over an hour and a half already gone. Stackpole and Ian Chappell batted until the close, with Australia 104-1, and perhaps even in sight of an unprecedented victory; there had been only one instance of a side batting fourth scoring more than 400 to win a Test match (Australia at Headingley in 1948) and that was only 404.

The story of the final day was one of Stackpole and Ian Chappell. Sensibly eschewing any attempt to go for the highly improbable winning target, they chose instead to bat England out of the game with a partnership which lasted for five and a half hours. Illingworth had been right about the pitch. It did start to take turn, but only slowly and only in the last couple of hours.

Illingworth's decision not to enforce the follow-on remains controversial, but in the light of how easily the pitch played thereafter, it seems difficult to believe that the result would have been any different. The draw meant that England went into the last Test – the extra one which had been arranged for Sydney – still one up, which also meant that Australia could still retain the Ashes with a victory to square the series.

England could draw a lot of comfort from the Adelaide Test. Fine centuries from Boycott and Edrich had cemented two more excellent opening partnerships. Their middle-order engine room had fired properly for once, though significantly without Cowdrey. Their bowlers had stuck to their task magnificently on an unhelpful pitch. Away from the action, there was good news about Luckhurst's finger – he might be able to play in Sydney. Two things were to occur in the next few days, however, which were to change things considerably for both teams.

First Boycott, batting in a one day match, had his arm broken by a delivery from a newly regenerated Graham McKenzie, who was staking a claim for recall to the Test side. England would therefore be without their best batsman. Second, it was announced that just as England would be without their most obdurate opener, so too would Australia. Bill Lawry was ruthlessly sacked as captain and, as is the Australian tradition, dropped from the side in consequence. Ian Chappell took over the captaincy, while the untried Ken Eastwood of Victoria was called up to open the innings with Stackpole. Like the hapless Ross Duncan, Eastwood would also prove to be a one cap wonder, scoring just five runs in two innings, though he did take the surprise wicket of Keith Fletcher when given a chance to display his chinamen.

Froggy Thomson was discarded, but McKenzie was felt by the selectors not yet to be fully fit enough for the rigours of a five-day Test match, so they plumped instead for the left-armer Tony Dell. He would go one better than Duncan and Eastwood, actually winning a second cap.

Though nobody could have known it at the time, this was a turning point in the fortunes of Australian fast bowlers. McKenzie, somewhat harshly discarded after 60 Tests and 246 wickets at the relatively early age of 29, would never play for Australia again. Nor would Froggy Thomson, though another bowler with the same surname would shortly emerge to form, with Dennis Lillee, the most feared bowling attack in the world.

Australia again shuffled their spin bowling, this time playing both Jenner and O'Keeffe at the expense of Gleeson. Thus they fielded what must surely have been their least experienced attack ever. Their four specialist bowlers shared just three caps between them.

Chappell performed his first duty for Australia by winning the toss and putting England into bat. It had been raining heavily for several days prior to the match, and the pitch, which had spent all that time under cover, was looking ominously green. Illingworth had also been planning to insert the opposition had he won the toss.[92]

The first half hour was all defence for England, with only five runs on the board, and Luckhurst, looking unusually hesitant, yet to score. Chappell gave Walters a try and the change of pace worked, with Luckhurst giving a catch to Redpath. It was a rare failure for Luckhurst in the series, but a vital breakthrough for Australia with no Boycott in the batting line-up.

Edrich and Fletcher grafted grimly into the third hour of the day, when suddenly three wickets fell in the space of twelve minutes: Edrich, Fletcher and D'Oliveira.

Now it was the Yorkshire pair of Illingworth and Hampshire who tried to dig in to defy Australia, but batting was still very difficult and Lillee made his first contribution to the proceedings by having Hampshire caught behind by Marsh to reduce England to 98-5. Knott replaced Hampshire, and captain and wicketkeeper now put on 47 vital runs in what was already looking likely to be a low-scoring contest. When Knott fell to O'Keeffe, however, the remaining wickets fell steadily and England were all out for 184, Illingworth top-scoring with 42. Interestingly, on

---

[92] *Yorkshire and Back* op. cit.

what was generally agreed to be a pitch helping seam bowling, Lillee and Dell took only three wickets between them, while the two legspinners took three each.

Australia were left with an awkward half hour or so to survive until the close, and the debutant Eastwood, and the more experienced Stackpole, failed to do so, falling to Lever and Snow respectively. With Australia 13-2 at the end of the day, Marsh having come in as a nightwatchman, England knew that they were back in the game, albeit still struggling to catch up.

The second day of the match was to prove a highly controversial one. Marsh fell to Lever and Ian Chappell to Willis, to leave Australia 64-4, but Walters and Redpath dropped anchor to form what was beginning to look like a match-winning partnership, until Derek Underwood got them both out, Walters to a brilliant stumping by Knott. Pegged back to 162-6, Australia were once again struggling. Greg Chappell had embarked on what would become a three-hour stay at the crease but one end was now open, and it needed the Australian bowlers to sell their wickets dearly, staying with the younger Chappell brother for as long as they could. O'Keeffe lasted for over half an hour as Australia moved slowly but steadily towards a total of 200, which was beginning to look like a very good score on this pitch.

Then the controversy began. Snow bowled a delivery to Jenner which was not a bouncer but, as happened with Snow from time to time, lifted sharply from just short of a length. Jenner, not being a specialist batsman, misjudged the length and, thinking that it was a bouncer, ducked. Had he been correct in his assumption, the ball would have sailed harmlessly overhead. However, as he was not, he simply ducked into it; the ball never got above chest height, but Jenner's head was now where his chest would have been, and he was struck a sickening blow. Unable to continue, he was helped from the field.

Umpire Rowan now made his final fateful contribution to the series. Before Snow could continue bowling to the new batsman, Lillee, Rowan gave him an official warning for intimidatory bowling.

Both Snow and Illingworth were naturally flabbergasted. Illingworth pointed out first that the delivery had not been a bouncer and second that, even if it had been, a warning could only be issued for 'persistent' bowling of bouncers, not a single one. As he made this latter point he raised a single finger in front of Rowan's face. This was misinterpreted in some quarters as having wagged his finger in admonition, or even having made an obscene gesture. Rowan attempted to enlist the moral support of the other umpire, Tom Brooks, who refused to get involved, a clear sign that he thought Rowan was wrong.

At the end of the over, Snow went down to his normal fielding position of fine leg; at this point bottles and cans started being thrown at him. Illingworth called him and the other England players back to the middle of the pitch, where they all sat down and waited for the police to restore order. After this had apparently been done, and the cans and bottles cleared away, the fielders went back to their positions, at which point not only did Snow once again become the target of missiles from the crowd, but one spectator, shouting menacingly, reached over the fence and made a grab at him as Snow tore himself free.

Illingworth now led the entire England team off the field. Incredibly, given that Cowdrey had twice quite reasonably done this in recent memory when he felt that the safety of the players was threatened, this action was roundly criticised in certain quarters, not least by David Clark, who angrily ordered Illingworth back onto the field. Illingworth robustly refused. Snow then intervened and told Clark forcibly what he thought of him – so forcefully in fact that Clark felt it necessary to beat a hasty retreat. Again, the fact that Clark, a man with very limited cricketing experience at the highest level, should feel entitled to countermand Illingworth's decisions, points to the fact that many gentlemen amateurs had failed to realise that the world had moved on.

Rowan came into the dressing room and threatened to declare the game forfeit. Illingworth was adamant that he would not return until there was no further disorder. Eventually the game did restart, and Australia finished the day on 235-7.[93] Illingworth makes two points, both of which deserve to

---

[93] This section narrative is based on Illingworth's account, which is consistent with those of Snow and Underwood, each of whom says independently that they thought Illingworth entirely justified to take the team off the field. See *Yorkshire and Back*, *Cricket Rebel* and *Beating the Bat*, all op. cit.

be noted before this sorry tale is consigned to history. First, no less than four former Australian captains in the press box approved his actions in their copy the next day. Second, he says how proud he is of England *as a team* (italics added) for having stood firm during this episode. It is clear that he includes standing firm against the England management in this statement, yet another example of how deep and complete the breach between Clark and Cowdrey on the one hand, and the professionals on the other, had become.

Bob Willis struck twice the next morning to dismiss Greg Chappell and Dennis Lillee. Jenner returned bravely to resume his innings and scored 30 valuable runs before being bowled by Lever. Australia had a lead of 80 on the first innings, a margin which looked like being decisive on this surface. For England to have any sort of total to bowl at in the fourth innings, they were going to need to score at least 300, which looked extremely unlikely, particularly in the absence of Boycott.

Edrich and Luckhurst, though, had resumed business as usual, and once again, as so frequently during this series, England got off to a good start. The opening pair batted for two hours, accumulating runs steadily, until Luckhurst was out to O'Keeffe with the score on 94. Fletcher then hung around for an hour without ever looking convincing, before becoming the one and only Test victim of the left-arm wrist spin of Ken Eastwood. The fact that he was one of seven bowlers employed shows imaginative captaincy on Chappell's part, but also that the English batsmen, particularly Edrich, had blunted Australia's inexperienced pace attack. However, O'Keeffe claimed Edrich and Hampshire, leaving England tottering at 165-4, only 85 runs ahead. All of the wickets had fallen to wrist spin.

Again D'Oliveira proved resolute, finding partners in both Illingworth and Knott. Snow batted for an hour and a half, and after Knott was dismissed at 276-7 put on more useful runs with Lever. England finally reached the unlikely heights of 302. It was still the fourth day, so time was not an issue, and Australia needed just 223 to win the game and retain the Ashes.

It did not look enough, but when Snow bowled Eastwood before a run had been scored, England's hopes rose. Two overs later Stackpole hooked a short ball from Lever down to fine leg. Snow made a heroic effort to get to the ball, but missed it, crashed into the fence, and broke a finger on his right hand. His injury was sufficiently serious to require an operation and, under the combined effects of the painkillers, the anaesthetic, and his accumulated physical and mental tiredness, he did not come round until late that evening. Thinking that he had been 'out' for only a short time, and sill somewhat woozy, he made a nuisance of himself by pestering the nurses to tell him the current score.[94]

When Stackpole had scored 13, he edged Lever to Knott. All the England players behind the wicket heard the snick, and bowler and wicketkeeper saw a clear deviation. Knott, who never appealed unless he thought the batsman was out, was dumbfounded when umpire Rowan gave Stackpole not out. He had now reprieved Stackpole no fewer than four times during the series.

This was an important let-off, because wickets were falling steadily at the other end. Both Illingworth and Underwood were finding turn from the pitch. Lever had Ian Chappell caught behind, and then Redpath edged Illingworth's arm ball to Hampshire at slip. However, Redpath and Stackpole had put on nearly 50 for the third wicket and, at 71-3, Australia only needed another 152 for victory. Walters never settled, though, and soon gave a catch to D'Oliveira off Willis. Then came the decisive moment when Illingworth finally dismissed Stackpole – clean bowled so that not even the umpire could save him.

Australia were now 96-5: 223 was looking further and further away. At 150-7 Illingworth brought D'Oliveira back into the attack. He quickly picked up the wickets of O'Keeffe and Lillee, Underwood dismissed Jenner, and it was all over. England had won an improbable victory without their best batsman and, for half the match, their best bowler (though the thought of what might have been had Lawry and McKenzie been playing for Australia is a tantalising one). They had clinched the series 2–0 and regained the Ashes.

For Illingworth, who was chaired from the field by his players, it was a

---

[94] *Cricket Rebel* op. cit.

personal triumph. As if it were not enough of an achievement in itself (no England captain had regained the Ashes in Australia for nearly 40 years), he had done so in the face of a stormy relationship with his tour manager, the total breakdown of his relationship with his vice-captain, some abject umpiring, and controversy aplenty on the field.

For Cowdrey, the pain must have been almost unbearable. Not only had he been forced to sit in the background and watch his own personal objective of the Five Tour Plan achieved by the man whom he must surely have felt had stolen the captaincy from him; he must also have realised that his own career as an England player was all but over. Three years previously he had flown back from the West Indies with his friend Jim Parks, knowing in his heart of hearts that, with the emergence of Alan Knott, Parks would never play for England again. This time the object of the embarrassed glances on the plane would be Cowdrey himself.

Not quite yet, though, for Cowdrey would be granted a final consolation match when the party moved on to New Zealand, at that time a traditional postscript to a tour of Australia.

In the first match, at Christchurch, England fielded what was essentially a second eleven, giving chances to all the players who had featured only marginally in the tour to date. Knott sportingly stood down to give Bob Taylor a Test cap, and Shuttleworth and Wilson also came into the side. Pointedly, though, there was no room in the side for Cowdrey. He had to sit in the pavilion and watch Hampshire, his main rival now, score 40 and 51 not out (Fletcher failed twice).

England won easily and moved on to the second and final Test in Auckland. Cowdrey did play, in place of Fletcher, and found his touch returning. He scored a slow 54 in the first innings as England struggled initially, Bob Cunis taking six wickets, and 45 batting down the order in the second. The game was drawn – the highlight for England was Alan Knott very nearly scoring two centuries in the match, falling four short in the second innings. This time it was Hampshire's turn to fail twice.

The winter tour had confirmed Illingworth's view that in Boycott, Edrich and Luckhurst, England had three batsmen who could be relied upon to get an innings off to a good start. It had also confirmed the class of Alan Knott and John Snow. Lever and Willis had shown promise in support of Snow, and Underwood had been his usual steady self. Only over the middle-order batting hovered unanswered questions. Cowdrey, Fletcher and Hampshire had all been tried, but found wanting. They had not scored a century between them in the Australian Tests, and only two fifties (one each for Fletcher and Hampshire at Adelaide). Comfortably outscored by D'Oliveira, Illingworth and Knott, all of whom were playing as all-rounders, it had been a wretched tour for all three of them. For Cowdrey, of course, there was also the question of his catching at slip which had begun to look distinctly fallible.

The England players must have returned home with mixed emotions. On the one hand was the understandable jubilation at having regained the Ashes in Australia for the first time since 1932–3. On the other hand, they must have felt a considerable amount of trepidation as the retribution that was likely to be visited upon them for their mid-tour mutiny against the powers that be. To their relief, they found that, apart from the individual bollockings for which Boycott and Snow were summoned as a result of their respective run-ins with umpires, there were no disciplinary consequences at all. Even their end of tour good conduct payments were duly made.

This was almost certainly due partly to the unparalleled success enjoyed by team and captain alike. For Lord's to sack Illingworth as captain after regaining the Ashes would have been as unthinkable as Alf Ramsey sacking Bobby Moore as captain after England had won the World Cup in 1966. In part, though, the players were rewarded for the remarkable solidarity which they all, other than Cowdrey, had displayed. Various participants refer repeatedly both to the way in which they bonded together as a team, and the remarkable degree of respect in which they, professionals all, held Ray Illingworth, a man whom they felt would do anything for his players, even putting his own career at risk if necessary.

The Australians would have an early opportunity to regain the Ashes themselves, since they were scheduled to tour England in 1972. In a sense, this was even sooner in sporting terms, since England had no winter tour scheduled, and thus had only six Test matches, three each against Pakistan and India, in which to find the answer to their middle-order batting problems.

It is worth pointing out that English cricket was at this time going through a period in which virtually no specialist middle-order batsmen were challenging for a place in the side. Though the top three places in the batting line-up were already occupied by openers, it would have been possible to pick four or five, since there was no shortage of other suitable candidates. Mike Denness, Alan Jones, John Jameson (whose robust approach reminded some of Ollie Milburn), David Lloyd, Barry Wood and Roy Virgin would all have considered themselves genuine contenders. Some blamed this paucity of stroke-makers on the growing number of overseas players in the game: the middle orders of county cricket would be filled, amongst others, by Greg Chappell, Clive Lloyd, Rohan Kanhai, Garry Sobers, Mushtaq Mohammad, Majid Khan, Asif Iqbal, Younis Ahmed, and Zaheer Abbas. Yet there were also plenty of foreign fast bowlers playing in the Championship, which did not seem to inhibit the development of English pacemen.

A more likely explanation is that a generational change had conspired with other factors to leave the cupboard temporarily bare. Of those who have already featured in our story, Barber, Barrington, Graveney, Dexter, Close, Smith, Milburn and Prideaux had disappeared from view. With Sharpe and Parfitt apparently no longer featuring in the selectors' deliberations, this left only a very restricted pack, which England had already repeatedly shuffled. If Cowdrey was now to be ignored too, this left only Hampshire, Fletcher and Amiss. Given this imbalance of riches, it remains one of the ironies of this most fascinating of games that it was only after reinventing himself as an opener that Amiss would finally win a regular place in the side.

CHAPTER 15

AT HOME TO PAKISTAN AND INDIA

Pakistan were England's first opponents of the summer; their touring party provided an intriguing mix of youth and experience. Imran Khan, cousin of Majid, was said to be a promising all-rounder, while in the traditional match at Lord's against the MCC a young Zaheer Abbas, playing a short innings on a cold, grey day, reminded some onlookers of the great Garry Sobers with the timing of his shots through mid-wicket. Promising newcomers aside, it was not widely predicted that Pakistan would provide much opposition for Illingworth's all-conquering heroes.

For the first Test England, perhaps surprisingly, went with Cowdrey in the middle order, less surprisingly restoring Amiss alongside him. On respective recent showings, Hampshire was surely unlucky to be overlooked. Boycott was not considered for selection, as he was not yet fully fit.

There was no place for Snow either, so the three-man pace attack had a rather strange look to it: Ward, Lever, and Shuttleworth. In fact, Snow would not feature in any of the three Tests against Pakistan. In addition to his injured hand, he had also developed a problem with his right shoulder.

More damagingly, however, he fell out badly with the Sussex captain Mike Griffith (son of Billy), whom various Sussex players ('us') saw as symptomatic of the 'gin and tonic' set who ran the club ('them'). Snow felt that the captaincy should have gone to the more experienced Tony Buss but, as he pointedly comments in his book, Buss was the son of a carpenter rather than the son of the secretary of the MCC.[95] This would not in fact prove a happy year for Snow, as he would be dropped by both England and Sussex for (different) disciplinary reasons.

Pakistan won the toss on a typically grey Birmingham day and batted. Almost immediately one of their openers, Aftab Gul, was hit on the head and forced to retire. Pakistan were now effectively 0-1, with the ball moving around both in the air and off the pitch. One wonders what odds bookmakers would have offered at that moment against them still batting on the third day, yet this is exactly what would happen. Zaheer turned in one of the great Test innings of 274 in what were initially very difficult circumstances, and Pakistan ended up declaring on the third morning at 608-7. Alan Ward, the great white hope, conceded over a hundred runs and finished wicketless.

Any belief that England might find batting on the third day as easy as Pakistan had done was promptly disproved as Edrich, Cowdrey and Amiss fell in quick succession to the young quick bowler Asif Masood. England, needing 408 to avoid the humiliation of following on, were 48-3. Follow on they duly did around lunchtime on the fourth day, but by then long vigils by D'Oliveira, Knott, Lever and Shuttleworth had given them hope and 353 runs. Knott batted three hours for a breezy century and looked by a long way England's best batsman. Amiss and Cowdrey had managed just 20 runs between them.

Following on, England made a better fist of things, Brian Luckhurst dropping anchor for a characteristically obdurate stay at the crease, batting through the entire five and a half hours of the England second innings, which finished at 229-5, having survived a bad scare.

The Lord's Test was ruined by the weather. Rain prevented more than

---

[95] *Cricket Rebel* op. cit.

two and a half hours' play on the first two days combined, and then completely washed out the third day. For England, Boycott returned in place of Cowdrey, and there was general sad acceptance that an outstanding Test career had now really drawn to a close.

There was little of significance about what was left of the game after the weather was finished with it, other than a first cap for Yorkshire's Richard Hutton (son of Len) – a bowling all-rounder, who played in that fateful 'Close affair' match at Edgbaston. Boycott made a century on his return; England's new-look bowling attack skittled Pakistan out for 148 (Zaheer top-scoring with 40), and the proceedings ended as an exhibition match, Hutton being promoted to open the batting with Luckhurst and scoring an undefeated 50.

The third and final match, at Leeds, was an oddity. Believing that the Headingley wicket would take turn, England fielded three specialist spinners for the first time in living memory, legspinner Robin Hobbs being recalled from obscurity to replace the fast bowler John Price. Disappointingly for those who thrilled to the possibility of legspin becoming a regular feature of the England side, Hobbs would bowl only 24 overs in the match and finish wicketless. No specialist legspinner would play for England again for over 20 years.

Another century by Geoff Boycott masked another batting collapse for England, with only D'Oliveira, Illingworth and Hutton of the lower order offering serious opposition. They finally subsided on the second morning for 316, a score which probably flattered their efforts. In reply Pakistan made exactly 350, again built around a top-score from Zaheer, who this time made 72. England's three-man spin attack failed to fire, only Gifford looking dangerous.

Now England desperately needed their trusty top three to dig them out of trouble, but they suffered a rare failure and Illingworth found himself at the crease with D'Oliveira with his team 142-5. Only a maiden Test 50 from Amiss had momentarily brightened the proceedings.

Illingworth and D'Oliveira would bat for two and half hours in adding just over a hundred together for the sixth wicket. Once they were both out, however, England's tail failed to wag and Pakistan were left needing only

231 to win. For a side which batted down to number eight, this did not seem like a great challenge.

Illingworth made his intentions clear by getting himself and Gifford into the attack almost at once. His readiness to bowl himself was rewarded by three early wickets: Aftab, Zaheer and Mushtaq. When Gifford had Saeed Ahmed caught by D'Oliveira, Pakistan were 65-4 and England scented an improbable victory. Meantime, however, opener Sadiq Mohammad, younger brother of Hanif and Mushtaq, was playing the innings of his life and he now found someone who could stay with him. Asif Iqbal played many glorious innings for Kent, particularly in one day matches, but had a reputation as a poor starter. Once he was set, though, he was as dangerous as any batsman in the world. He was also a good enough medium-pace all-rounder to take 53 Test wickets at an average of only just over 28.

On this occasion restraining his natural attacking instincts, Asif concentrated on occupying the crease, knowing that in time the runs would come, particularly with his partner in such fine form. Neither batsman looked like getting out. Finally, it took a piece of sheer brilliance from Alan Knott to break the stand. Asif stretched forward to a delivery from Gifford, attempting to smother the spin. His back foot dragged over the line, and quick as a flash Knott had the bails off. Pakistan were now 160-5, needing just 71 to win.

Now it was Intikhab's turn to try to stay with Sadiq. Ignoring the temptation to give Hobbs a bowl against the new batsman, Illingworth threw the ball to D'Oliveira. It was to prove an inspired move, as D'Oliveira took two crucial wickets to turn the match decisively in England's favour. First he had Intikhab caught by Hutton. Then he held one back and induced Sadiq to give a caught and bowled. Young Sadiq, dismissed nine short of what would have been a magnificent century, and less than 50 runs away from the victory target, returned to the dressing room distraught and inconsolable.

Illingworth now turned to Peter Lever, who in the space of just a few minutes produced two outswingers to have Wasim Bari and Asif Masood caught behind by Knott, and then an inswinger to have Pervez lbw. So England won a match which they might very easily have lost. In both Test matches which had gone the distance, Pakistan had served notice that they were now a force to be reckoned with.

The Indian touring side offered a rather unique package. India had at this time nobody even resembling a fast bowler, and their attack relied almost entirely on a three-man spin attack usually formed by the legspinner Chandrasekhar ('Chandra'), the left-arm Bishan Bedi, and whichever one of the two offspinners, 'Venkat' (Venkataraghavan) or Prasanna, happened to be in favour. This summer it was Venkat, who went on both to captain India and to become a much respected Test umpire. The side also usually included two medium-pace all-rounders, whose role was partly to bowl a few overs to take the shine off the ball, and partly to stiffen the batting of the tail. This balance was made possible by the fact that their wicketkeeper, Farokh Engineer, who played for Lancashire during the English summer, was almost good enough to warrant a place in the side as a batsman. In fact, he frequently opened the batting for Lancashire in one day games.

The side also included one of the greatest opening batsmen ever to play the game. Sunil Gavaskar had just begun his Test career during India's recent winter tour of the West Indies, when he had scored no less than four centuries, including a century and a double century in the same match. Given this, great things were expected of him. His brother-in-law, Gundappa 'Vishy' Viswanath, was the only other class batsman in the side. He might be best described as an Indian Rohan Kanhai, playing in similarly cavalier fashion outside the off stump, and capable on his day of taking any attack in the world apart. He would be remembered in particular for many heroic knocks against the superb West Indian fast bowlers of the mid to late 1970s.

England recalled Snow to the side in the first match at Lord's alongside Hutton and Price, and it was to be Snow's batsmanship for which England would be most indebted to him. After the military-medium pace of Abid Ali had accounted for Boycott, caught behind, India's spinners got to work and England quickly lost their first five batsmen for just 71 runs in another of the batting collapses that were starting to be an unwelcome feature of their game.

It was left to Illingworth, Knott, Snow, Hutton and Gifford to pull England's irons out of the fire. The last five wickets added 233 runs, Snow top-scoring with a classy 73. India then surpassed England's total, making 313. Though their opening partnership of Mankad and Gavaskar failed, the rest of the batsmen contributed all the way down the order, led by a fighting captain's innings from Wadekar. Solkar, the other medium pacer, occupied the crease for over five hours in making 67. He was destined to become a major thorn in England's side.

Largely because he had batted so slowly, India's first innings did not end until the stroke of time on the third day. When play began on the Monday, England needed to build a respectable total quickly and then declare. Sadly it did not quite work out this way as only 50 overs were possible in the day, during which England limped, rather than scampered to 145-5. Most of the scoring had been done by Boycott and Edrich, and even after flurries by Knott and D'Oliveira, the scoring rate was still well below two an over.

So Illingworth could not declare overnight, as he must have hoped to, and was forced to bat on the next morning. However, thoughts of a declaration quickly became irrelevant as first Knott was out to Chandra and then the remaining wickets toppled, leaving England 191 all out, and India needing only 183 with about 50 overs left in the game.

Again Mankad went early, and this time Wadekar could not put his foot in the door. When he was caught by Boycott off Price with the score at 21, however, in came Engineer, promoted up the order. With the dangerous Viswanath yet to come, this sent a clear message. India thought they could get the runs, and were going to try to win the game.

With Gavaskar batting steadily at the other end, Engineer scored 35 at almost a run a ball until he was stumped by Knott off Gifford, another smart piece of work by the Kent keeper. Viswanath came in to pick up where Engineer had left off, but almost immediately perished, caught close in by Amiss off Gifford. Then the new man, Sardesai, was clean bowled by Illingworth and the crowd realised they now had a one day style tight finish on their hands. With the hero of the first innings now partnering the great Gavaskar, however, the odds were still on India, who only needed 75 more runs to win. Then disaster struck for India. Gifford got one to turn away from Gavaskar and he edged it to Edrich, who made no mistake.

Now the two all-rounders were on their own, with only the spinners, who had no pretensions as batsmen, left to come. Solkar, however, seemed still to be stuck in his defensive groove from the first innings, and though he seemed in little trouble, India were in danger of running out of time. Now a third result, previously discounted, began to come into play. Perhaps India would fail to make the runs, but England would fail to bowl them out.

Abid Ali was still doing his best to go for the runs, but when he was caught by Snow having a heave at Illingworth, the shutters went up for good. Venkat came in with orders to defend. When he was caught by Hutton off Gifford there were still nine minutes left. Solkar obviously trusted Bedi, because he made no effort to farm the strike, and the match duly ended in a draw. Solkar had batted over an hour for six runs.

In the end, a draw was probably a fair result, and while both sides doubtless felt they had done enough to claim a moral victory, the truth is that each in turn had been lucky to escape, particularly on that riveting last day. Like Pakistan earlier in the summer, India, previously regarded as rather soft opposition in English conditions, had served notice that they deserved to be taken seriously.

By the time the Lord's Test match ended, it had provided yet another episode in John Snow's chequered record with the game's authorities. During the last over before lunch on that dramatic last day, Snow and Gavaskar collided in mid-pitch while the bowler was trying to field the ball and attempt a run-out off a quick single. Most of those who watched the incident repeatedly in slow motion agreed that Snow made more of the collision than was strictly necessary. In fact Gavaskar, who was not a big man, was sent sprawling wearing an understandably startled expression. Snow then picked up Gavaskar's bat and tossed it to him. This fact merits specific mention because various newspapers later portrayed it as a further sign of thuggishness on Snow's part. A gentleman, it was implied, would have handed the batsman back his bat while enquiring politely after his condition.

As the players came into the dressing room, Snow apologised to Alec Bedser, the chairman of selectors, and promised to go along to the Indian dressing room to apologise to Gavaskar as soon as he had changed his shirt. While he was putting a fresh one on, however, Billy Griffith stormed into the room and started shouting at him. In view of Snow's well publicised differences of opinion with Sussex's captain, Griffith *père* was of course hardly a disinterested observer. Snow told him that he had already settled the matter with Bedser, but Griffith brushed this aside, and a heated argument ensued which ended only when Illingworth asked Griffith to leave the room.

Snow was duly dropped from the England side for the next Test, Bedser issuing a statement that this was for disciplinary reasons. In phoning Snow to convey the news, however, he said that it had not been the selectors' decision, but 'a direct order from above'. Snow gave him a terse message to relay to 'above'.[96]

For Old Trafford, England shuffled their batting again for the second match. Fletcher came back into the side in place of Amiss, and John Jameson was awarded a first cap in place of Boycott. Lever replaced Snow. The revamped line-up could not save them from another batting collapse but, putting the efforts of the specialist batsmen to shame, Illingworth and Lever then embarked on a mammoth stand which would last for three hours and add 168 for the eight wicket. England's final total of 386 was very much more than they had looked like making when they had ended the first day's play at 219-7.

Batting hero now became bowling hero as Lever started to make inroads into the Indian batting. All four of England's seamers bowled accurately, and Illingworth was able to place India under the sort of pressure which he loved to apply, strangling the run rate and taking wickets on a regular basis. Only fifties from Gavaskar and Solkar (though he batted for only two hours this time) ensured that India had any sort of respectable total at all. They were dismissed for 212, still 174 behind. Peter Lever finished with 5-70.

---

[96] *Cricket Rebel* op. cit.

When England batted again Illingworth was able to declare on 245-3, setting India 420 to win, with well over a day left to play. England's pace attack had taken the first three Indian wickets by close of play, including the hugely valuable one of Gavaskar, but rain intervened overnight and no further play was possible in the match.

So the sides went to the Oval with the series still level. Presumably believing that the pitch would take turn, the selectors restored Underwood to the side in place of Gifford, while Snow also returned. After Lever's heroics at Old Trafford, both Price and Hutton were lucky to keep their places, since Lever was now unfit.

England's first innings total of 355 was built around three fine fifties. Jameson scored a breezy 82 at the top of the order but was run out. Knott missed out on a century when he gave Solkar a return catch on 90, and Richard Hutton showed his all-round potential for England for the first time in scoring 81.

India began their first innings on the third day, the whole of the second day having been lost to rain. They looked in good shape at 114-2 with both Wadekar and Sardesai batting comfortably, but then Illingworth took three quick wickets to reduce them to 125-5. Now it was down to Engineer, Solkar, Abid Ali and Venkat to bat long and defensively. India eventually prolonged their innings into the fourth day, but could muster only 284.

Jameson again began brightly but was again run out – this time in the cruellest way imaginable as Chandra deflected the ball onto the stumps at the non-striker's end – to become the first ever English batsman run out twice in the same Test match. As if inspired by this fortunate happen-chance, Chandra now embarked on a remarkable spell of 6-38, simply destroying the England second innings. When Luckhurst became his fourth victim at 72-7, the writing was on the wall, and England could manage only 101, their lowest total ever against India. England's latest middle-order reshuffle had failed dismally, Fletcher scoring only one run in the entire match.

The pitch was now taking considerable turn, as Chandra's remarkable figures demonstrated – his buzzing legspinners had been simply too much for

177

the English batsmen. Could Underwood and Illingworth achieve something similar, despite India needing only 173 to win?

Hopes were raised briefly when Snow had Gavaskar lbw for a duck, and then Underwood had the other opener, Mankad, caught by Hutton. The rest of the innings now became a battle of attrition, with India determined to survive and wait for the runs to come, while England desperately tried to chip away at the wickets. It took India three hours to make the last 97 runs, but make them they did, to score a historic first victory on English soil. England had flirted with disaster once too often.

In handing Illingworth his first defeat as captain against an opposing country, India ensured that England's season ended on a rather flat note. There was not even the suspense of a squad to be picked for the winter, as there was no tour scheduled. England's next taste of international opposition would be Australia the next summer, grimly determined under Ian Chappell's leadership to win back the Ashes.

CHAPTER 16

THE 1972 ASHES

When the Australian party was announced, it had an unfamiliar ring to it. The selectors' rather ruthless blood-letting had continued, with Ian Redpath apparently joining Lawry and McKenzie on the scrapheap. With Eastwood also denied another chance, Bruce Francis, who had played for Essex as an overseas player, was picked to open the innings with Stackpole. Alongside the Chappell brothers, the specialist batsmen were Walters, Sheahan and Inverarity, all of whom had toured with Lawry in 1968, and Ross Edwards, who had not. In addition to Walters, Greg Chappell and Inverarity, all of whom were legitimate bowlers, Australia picked one genuine all-rounder, Graeme Watson, who was both a back-up opening batsman and a medium-pace bowler. There were no surprises in the spin department, the selectors returning to the tried and tested combination of Gleeson and Mallett.

There were, however, surprises aplenty in the fast bowling line-up. Australia had dispensed with the experience of McKenzie and Connolly during Illingworth's tour, but they went further after it. With the sole exception of Lillee, not a single one of the fast bowlers employed in that series ever played another Test for Australia. Thus when the squad was named it emerged that Lillee would be supported by three other bowlers, none of whom had ever played Test cricket before. It was a bold move, but would boldness be rewarded? Time would tell.

Jeff Hammond was known to be fast, and in addition to playing cricket was a successful baseball pitcher. David Colley was thought to be the sort of fast-medium workhorse who might excel in English conditions, and was a decent batsman with a first-class century to his name. Little was known of Bob Massie, except that he was said to be able to bowl long spells and swing the ball both ways. Wicketkeepers Marsh and Taber completed the party.

The traditional MCC v tourists game, occurring early in the tour, is normally useful for the tourists as a Test trial. This time, not having had the advantage of a winter tour, it was so for England too. Interestingly, both sides needed answers to the same questions: who should bat in the middle order, and who should open the bowling?

In an attempt to find the answer to the first question, Australia picked both Inverarity and Edwards. The implication was that they might be competing for a single vacancy. The MCC invited Tony Greig and Graham Roope, the exciting young Surrey batsman, to Lord's. However, the demon that was the Benson & Hedges Cup, now in its inaugural season, proved the traditionalists to have been right, as both were promptly summoned back to their counties, playing for the MCC against Australia now being deemed less important than playing in a first-round limited overs match.

This largely deprived the match of any significance for the England selectors even before it had begun. The paucity of middle-order candidates was demonstrated all too clearly when two opening batsmen were summoned as late replacements. The MCC side thus had an extremely bizarre look to it: Boycott, Jameson, Luckhurst, Denness, Virgin, Wood … can any first-class side ever before have featured six opening batsmen?

Willis and Ward were chosen to try to settle the MCC's bowling attack, again presumably on the basis that they might be competing for a single place in the Test team alongside Snow. Lillee and Massie played for Australia; it was generally believed that this pairing was in fact their preferred combination, so they were being given their first taste of big match atmosphere as a partnership. In the event, it was to be a brief partnership. Having bowled one maiden over, Massie pulled a muscle in his side and had to leave the field. He was unable to bowl again in the match, and spectators were treated to Greg Chappell and Doug Walters sharing the fast bowling duties with Dennis Lillee.

For those who had not seen Lillee in action before, it was an experience not to be forgotten. He sprinted to the wicket flat out and with no apparent acceleration, released the ball and was then carried by his momentum a considerable way down the pitch, ending up only a few yards from the batsman. He was fast. Blisteringly fast. Just after Massie went off, he bowled one that Boycott clearly never saw, and dismissed him lbw.

Fortunately for the MCC batsmen, though, he was very fast but not yet very accurate. That would come a little later in his career, when he would mature into the truly great fast bowler of legend. So, while there was a lot of playing and missing, a lot of balls went hurtling harmlessly down either side of the wicket.

MCC in truth did not bat very well, perhaps unnerved by the early loss of Boycott. Luckhurst and Denness both scored fifties, but Denness did not impress. He was clearly nervous and out of touch, and looked ill at ease against Lillee. Rain then intervened and, after a great deal of contrivance by the captains, Australia were set a target on the last day, and won. It was announced shortly afterwards that Massie would definitely be unfit for the first Test, due to start two weeks later at Old Trafford.

Australia had committed to playing Watson in the middle order instead of a second spinner, and thus had three clear decisions to make. They chose Inverarity over Edwards, Gleeson over Mallett, and Colley over Hammond.

England had already signalled their renewed interest in Tony Greig, and so his recall drew little comment. Less so, their choice of M.J.K. Smith to bat at number four.

Geoff Arnold was picked to partner Snow, which seemed straight-forward as he had been bowling well for Surrey, and both Lever and Ward were now injured. Mike Smith, however, was a real wild card. As discussed previously, he had actually retired from first-class cricket in 1967, but had returned to the scene in 1970. The fact that he was chosen is cogent evidence of the lack of any other credible contenders (though John Arlott thought Barry Wood was unlucky not to be given a chance after his 50 at Lord's for the MCC, despite playing for Lancashire as a specialist opener).[97] In fact, before the end of the series more than one journalist suggested that Brian Close, who had been in good form for Somerset, was as good a candidate as any.

Somerset? Yes, controversy and Brian Close had become reacquainted with each other in 1970 when Close had been sacked as captain of Yorkshire. One reason was that Yorkshire, who operated a birth qualification which excluded them from using overseas players, had realised that they were unlikely to be able to win the Championship against teams including the likes of Garry Sobers or Barry Richards, and had decided to take limited overs cricket very seriously in future, whereas Close was a vociferous opponent of it, particularly the Sunday League. The immediate cause of Close's downfall, however, seems to have been that he was less than polite to Lancashire's president, Lionel Lister, after a Sunday League match (which Lancashire, fast becoming the best one day side in the country, had won). Obviously not the forgiving sort, Lister complained to Yorkshire about Close's lack of respect.

Close had immediately been offered terms by several clubs, but had chosen to go to Somerset as captain. Playing alongside Tom Cartwright, who had moved there after a disagreement with Warwickshire, the two of them would mentor two of the most significant players of the next generation: Ian Botham and Viv Richards.

The fact that a 39-year-old should be picked for England, and a 41-year-old seriously considered, speaks volumes for the lack of decent middle-order batsmen in the country. The selectors clearly thought, with every justification, that both Fletcher and Amiss had been given ample opportunities to impress, and had failed to take them. Presumably, but perhaps with slightly less justification, they also felt the same about Hampshire, Sharpe and Parfitt. As for the Australians, they had been

---

[97] John Arlott, *The Ashes 1972*, Pelham Books, London, 1972

mightily impressed by David Turner of Hampshire, who had scored 131 against them in fine style before the MCC match, and were puzzled that he did not seem to form any part of England's plans.

There may, however, have been another motive behind the selectors asking Smith to return. The selectors may well have been looking for someone to replace the plain-talking and occasionally rebellious Illingworth as captain. When he had returned victorious from Australia he had been in an unassailable position, but defeat by India at the end of the previous season had dented his aura of invincibility. With Cowdrey's Test career acknowledged to be over, and Denness as yet unable to establish himself in the side as a batsman, perhaps they felt that the gentleman amateur Mike Smith would be a safe pair of hands for a year or so if only he could cement himself a place in the team. It is common knowledge, for example, that Smith had been the selectors' alternative choice to Close for the 1967–68 West Indies tour, and, perhaps significantly, Illingworth had not been appointed as captain for the present series, but only for the first two Tests.

If so, then Smith is adamant that nothing was said to him. He also points out, not unreasonably, that Illingworth was a member of the selection committee, so that any open discussion of the captaincy would have been unlikely to feature when the team was chosen.

Greig's selection was itself a matter of some controversy. A South African, he did not as yet satisfy the ICC's residence qualification and played in this series only because the Australians were asked the question, and sportingly agreed to waive any objection.

The Old Trafford Test match proved a one-sided affair. Australia never recovered from being skittled out for 142 in their first innings by Snow and Arnold, losing all ten wickets for less than 80 runs after a bright start by Stackpole and Francis. They did better in their second innings, largely thanks to a robust 91 from Rodney Marsh. For England, Greig scored a 50 in each innings, which may perhaps have given the Australians cause to rue their generous gesture.

While scoring runs in each innings, Smith had never looked comfortable. In fact, his old fallibility against short-pitched bowling was all too evident. Once in the second innings he failed to pick a bouncer from Lillee, which only just missed his head.[98]

So England started the series with an easy win. There was, however, one detail which they had overlooked. With the exception of Greig, the team did not contain a single specialist slip fielder and, with even Snow being summoned for emergency duty in the slips, they had dropped a number of catches, including no less than four off Geoff Arnold during the first hour or two of Australia's first innings.

Australia seemed to be having problems with their own middle order, and would surely consider changes. Watson, in particular, had seemed impressive neither as a batsman nor as a bowler. There was good news about Massie, though, who would apparently be fit for Lord's, and thus ready to gain his first cap. To play even a single Test at Lord's is every player's ambition, and to make his debut there the stuff of dreams. Robert Arnold Lockyer Massie of Subiaco, Western Australia would be able to look back in later years and relish the memory of the Lord's Test match of 1972 with more justification than most.

When England batted first at Lord's, Massie, opening the bowling with Lillee, beat both Boycott and Edrich with late swing both ways before Boycott misjudged an inswinger and was bowled. Then Lillee beat both Edrich and Luckhurst for sheer pace, dismissing them lbw and bowled respectively. England were 28-3 and the rest of the innings was destined to be a long, hard grind.

While looking like getting out from one ball to the next, Smith somehow managed to cling on for over an hour and a half for 34. D'Oliveira batted less time for 32. Both were dismissed in quick succession by Massie, both by big inswingers. England were now indebted to two breezy partnerships, both defying the difficult conditions and going for their shots. First Knott and Greig put on nearly a hundred for the sixth wicket before both being dismissed within a few minutes of each other by Massie, who had now taken five of the seven wickets to fall. Then Illingworth and Snow added another 60 in even time. England finished the day on 249-7 but were

---

[98] *The Ashes 1972* op. cit.

bowled out the following morning for 272. Given that the ball had been moving around consistently, batting had not been easy, but it was felt that another 50 or so would have been necessary for a par score.

The big news of the match so far was that Bob Massie, bowling in his very first Test innings, had taken 8-84. Only Alf Valentine had ever equalled this feat in the whole history of Test cricket, and his eight wickets had come more expensively (8-104).

As Francis and Stackpole came out to open the batting for Australia, England wondered how much they were going to miss their own leading swing bowler, Geoff Arnold, who was injured and had been replaced by John Price on his home ground. 'Not very much' was the apparent answer after both openers were back in the pavilion with only seven on the board, undone by Snow and Price respectively. The Chappell brothers were now together, and Ian attacked, hooking several bouncers to the boundary, while Greg grafted. In fact, Greg Chappell would bat for much of the Australian innings while a succession of partners tried to stay with him, with varying degrees of success. He was finally out for 131 with the score at 250-7. The tail then wagged, built around a boisterous 50 from Marsh with good support from Colley, advancing Australia to 308 all out, with Snow's 5-57 the pick of the bowlers. They were only 36 ahead, but the ball was still moving around and it looked like being the sort of match where runs in the bank might count for a lot.

Greg Chappell came of age as a Test batsman in this innings. His century was classy and composed. Batting was never easy, and early on he had to battle hard to survive, but without his contribution the Australian innings might well have folded; after all, when Walters was caught by Illingworth off Snow, they had been 84-4.

When England came into bat for the second time the sun had broken through, and it seemed unlikely that Massie would find the same degree of swing he had produced in the first innings, but in fact, if anything, he seemed to be swinging the ball more, not less. A few of his inswingers moved so much that Marsh had to go hurtling across to the leg side with his goalkeeper dives to stop them. After a mid-wicket conference, Massie went round the wicket. The rest is history.

Having the effect now of a left-armer moving the ball into the right-handed batsman, always a horrible line to handle, the English batting line-up was simply destroyed.

Before too long they were 74-8. Again, only Mike Smith had managed to survive, but he was the ninth man out just before the close. England finished the day 86-9, their innings in tatters. Apart from Boycott and Luckhurst, both of whom had been beaten by Lillee's sheer speed, every other wicket had fallen to Massie's swing.

Some agricultural hitting from Price and Gifford briefly entertained the crowd the next morning but before long Massie, inevitably, took the last wicket and Australia were left needing just 81 to win, which they duly knocked off. With five runs left, Illingworth conceded defeat and brought on Luckhurst.

Unsurprisingly, the match has gone down in history as 'Massie's Match'. His final tally was 16 wickets. Only Jim Laker and Sydney Barnes had ever done better. Australia, it seemed, had found a potent match-winner who, now that he was fit, could sweep England away in every remaining match of the series.

From Lord's the Australians went to Somerset, where the evergreen Tom Cartwright impressed with his bowling, and then to play Middlesex at Lord's, Parfitt, Radley and the other Mike Smith all making runs. The Australian tour selectors saw nothing that might have persuaded them to change a winning side, and so named the same eleven for Trent Bridge as for Lord's.

As for England, they had some tough choices to make, at least one of which was forced upon them. Geoff Boycott sustained a serious finger injury when hit by a rising ball from Bob Willis during a county match. The selectors decided upon Parfitt as his replacement, perhaps on the basis that he was next in line on the batting carousel, but perhaps also in the knowledge that he would at least strengthen the slip cordon, which had proved fallible.

John Price, who had disappointed at Lord's, was dropped, and since Arnold was still unfit, Peter Lever came back into the side. Though Price would remain on the fringes of selection for a while, he would never play for England again.

As for the captaincy issue, it turned out to be a damp squib, with the selectors duly reappointing Illingworth for the remainder of the series. It remained an active question, however, since England were due to tour India and Pakistan in the winter, and Illingworth was already known to be unlikely to make himself available, for reasons partly of family (he had two young daughters) and partly of health (he had digestive problems that were aggravated by exposure to spicy food, perhaps a legacy of a liver infection when he was younger). If the selectors had been considering a change, Smith's batting form had not been sufficiently exciting to hint at a prolonged run in the team, though in fairness he had done little wrong, batting for lengthy periods and holding some good catches.

They were presumably also influenced by the fact that to have dumped Illingworth as captain after the crushing defeat at Lord's might have smacked of panic, whereas they were determined to show faith in their players, as evidenced by their retention of everyone in the Lord's eleven, save Price.

Trent Bridge has always had a reputation for assisting seam bowling, so Illingworth, on winning the toss, asked Australia to bat. This tactic briefly seemed to be paying off, when Lever had Francis caught by Smith off a loose shot after half an hour, but England would be frustrated by Keith Stackpole, who batted into the final half hour of the day in making a patient 114. Ironically, Parfitt, brought into the side partly because of his slip catching, dropped him when he was 46.

Stackpole was the sixth man out, but by then England's gamble in inserting the opposition had clearly failed, since Australia ended the day on 249-6 with Marsh and Colley at the crease, already threatening to repeat their batting successes at Lord's.

So it was to prove the next morning, as they put on 62 for the seventh wicket. Colley was slotting almost into an all-rounder's position in the Australian side, rarely looking threatening as a bowler, but making useful runs down the order. He made 54 in this innings.

However, once Marsh became Gifford's sole victim the innings ended quickly. Australia had scored 315.

For England, Edrich and Luckhurst began slowly but steadily, taking over two hours to score the first 50 runs. Then Luckhurst was lbw to Lillee and wickets began to fall steadily. Again, Smith proved obdurate, but only at the expense of being largely strokeless. By the end of the second day England were struggling at 117-4, Gifford having come in as nightwatchman to bat out the day with D'Oliveira when Smith was finally dismissed just before close of play.

Norman Gifford could be quite a useful batsman, particularly in limited overs cricket, and he demonstrated this the next morning by surviving for well over an hour against Lillee and Massie. D'Oliveira was first to go, lbw to Lillee, which prompted a steady fall of wickets to leave England 189 all out, Lillee and Massie with four wickets each.

There was drama off the field between the innings. Bruce Francis, who had been unable to field owing to one of his periodic migraines, was replaced as opener by Ross Edwards. Edwards, who had been delighting the crowd with his athletic fielding in the covers, and was also an occasional wicketkeeper, would now demonstrate his versatility by proving a very successful opening batsman, ending the Saturday 90 not out.

When he resumed on Monday he showed that despite over 36 hours to reflect on the prospect of his first Test century, nerves had not set in, and he quickly passed this landmark. Though Snow had dismissed Stackpole early on the Saturday afternoon, this availed England little, since first Ian Chappell and then his brother dug in alongside Edwards, and Australia were able to declare in the afternoon on 324-4 with Edwards undefeated on 170, a magnificent effort as an emergency opener. England now had to make 451 to win or, more realistically, survive about 150 overs for a draw.

England desperately needed a solid start to their second innings – once again Edrich and Luckhurst, who seemed to have recovered something of their old form, supplied it. However, Edrich was out after an hour and a half and England left the field that evening at 111-1, still with a mountain to climb.

The next day Luckhurst and Parfitt stayed together for over three hours, though Luckhurst was cruelly robbed of a well-deserved century when he was dismissed for 96 by the part-time legspin of the Australian captain, upstaging Gleeson, who would go wicketless. The match was still there for Australia to win, as they proved by now getting Parfitt and Smith out within a run of each other, an unusually short stay at the wicket for the latter.

England were 201-4 but the runs were irrelevant. They still had two and a half hours to survive. Australia scented victory and crowded the bat. It was left to the two all-rounders, the veteran D'Oliveira and the young blood Greig, to bat out the match calmly, putting on another 90 runs in the process, though by the end much of the bowling was being done by Stackpole.

England had survived, though save for their inspired rearguard action on the last day they had been comprehensively outplayed. The one positive which they could take away from the game was that in the second innings the English batsmen had seemed at last to adjust to the swing of Massie and draw his sting. Though he bowled 36 overs he took only the solitary wicket of Edrich, and none at all on the vital last day.

For the fourth Test, at Headingley, Australia decided, not unreasonably, that Edwards had done such a great job as an opener at Trent Bridge that he should keep the position, the unfortunate Francis losing out. His was to prove a brief international career since he, like John Price, never played Test cricket again.

The soil at Headingley had been infected shortly before the game by a fungus called fusarium, which had killed most of the grass. Without grass to hold it together, there was always the danger that the surface would break up and take excessive spin. Having seen the pitch, England called up Underwood in place of Gifford. Arnold, who was now fit again, reclaimed his place in the side from Lever.

The other change was more controversial, Fletcher being recalled in place of Smith. Fletcher was entitled to feel very fortunate, and Smith aggrieved, but Smith himself accepted the decision stoically, then as now. 'I hadn't made enough runs', he says simply.[99]

Australia won the toss and faced a difficult choice, since nobody had any idea how this very strange-looking pitch was likely to play. They chose to bat,

---

[99] MJK op. cit.

which was understandable enough, but passed up their last opportunity to bring Gleeson back into the reckoning. In the light of what was to occur, this was to prove an important decision, though probably not one which would have altered the eventual outcome.

Illingworth turned to Underwood early on. Immediately he found spin, so the crowd were treated to the unusual spectacle of two English spinners bowling in tandem to attacking fields before lunch on the first day of a Test match. Five wickets then fell for five runs on the first afternoon and the match was effectively over as a contest. Australia were all out for 146.

England appeared to cope with the pitch better than Australia, though to be fair they did not have to face Underwood, and their final total of 263 looked to have put the match beyond doubt as the pitch was now taking quite savage turn.

When Australia batted again on the third morning Underwood was quickly into the action, and wickets again fell rapidly. This time Australia could only muster 136, leaving England only 20 to win. Again Underwood proved close to unplayable, finishing with 6-45 in the innings and 10-82 in the match.

At the Oval England's revolving door turned once more for the consistently disappointing Keith Fletcher, the baton passing again to Jackie Hampshire. More surprisingly, Barry Wood came in for Brian Luckhurst, who had experienced a disappointing series by his own standards, but might have expected his track record to earn him another chance.

Australia made only one change, bringing back Watson in place of Doug Walters, who was in wretched form (in the Tests to date he had scored 54 runs in seven innings), and announcing that he would open, with Ross Edwards dropping back down the order.

England won the toss and batted, only to find themselves 145-6 – the rest of the innings would be a story of the English tail-enders trying to resist Lillee, while Knott scored runs at the other end.

This was to prove one of the elfin Knott's best innings. Farming the strike and scoring briskly, he received solid support from Geoff Arnold, who stayed with him for over an hour. Knott was eventually the last man out, eight runs short of a well-deserved century, and thanks to his efforts

England had clawed their way to 284. Lillee finished with 5-58 but already there were signs that the wicket was starting to take turn; Mallett had a long bowl and took three wickets on the first day.

Arnold and Snow dismissed Watson and Stackpole respectively to leave Australia 34-2, raising English hopes, but this was the last wicket to fall for over four hours as the Chappell brothers embarked on a stand of over two hundred. Greg was out just before the close on the second day, but the next day Edwards and Ian Chappell carried on where they had left off. Geoff Arnold finally had Ian Chappell out for a dogged 118 scored over five and a half hours.

After Australia were all out for 399 it was England's turn to grind out the runs. It had already been announced before the match that it could run to a sixth day in order to produce a result, which explains why both sides were content to score their runs slowly.

Despite the fact that it was looking increasingly like a spinner's wicket, Lillee again proved the main threat. He stuck to his task magnificently, taking another five wickets to give him ten for the match. England's reply was built around a fighting 90 from Barry Wood, who was eventually dismissed by Bob Massie, a rare wicket for a bowler who had looked decreasingly dangerous in the last couple of Tests.

England scored runs all down the order, Knott again a major contributor, this time with 63, and were finally dismissed for 356, leaving Australia 242 to win. On what was still quite a good batting pitch, Australia were favourites, but with it taking turn there was still the chance that Illingworth and Underwood could force an upset. Two of their other bowlers were injured, however. D'Oliveira, with back trouble, was unable to take the field, while Snow had hurt his wrist and would manage only six overs in the innings.

It was not to be. On the fifth evening Illingworth, who had been bowling beautifully and looking threatening, turned his ankle in the delivery stride and had to be carried from the ground. Edrich, who took over as captain, turned to Greig to replace him rather than the second offspinner, Parfitt. Stackpole and Ian Chappell now began to score freely and Edrich brought back the quick bowlers to encourage the umpires to end play early for bad light, which duly transpired.

There was no good news for England the next morning. None of their walking wounded had recovered. Indeed, Illingworth was now on crutches and apparently out for the rest of the season. This left Edrich with only two first line bowlers at his disposal: Arnold and Underwood. Early that morning, Arnold had Stackpole dropped by Hampshire at slip. It was a straightforward catch: England's last chance had gone.

Though it was a grim fight against Underwood on a turning pitch, the ball was turning slowly, so for any class batsman content to defend, even Deadly himself was a manageable proposition. When Greg Chappell was out to Underwood with the score on 171-5 England briefly felt they were back in the game, but Sheahan and Marsh brought Australia to their target. It was a worthy victory; the batting of the Chappell brothers in the first innings and the bowling of Dennis Lillee throughout the match had proved decisive. Nonetheless, England had retained the Ashes as a result of a drawn series.

CHAPTER 17

ENGLAND'S TOUR OF INDIA AND PAKISTAN, AT HOME TO NEW ZEALAND AND THE WEST INDIES

Off the field, the selectors had been busy choosing the squad for the winter tour of India and Pakistan. It had already been known for some time that Illingworth would not be going. In addition, Snow, Edrich, Boycott and Hutton had all declared themselves unavailable.

This was in fact not surprising, as it was common practice at the time. Pakistan in particular was an unpopular destination, with primitive living conditions, tummy bugs and civil disturbance all practically guaranteed. Finance also played a part; unbelievable though it may seem, Illingworth was able to make twice as much money from his winter job as a fireworks salesman than he would have earned captaining England on a winter tour. The England squad on these occasions thus often had something of a second-eleven quality about it; Bob Cottam, for example, played all of his Test matches in India and Pakistan.

If the selectors had been looking for a captain who had originally played as an amateur in M.J.K. Smith, they found another in Tony Lewis. A grammar schoolboy, Lewis had been a double blue at Cambridge (cricket and rugby), becoming an honorary gentleman in the process. An intensely likeable man, he would go on to hold just about every prestigious position that Wales had to offer, ranging from captain of Glamorgan to chairman of the Welsh National Opera. One position for which he had never been seriously considered though was as a Test cricketer (other than a brief period in the mid-1960s) and a first-class batting average of 32 helps to explain why. He was, in short, a throwback to the gentlemen captains of yesteryear, and would be the last man to be chosen as England captain never having previously played Test cricket.

In the event only five players from the team at the Oval would feature in the winter squad, which listed in full was: Lewis, Denness, Wood, Amiss, Fletcher, Roope, Greig, Birkenshaw, Knott, Taylor, Underwood, Gifford, Pocock, Arnold, Cottam and Old.

Surprise omissions were Brian Luckhurst and Peter Lever. D'Oliveira had made little impact on the Ashes series: in fact the Oval Test was his last. Fletcher and Amiss were lucky to be preferred to Hampshire and Parfitt, neither of whom had done anything wrong at the Oval.

The one really significant move, though, was the choice of Mike Denness as vice-captain. He had enjoyed a solid season but even so, his county teammates Luckhurst, Knott, Cowdrey and Asif Iqbal all had better season averages, as did contenders from other counties such as Roope. He was therefore a borderline candidate as a player. That he should have been chosen at all, let alone as vice-captain, was highly suggestive that in the minds of the selectors he was still a favoured alternative captain. It is interesting to conjecture, though, what might have happened had Geoff Boycott been available to tour; it would have been difficult not to name him vice-captain.

With four specialist spinners in the side and only six specialist batsmen, it seemed clear first that England were prepared for long hot days on slow-turning wickets, and second that they were planning to give Fletcher and Amiss extended runs in the side. Both assumptions were to be proved right. Incidentally, this tour was to be significant in shifting Amiss from the middle order to open the innings, and from an unlucky hopeful to a successful regular member of the team.

There was to be a final ironic twist to the 1972 season. It marked the first instance of a scheduled series of what would become known as ODIs (One

Day Internationals), which also marked Christopher Martin-Jenkins' debut as a commentator on TMS. Since Illingworth was injured, the selectors needed to find a new captain in a hurry, and settled on … Brian Close. That he should previously have been dismissed from the Test captaincy supposedly in disgrace, and that he should be the most vociferous critic of limited overs cricket in the country, at least suggested that the selectors had a sense of humour.

Against India that winter, England won the first Test match but lost the series two–one. The fact that England registered only three centuries in five matches (Lewis, Greig and Fletcher) is evidence that England were still some way from finding the answers to their batting problems, while the trying of Lewis, Roope, Birkenshaw, and Denness as openers is testament to the failure of Wood and Amiss as a combination at the top of the order.

Against Pakistan all three matches were drawn. In the first, at Lahore, both Amiss and Denness came good as openers, Amiss scoring a century, but this was a high-scoring game on a dead pitch. In the second, at Hyderabad, Amiss scored another century in similar conditions, but Denness failed twice. At Karachi, with Denness dropping back down the order, Amiss nearly made it three in a row, being dismissed for 99 in the first innings.

So the winter tour told the selectors little of value. Fletcher, with one century from eight matches, could hardly be said to have answered any of his doubters. Nor could Denness, without even the comfort of a single century. The only bright spots had been the consistently steady bowling of Arnold and Underwood, well supported by Pocock, and the apparent emergence of Dennis Amiss as a credible Test opener.

There was, however, the burning matter of the captaincy to resolve. As Illingworth himself admits, since he had made himself unavailable to tour and Lewis had led the side well and batted steadily, the selectors would have been entirely justified in confirming him in the post for the forthcoming 1973 summer series against New Zealand and West Indies. On the other hand, Illingworth had often looked England's best player, and had an outstandingly successful record as captain. He had lost only three Tests, and for one of those had spent the crucial part of the match off the field injured.

In the event, the selectors adopted the somewhat cowardly compromise of a Test trial, with 'the player' Illingworth and 'the gentleman' Lewis captaining the two sides. Understandably, this pleased nobody. Did the selectors really think that the issue of who was the better captain could be settled by the events of a single match? Illingworth frankly described the situation as 'ludicrous'.[100] Lewis got a first-ball duck, but captained his side well. The selectors, still collectively in search of a backbone, now decided on a further compromise, making Illingworth captain but Lewis vice-captain. Just like the Test trial, this was supremely irrational. As a player, Lewis was struggling to justify a place in the side, so if he was not going to be captain he should not have been selected.

The first match against New Zealand at Trent Bridge saw the first glimpse for English crowds of Dayle Hadlee's younger brother Richard, who opened the bowling alongside Dick Collinge. England's batting line-up had an unfamiliar look to it: Boycott, Amiss, Roope, Lewis, Fletcher.

England's three seamers, Snow, Arnold and Greig, skittled New Zealand out for 97 to give England a first innings lead of 153; Amiss and Greig then both scored centuries to set the Kiwis an improbable 479 to win. When New Zealand reached 400-5, though, England were seriously worried. Bev Congdon, who was dropped by Fletcher early on, scored 176 while Vic Pollard batted over seven hours for 116, occasionally leaving his crease to come down the pitch to the fast bowlers. England's blushes were spared by Tony Greig, who dismissed Pollard lbw, and New Zealand finished 39 runs short of what would have been a truly heroic victory.

By the time the teams reconvened at Lord's, Tony Lewis had suffered the leg injury which would end his career. This of course raises another fascinating 'what if?'. If Lewis had been captain, who would the selectors now have appointed in his place? Again the name of Geoff Boycott looms large.

In his place England decided to play an extra bowler, Chris Old, but would shortly regret this decision when a good bowling display by New Zealand held them to 253 in their first innings. Only four batsmen got

---

[100] *Yorkshire and Back* op. cit.

into double figures, and in the middle of their innings England lost three wickets for ten runs.

The New Zealanders now carried on where they had left off at Nottingham, Congdon, Burgess and Pollard all making centuries in compiling a massive 551, leaving England to score nearly 300 just to make New Zealand bat again. England began their reply on the Monday morning needing to bat for nearly two days to save the match.

That they managed to do so was due largely to Keith Fletcher, who finally compiled the big innings that had been so long overdue, batting six and a half hours for 178. Boycott, Amiss and Roope all made long defensive fifties, and Illingworth batted for over an hour and a half on the last afternoon. So the match was drawn but England had again been given a bad scare.

Normality was, however, restored in the third match at Headingley which England won by an innings, the main contributors being the two Geoffs. Arnold took eight wickets in the match, while Boycott scored a century in the first innings. The great Glenn Turner, who once again had been strangely subdued in the Test matches, very nearly carried his bat in the second innings, being last man out after a four and a half hour 81.

So, the summer's curtain-raiser was over, and cricket enthusiasts looked forward eagerly to the main event: a three-Test series against the West Indies, whose side was a fascinating blend of youth and experience. Alongside the great but ageing Sobers, Kanhai (who had taken over as captain) and Gibbs, were the brilliant Roy Fredericks and two fast bowlers who were also big hitters: Bernard Julien, who played for Kent, and Keith Boyce, who played for Essex.

For the first match, played unusually at the Oval, England dropped a bowler, Old, and brought in a batsman, Frank Hayes of Lancashire, to win his first cap.

With the exception of the ever-reliable Arnold, who took five wickets, England's bowlers struggled to make an impression during the West Indies first innings. It was not that they bowled badly, but rather that the West Indies batting line-up was one of the most talented ever to take the field together. Partly due to Arnold's sterling efforts and partly due to Sobers being run out early in his innings, West Indies 'only' made 415, Clive Lloyd making a century, and Keith Boyce 72 including seven boundaries, one of them a six. Even the miserly Underwood conceded nearly three an over.

As he often did when he had been dismissed cheaply, Sobers opened the bowling, taking a superb 3-27 from 22 overs. It was Boyce, though, who took the first wicket, Amiss, but by then England at 50-1 had been given a fine start. However, the seam trio of Boyce, Sobers, and Julien chipped away, steadily taking wickets, and only Boycott, with 97, provided any serious resistance, though Greig and Illingworth showed some sound defence down the order. They finished on 257, a first-innings deficit of 158.

When the West Indies batted again they were restricted to 255, leaving England a notional 414 to win. 'Notional' because, with the exception of a fine century on debut by Frank Hayes, England never looked like getting anywhere near their target, despite a typically dogged two-hour knock from Illingworth. Boyce was particularly impressive, finishing with eleven wickets in the match. Lance Gibbs, approaching the twilight of his career, also reminded the crowd of just what a class performer he could be, taking three wickets and giving away less than two runs an over. West Indies had evidently been the better side, the batting of Lloyd and Kallicharran (who scored precisely 80 in each innings) and the bowling of Boyce standing out in particular. For England, the arrival of Hayes and the steadiness of Arnold were the only real points of comfort.

For the second match at Edgbaston, West Indies changed the balance of their side, bringing back the veteran seamer Holder in place of the spinner Inshan Ali, who had not impressed at the Oval. For England, Luckhurst came back for Roope, while Old returned in place of Snow.

Snow's omission was controversial. He believed that he was being punished for past misdemeanours, rather than present form, and claims that Illingworth later told him that, with his own position as captain coming under threat, he no longer felt able to insist categorically on his inclusion.[101] Even today the decision seems a strange one. Whatever the rights and wrongs of Snow's temperament and behaviour, he was the

---

[101] *Cricket Rebel* op. cit.

greatest English fast bowler of his time, and had not bowled nearly badly enough to be overlooked.

Sadly, the Edgbaston Test would be memorable chiefly for a controversial incident when Kanhai showed open and repeated dissent against a decision of umpire Fagg, as a result of which Fagg went on strike the next morning for a token one over to make his feelings clear. The West Indies issued a statement supporting Fagg's abilities, but no apology. It was yet another sign of a different attitude creeping into the game, a trend that would see its brutal dénouement under Kanhai's successor, Clive Lloyd.

As far as the game of cricket was concerned, the tone was set by a marathon innings from Roy Fredericks during which, eschewing entirely his normal attacking instincts, he batted for eight and a half hours to make 150 – an innings of which Boycott or Barrington would have been proud. It was what was needed, though, since for once the West Indies struggled against steady and accurate bowling, in particular from Arnold and Underwood.

This was very much Illingworth's trademark: to apply pressure to the batsmen with tight bowling and keen fielding until they lost patience or concentration and did something silly. It took the normally fast-scoring West Indies five sessions to make just 327. It was a tactic which future England captains would also attempt against an increasingly dominant West Indies side, but usually with much less success.

Ironically, England were then subjected to their own tactics. Despite three players reaching 50 (Boycott, Amiss and Fletcher) they were unable to get beyond 305, and so much time had been used up that the match was now well into its fourth day, with a draw looking the only likely result.

So it was to prove, England being set 325 to win in about four hours but choosing unsurprisingly to bat out time instead.

After the draw at Edgbaston there seemed to be light at the end of the tunnel for England, but as so often it turned out to be on the front of an express train coming towards them.

Things started badly at Lord's and rapidly got worse. First Old announced on the morning of the match that his ankle was troubling him, and withdrew. Bob Willis had already been called into the side to form a three-man pace attack. This now became a two-man attack with Geoff Arnold. Against his better judgement, Old's retirement pushed Illingworth into naming Greig in the side. It had been intended to leave him out, as he was exhausted and a stone and a half underweight, but now being down to two fast bowlers, Illingworth needed him to cover as first change.

Two fit fast bowlers then became one as, after a few listless overs, Illingworth confronted Arnold only to be told that he too was exhausted from having bowled so much in recent weeks. Understandably, Illingworth was not amused.[102] He was forced to bowl Greig instead, with predictable results. West Indies compiled a massive 652, scoring throughout at nearly four an over, unheard of in those days. Kanhai, Sobers and Julien all scored big centuries.

Sobers was particularly impressive as he was suffering both from a leg injury and a stomach upset (possibly exacerbated by an all-night party, according to the man himself), having to retire and return at one stage, and would certainly have scored more than 150 not out had he not been so slow between the wickets. Nearing the age of 40, everyone was well aware that this would surely be the great all-rounder's last appearance in England, and he did not disappoint.

Nor did Julien, whose century was the cricketing equivalent of gratuitous violence. He scored 121 runs off just 143 deliveries against a dog-tired attack, including 20 boundaries, two of them sixes.

So quickly had West Indies scored their runs that there was still time for England to have to bat on the second evening. By close of play they were 88-3, and, in the absence of rain, the outcome looked already beyond doubt. Even the normally dependable Boycott had let them down, going for the hook shot against Holder only to top edge a catch to Kanhai at slip. England would be dismissed on the third day (Saturday) for 233 and be asked to follow on, though not before a very unwelcome first, when Lord's had to be cleared as a result of a telephoned bomb warning (this was at the time of an IRA terrorist campaign and the ground authorities rightly decided not to take any chances). It fell to Don

---

[102] All from *Yorkshire and Back* op. cit.

Mosey, commentating on his first Test match, to face the challenge of describing what was effectively a very extended drinks interval to TMS listeners. Eventually he was put out of his misery, being ordered from the commentary box by the Metropolitan Police.

This series also saw for the first time a pattern of regular idiotic pitch invasions, usually led by exuberant West Indians in brightly coloured hats waving cans of Red Stripe. Sadly, this led to the abandonment of the traditional practice of allowing people, mostly schoolboys, to pay at the gate and sit on the grass behind the boundary boards.

Following on that Saturday evening, there was still time for England to lose three wickets, all to Keith Boyce, including Knott who had gone in as nightwatchman. So Luckhurst had to come in after all and, since Boycott had been batting for nearly a hour and a half and so presumably had his eye in, Luckhurst asked him if he would take the last over of the day. Boycott agreed, only to fall to a sucker punch. Boyce dropped one short, Boycott hooked, failed to get hold of it, and was caught.

Furious with himself for getting out tamely to the hook twice in one match, he pitched into Luckhurst in the dressing room afterwards, only to be told by Illingworth to shut up. He then started again, at which Illingworth told him again to shut up, only this time more forcefully. That night Boycott, presumably still in agonies at having thrown away his wicket, was taken to hospital with a bad nosebleed, a condition to which he was prone when highly stressed.

So upset was Boycott the perfectionist by this experience that thereafter he entirely renounced the hook shot. Indeed, he gradually gave up any shot to which he got out, eventually proving that it was entirely possible to go to a century (though admittedly over the course of many hours) entirely with the aid of a solid forward push. This is not, though, to belittle his contribution in any way. The figures correctly show that he was one of England's most successful batsmen ever, and he is the holder of a proud statistic: on no occasion during his Test career did he score a century and England go on to lose the match (presumably because there was never enough time left).

England were bundled out on the Monday for 193 to lose by an innings and 226 runs, their biggest margin of defeat since Brisbane in 1946–47. Frank Hayes, incidentally, had failed twice in the match – his century at the Oval was beginning to look increasingly like a flash in the pan.

Before the match had even finished, it was announced that Ray Illingworth had been sacked as England captain. When Geoff Boycott learned that Illingworth's successor would be not the northern working-class G. Boycott (captain of Yorkshire, 57 Test caps, 11 Test centuries) but the southern middle-class M.H. Denness (captain of Kent, nine Test caps, no Test centuries), he suffered a severe nosebleed.[103]

---

[103] *Yorkshire and Back* op. cit.

CHAPTER 18

ENGLAND'S 1973–74 TOUR OF THE WEST INDIES

As Illingworth himself says, he had always recognised that there would come a time when it was right for him to relinquish the captaincy. To be summarily dismissed without any explanation, especially when he had apparently been given to understand that same morning by at least one selector that his reappointment would be automatic, must on any view rank as appalling treatment of someone who had been not only one of England's most successful captains, but had frequently looked one of the best players in the side.

He had won 12 of his 30 Tests as captain, and lost just five, two of them to the rampaging, brilliant West Indies side that summer of 1973. One of his five losses had come when he was off the field injured, and another with just one fit seam bowler to call upon. In addition to being a front line bowler he had developed into a genuine all-rounder who averaged 28.62 with the bat, even if his heroics against the Rest of the World are left out of account.

He has a genuine claim to be considered as one of England's greatest captains: his only fault on the field was a tendency to underbowl himself, and surely everyone is allowed one weakness. Off the field, he had a disconcerting tendency to give a straight answer to a straight question, not a trait that endeared him to the more political world of the cricket establishment. By any standards, he was shabbily treated by the selectors throughout his career as captain, and at no time more shabbily than in their ending of it.

He believes that his sacking was for political, not cricketing reasons. It was felt that he was getting his own way too often in selection meetings,[104] and surely his mutiny in Australia cannot have been forgotten or forgiven. It seems likely that ever since he returned victorious with the Ashes, there was an element within the establishment who wanted him gone and were awaiting their chance.

With their choice of Mike Denness, the establishment once again signalled their desire for a gentleman captain, one who would know how to behave and not step out of line; someone who was 'one of us', a fresh-faced young subaltern who would unquestioningly lead his platoon of chirpy working-class lads out of the trenches and towards the machine guns. In fact, Denness had enjoyed a relatively ordinary middle-class upbringing in Scotland, where he was as well known as a rugby player as he was a cricketer. He played at Ayr Academy alongside future Scotland captain Ian McLauchlan.

He had, however, been Colin Cowdrey's protégé for many years, captaining Kent when Cowdrey was unavailable and taking over the job full-time after Kent won the Championship in 1970. Doubtless there were those who believed he might carry on the Cowdrey tradition of breezy bonhomie. He was in fact a very likeable man.

As described earlier, while he had achieved a few good individual knocks in 1973, he certainly was not in the sort of form to challenge seriously for a place in the Test side. He had been given various chances and, apart from briefly in Pakistan under Tony Lewis on a dead wicket, had not really impressed. In fairness, the same could be said of various other batsmen who would go on to become fixtures in the side, notably Fletcher and Amiss, but the fact that the selectors had persevered with them despite

---

[104] *Yorkshire and Back* op. cit.

their disappointing performance and yet not with Denness speaks volumes as to how their relative talents were viewed.

The obvious choice to succeed Illingworth, and presumably his own preferred candidate given that they were old friends and teammates, would have been Boycott, though interestingly Christopher Martin-Jenkins, writing shortly afterwards,[105] does not mention him at all, while giving a canter to less likely candidates such as Cowdrey, Brearley, Richard Gilliatt of Hampshire, and even Brian Close. It seems clear from this that there was already a prevalent view in establishment quarters that Boycott's temperament ruled him out of contention, particularly as he was not even named as vice-captain (Greig was). The problem was that nobody ever had the consideration to take him quietly to one side and explain this.

Boycott had been captain of Yorkshire since 1971; the limitations to his performance of that role that his character presented had already started to become evident. Yet as the most experienced member of the team, and by far the best batsman of recent years, he must surely have felt mightily aggrieved to be overlooked. One feels that had Denness been an expert psychologist such as Brearley, Boycott's feelings could somehow have been better managed, perhaps by making a great show of consulting him on the field and in the nets. As it was, Denness was just a very nice man, and understandably insecure in his new job, so England's clumsy man-management once again came back to haunt them.

By some genius of planning, that winter's tour was to the West Indies, and so England (or rather the MCC as England were still referred to when touring overseas) faced the prospect of immediately facing again the side which had just trounced them, but this time with home advantage reversed. One year hence, after what promised to be fairly gentle opposition over the summer from India and Pakistan, would come another stern challenge: defending the Ashes in Australia.

England picked four batsmen who could open the batting: Denness himself, Boycott, Amiss and what many felt to be a long-overdue recall for the rumbustious John Jameson. Fletcher and Hayes were the specialist

---

[105] Christopher Martin-Jenkins, *Testing Time*, Macdonald, London, 1974

middle order, Greig and Birkenshaw (presumably viewed as a like-for-like replacement for Illingworth) the all-rounders. Pocock and Underwood completed the spin department. Within the complement of seamers, there was no place for Snow. Arnold and Willis, who had both bowled well during the summer, were joined by Chris Old and new boy Mike Hendrick. Snow says that Denness wanted him both on this tour and on the following Ashes tour, and called him to say so, but then faced stiff opposition to the idea within the selectors.[106]

Having just been beaten in England by the West Indies, the omens did not look good. Boyce and Julien formed a lively new-ball attack, while Sobers remained a class left-arm seamer. As for Lance Gibbs, Ray Illingworth would say sardonically, 'he was not exactly the world's worst'.[107] In fact, not until Harbhajan Singh and Muttiah Muralitharan many years later would any offspinner take more wickets in a career, and Gibbs held for quite a while the career record for any type of bowler (succeeding Fred Trueman and preceding Dennis Lillee).

The fact that Julien and Boyce, both tremendous late-order batsmen, batted at eight and nine in the first Test, speaks volumes for the batting strength of the side as well. Only in the as yet unresolved quest for a successful opening partner for Roy Fredericks could there be said to be the merest hint of a chink in the Caribbean armour.

Ironically, it was this apparent weakness which was to turn out to be the West Indies' greatest and most unexpected strength.

Lawrence Rowe had exploded onto the Test scene in 1972 against New Zealand, a series that is more usually remembered for the exploits of another great batsman, Glenn Turner. Not content with scoring a century on Test debut, he turned it into a double century, and then followed this up with an unbeaten century in the next match. However, his form then fell away over the next three matches, and he was disappointing the following winter against Australia, so was not chosen for the 1973 tour of England. In addition to his poor form, there were also concerns about his health.

---

106 *Cricket Rebel* op. cit.
107 *Yorkshire and Back* op. cit.

Most inconveniently for a cricketer, he was found to have an allergy to grass, leading one of his teammates to tell Garry Sobers 'if Lawrence sneezes, put the other side in, skipper'.

He was, however, recalled to the side for the first Test to open with Fredericks, and would play a significant role in the series.

For England, the tour was dominated by two figures: Dennis Amiss and Tony Greig. Amiss would truly come of age as a Test opener on this tour, scoring 663 runs at an average of nearly 83, with three centuries including an unbeaten 262 in Jamaica. Boycott, with 421 runs at an average of 47, would normally have expected to top the averages, but had to be content in the event with third place behind Amiss and Greig.

For Tony Greig, this was the series when all the youthful promise was fulfilled, and he showed the first glimpses of becoming just possibly one of the great all-rounders of all time. Not only did he come second in the batting averages ahead of Boycott, but he dominated the bowling as well, taking an amazing 28 wickets at an average of just under 23. To place these figures in context, this was as many wickets as the next four most successful England bowlers took between them. Interestingly, Greig had become captain of Sussex during the summer, bringing the troubled reign of Mike Griffith to an end, so it is surprising that he, like Boycott a county captain, was overlooked for the England captaincy: the England selectors were determined to have Denness, an appointment with which they had clearly been toying for some time.

For Denness the tour was not a success. He averaged less than 26, with a highest score of 67, though he was unlucky to be twice run out. Only Jameson, who also had a disappointing tour, playing in only two matches, fared worse, suffering the ignominy of ending below Bob Willis in the batting averages. Of his captaincy, Christopher Martin-Jenkins would later say:

> … one felt that the confidence Denness had outwardly shown was in fact a kind of whistling in the dark. It appeared he was being carried along by events and, to a certain extent, by his team.[108]

---

[108] Christopher Martin-Jenkins, *Assault on the Ashes*, MacDonald, London, 1975

In the first match at Trinidad, England were bowled out for 131 in their first innings, and were destined to lose by seven wickets despite a fighting double century opening partnership by Boycott and Amiss second time around. For the West Indies, the recalled Rowe failed twice with the bat.

The match was chiefly memorable for a controversial incident at the end of the second day. After the last ball of the day had been played, but before the umpire had called 'over' or 'time', Kallicharran started to walk towards the pavilion, and was promptly run out by Greig. Predictably, the crowd erupted. Garry Sobers, though he disapproved strongly of Greig's actions, showed his sportsmanship by sitting with Greig in the England dressing room for two hours after play had ended and then escorting him personally through the crowd. Fortunately good sense prevailed and England withdrew their appeal overnight, allowing Kallicharran to resume his innings in the morning.

The second Test at Jamaica was a high-scoring draw, and included a century from Rowe in West Indies' mammoth total of 583 (at one stage they were 400-3). Not to be outdone, Dennis Amiss then batted for nine and a half hours for 262 not out, very nearly carrying his bat (the match ended with England only nine wickets down). It was not a good match for bowlers and, perhaps in recognition of this, Kanhai achieved the captain's grand slam by giving all ten fielders a bowl.

The third Test in Barbados was another high-scoring draw, featuring 302 from Lawrence Rowe, and centuries for Kallicharran, Greig and Fletcher. One event of significance occurred, however. Greig, who had never before tried doing so in a Test match, switched from fast-medium to bowling offspinners (though in fairness to the likes of Laker and Gibbs, they could perhaps more fairly be described as medium-pace offcutters). Whatever their most appropriate description, they were successful: Greig finished with six wickets. However, since West Indies declared at 598-8, and 164 of those runs were conceded by Greig, any 'success' was clearly relative.

The fourth match in Guyana was also a draw: a good batting wicket combining with the loss of about a day and a half's play to rain. Amiss and Greig made centuries for England; Fredericks just missed out on one for West Indies.

For the final Test, the tour came back to Trinidad with the West Indies one up.

In their first innings England fared better than they had in the first Test, managing to score 267, built around a dour six-hour 99 from Geoff Boycott. He was not a happy man when he was caught at the wicket off Bernard Julien. It did not feel enough, a feeling that was confirmed when Fredericks and Rowe put on over a hundred together for West Indies' first wicket. Then Pocock had both Fredericks and Kallicharran out quickly, but Rowe and Lloyd carried on serenely, taking West Indies over 200 and close to England's score.

That England had gone into the match with only one specialist fast bowler, Arnold, but three specialist spinners, was clear proof that they were expecting the wicket to turn, but so far Pocock, Birkenshaw and Underwood had enjoyed limited success. It was Greig, switching again to his offcutters, who made the vital breakthrough, having Lloyd caught at the wicket, and West Indies now collapsed from 224-3 to 305 all out, Greig taking every single remaining wicket, including Sobers for a duck. That Derek Underwood, a much more celebrated purveyor of much the same style of bowling, should finish wicketless, is perhaps the greatest testament to just how great Greig's performance was that day. He finished with 8-86. Alan Knott, who had kept to Titmus and Illingworth, and batted against Gibbs, would later say that during this one individual game Greig was the greatest offspinner he ever saw in action.[109]

Though England were now behind on the first innings, Greig's performance sent a surge of morale through the side. Suddenly it appeared as if anything might be possible. However, they were again disappointed by their performance when they batted. Once more Boycott was the cornerstone, achieving a well-deserved century, with dogged support from first Fletcher and then Knott. They could manage only 263, setting West Indies 226 to win.

This time Arnold bowled only a token couple of overs before giving way to an all-spin attack. Again Rowe and Fredericks looked relatively

---

[109] Rob Steen, 'Why does Greig get a raw deal?', www.cricinfo.com, May 2011

untroubled, but with the score on 63 Birkenshaw dismissed Rowe, and Kallicharran bagged a pair, edging Greig to Fletcher at slip. Then Fredericks was run out, a disaster for West Indies, and suddenly they were 65-3. Kanhai and Lloyd survived, but looked in constant trouble against Greig – he dismissed them both before long to leave West Indies 85-5. However, with Sobers at the wicket nothing was ever impossible.

It was a strangely muted Sobers, though, who seemed content to graft for victory, with Deryck Murray, an underrated batsman in this team of stars, employing similar tactics at the other end. Successful tactics too, bringing them a 50 partnership. Still only five wickets down, they were less than a hundred from England's total.

Then Sobers misjudged a ball from Underwood and was bowled. Underwood had not had a successful tour, but had impressed with his perseverance, so it was fitting not only that he should make the key breakthrough, but that it should be the wicket of Sobers, his personal bogeyman. Always less comfortable bowling to left-handers, he took the wicket of the great man only twice. This time it was vital, almost certainly changing the outcome of the game.

Julien lasted only five balls before falling to Pocock, and now there was light at the end of the tunnel. Yet it would take England a nerve-jangling hundred minutes to take the remaining three wickets, with Keith Boyce batting immaculately and responsibly to take West Indies ever closer to their target. Once Murray fell to Greig, though, it was asking too much of Inshan Ali and Lance Gibbs to survive for long. Denness finally brought Arnold back to take the last wicket, and England had won by 26 runs to square the series. Greig had taken five wickets to add to his eight from the first innings.

Despite the batting heroics of Geoff Boycott, it was perhaps inevitable that the game should become known as 'Greig's match'. Only ten players had ever taken more wickets in a Test match for England – it was a performance that put him amongst the bowling greats such as Jim Laker, Sydney Barnes, Hedley Verity and Wilfred Rhodes.

On a much sadder note, the game also marked the end of perhaps the greatest Test career of all time: that of Garry Sobers, who had graced the cricketing stage since making his international debut at the age of just 17 in 1954. His record score of 365 not out would endure for 36 years until being beaten (twice) by Brian Lara. At the time of his retirement he also held the record for runs in a Test career, and even the likes of Hobbs, Tendulkar, Hutton, Ponting and Lara have failed to match his career batting average. Oh yes, and he took 235 Test wickets in three different bowling styles. It seems bathetic to add that the game also brought to a close the brief Test career of Jackie Birkenshaw.

Sadly, too, it marked the last time that England ever fielded a bowling attack including three specialist spinners (as an additional oddity, so did the West Indies). From now on the role of the spinner would decline steadily, as they became increasingly seen as defensive stock bowlers rather than attacking shock bowlers, and struggling to justify even one place in a side. It would take the likes of Warne, Kumble, Harbhajan and Muralitharan to prompt a glorious revival, but for the next decade and a half, all-seam attacks would gradually become the new model, at least outside the Indian subcontinent.

From the tour as a whole, the English selectors could take great comfort from the performances of Greig, Amiss, and Boycott. Yet the success of the former merely highlighted how disappointing both the middle-order batting and the spin bowling had been. Fletcher, Denness, Jameson and Hayes had managed only two scores of over 50 between them, Pocock, Birkenshaw and Underwood just 16 wickets. Without Snow, the fast bowling too had lacked penetration. Though Arnold had been steadiness personified, he had been much less effective when removed from English conditions.

For the final match itself, the selectors must have been supremely grateful. Had England lost it rather than won it, then it is unlikely that Denness could have survived as captain, and their choice would have been exposed as the non-cricketing decision that it clearly had been. Deprived of the captaincy, Greig or Boycott would still without question have commanded a place in the side as a player. Denness, equally without question, would not.

In the event, the selectors' blushes were spared. Yet again, though, it is interesting to conjecture what might have been. Had Denness been discarded, there would have been only two possible candidates: Greig and Boycott. Cowdrey was now 41, had not captained Kent for the last three seasons, and his Test career had ended in 1971. Injury had forced the retirement of Tony Lewis. M.J.K. Smith had not been able to re-establish himself as a player in 1972. In fact, by far the best candidate would almost certainly still have been Ray Illingworth, who would go on playing county cricket until 1976, but to go back to him would have required impossible levels of honesty and contrition. Whoever had been chosen, Denness's original selection would have been ruthlessly exploited by the press as a fiasco, and probably at least one of the selectors (presumably the chairman, Alec Bedser) would have felt compelled to resign.

CHAPTER 19

THE SUMMER OF 1974

As it was, Denness could be left safely in charge for the coming summer against India and Pakistan. Yet this was a matter of the gravest significance. Coming up that winter was a crucial Ashes tour in Australia; clearly it would be a nonsense to allow Denness to captain England during the summer and then appoint someone else for the winter tour. If a change was to be made, it had to be made now, to give the new man a decent chance to get used to the job. So, despite the reservations they must have had about his batting, the selectors were effectively confirming him in place for the next 14 Test matches (including six in Australia and two in New Zealand). It is deeply symbolic of the selectors' attitudes that they were prepared to make a much greater commitment to the struggling young officer, Denness, than they had ever been prepared to make to the experienced and successful platoon sergeant, Illingworth.

Perhaps if anything was weighing in the selectors' minds other than a strong desire not to look foolish, they might have reflected that Denness's shortcomings as a Test batsman seemed to be exposed most cruelly by extreme pace, which was unlikely to be forthcoming that winter. Dennis

Lillee had suffered a stress fracture of the spine early in 1973, and nobody came back from one of those, certainly not a fast bowler.

Australia had not yet found anyone else to compare either with Lillee or even the unfairly discarded McKenzie. Over the winter their opening bowling had been entrusted to Max Walker and Geoff Dymock, neither of whom would claim to be a fast bowler, with either Walters or Greg Chappell operating as first change. The fast-medium left-arm Gary Gilmour, who bowled rather like John Lever of Essex, had enjoyed some success in their last Test match against New Zealand, but again was hardly likely to trouble anyone for pace. Against such an emasculated attack, Denness, a good county batsman, could safely be expected to chip in with some runs.

The Indian touring team of 1974 were to prove a disappointment after their victory in 1971. In particular, their two medium pacers (Abid Ali and Solkar) must qualify as the friendliest opening attack that Test cricket has ever seen, designed simply to take the shine off the ball before the spinners began the serious business of trying to bowl out the opposition. They were not even taken over-seriously by their own team; there were from time to time suggestions that one of them should drop out, and allow Sunil Gavaskar to open the bowling (Gavaskar, while undeniably a great batsman, would take just one wicket in his Test career).

One of the Indians' early tour matches was against Yorkshire. The match ended in a draw, and the only event of note was that Geoff Boycott, the great technician, the man who had faced the world's fastest bowlers, was twice out cheaply lbw: to Abid Ali in the first innings and Solkar in the second.

Less than a week later, India played MCC in the traditional fixture at Lord's which was often used by England as a Test trial. Interestingly, this match marked the representative debut of Phil Edmonds, as well as the rather less likely England candidates Harry Pilling and David Acfield. The match was inconclusive, save that Denness encouragingly scored a century against admittedly lacklustre bowling. Geoff Boycott, however, having fallen twice to the inswinger at Bradford, now fell twice to the outswinger at Lord's, each time caught by Gavaskar at slip off Solkar. He made a total of 13 runs in the game.

Nothing that happened in this game was to influence selection for the first Test at Old Trafford, though there was a welcome return to the England side for John Edrich, with Denness batting at four. The MCC won the match easily, with centuries from Fletcher in the first innings and Edrich in the second. Gavaskar scored a century on the losing side for India.

Again there was a touch of tragicomedy about Boycott's involvement in the game. In the first innings he was out lbw to Abid Ali for 10. In the second innings, against the equally gentle medium pace of Solkar, he was caught behind by Engineer for 6. He had now fallen cheaply six times in succession against India in the course of just a few weeks, lbw twice to Abid Ali and the other four times falling to Solkar. Cricketers' humour is not always of the gentlest variety, and one can perhaps imagine some of the remarks which may have passed as he trudged back into the dressing room each time.

Between the first and the second Test matches something occurred which was to have great significance for the future of English cricket. Geoff Boycott made himself unavailable for England until further notice.

Since Boycott himself has always preserved a diplomatic silence about his reasons, one is forced to resort to speculation about his motivation. There have been no shortage of theories put forward, most notably (1) that his withdrawal was a protest against having Mike Denness as captain and (2) that when this grew into an extended absence, it was through not wanting to have to face the hostility of Lillee and Thomson that winter.

Don Mosey, Boycott's biographer, quickly disposes of theory (2), and rightly so.[110] During his career Boycott faced some of the fastest bowling the world has ever known, and stood up to it. He was targeted by hostile West Indian bowlers such as Holding, Garner and Roberts, yet never gave ground. To suggest that he was in any way motivated by apprehension of facing fast bowling is surely nonsense. Also, this theory is exploded by another factor which Mosey does not mention: during the summer of 1974 nobody had the slightest idea that England were going to face Lillee and

---

[110] Don Mosey, *Boycott*, Methuen, London, 1985

Thomson that winter. Dennis Lillee was known to be out of the game, probably for good, and Jeff Thomson was just a name, who had played a solitary Test against Pakistan in 1972 and finished wicketless (though, unbeknownst to outsiders, with a broken foot).

There are problems with theory (1) as well, at least as stated. If Boycott was aggrieved at being passed over for the captaincy, and he was certainly entitled to be, then surely the time to have taken a stand would have been the previous autumn, by announcing himself unavailable to tour the West Indies under Denness. He might even have done so, with all the moral strength of a superb tour of the West Indies behind him, at the beginning of the current summer when Denness, having failed as a batsman in the West Indies, was reappointed as captain against India. To do so now made little sense.

What both these theories ignore is that human beings are complex mechanisms, and that in consequence human decision-making tends to be a complex process. Mosey understands this, musing that probably different factors weighted with Boycott at different times.

Boycott had been a moderate player initially. In his early days in the Yorkshire League he used to bat below future Test umpire Harold 'Dickie' Bird, and his friend, the journalist Michael Parkinson. By dint of great hard work and discipline he turned himself not just into a good player, but into a great one. Quite possibly he is unique; it is difficult to think of anyone else in the history of the game who has achieved anything comparable.

One consequence of this is that Boycott, as a manufactured player, was always prey to insecurity, requiring constant reassurance that he really was a quality batsman.[111] Another is that he was fiercely proud and protective of his technique, which he had meticulously crafted over the years. Should any crack, real or imagined, appear in it, then his reaction would probably be similar to a top golfer losing both his form and his favourite putter at the same time. When he was being captained by Close or Illingworth, such reassurance was always on hand. Once he was captaining Yorkshire himself, he not only lacked any friendly shoulder to

---

[111] Mosey, Close and Illingworth all agree on this.

cry upon, but he also overlooked the fact that other members of the team might have similar needs. Instead his attitude that 'if I can do it, you can do it; all you need to do is to work harder' drove a wedge between him and the rest of the team, resulting in a very troubled dressing room. In the eyes of many, this would prove his hamartia, the character flaw which would tragically blight his captaincy at Yorkshire, and lead to years of divisive infighting at the club.

Mosey suggests that with his beloved technique apparently being mocked by the most modest of bowling, and deprived of someone such as Illingworth to whom to turn for advice, Boycott found himself in a position where mentally he simply could not cope any more. If one considers that he was already under pressure because of the first internal rumblings about his captaincy at Yorkshire, that this was his benefit season and he had already fallen out with the head of his benefit committee, and that in such circumstances his repressed resentment at the selectors over the captaincy may well have come bubbling back to the surface, this is an entirely credible view.

It seems inconceivable that Boycott, for whom scoring runs for England was almost an obsession, should ever have intended his absence to last for more than a couple of games. It is therefore truly difficult to explain why it should have lasted as long as it did. Staying with a purely objective view, the fact that it did so was clearly Boycott's own fault. He was asked by Alec Bedser to contact the selectors when he was ready to play again, but failed to do so. Notwithstanding his silence, the selectors contacted him to ask if he would be available to tour Australia that winter, but by then they had already announced that Denness would captain the side, with John Edrich as vice-captain. With echoes of Cowdrey in 1970, Boycott delayed a long time. Then, unlike Cowdrey, he said 'no'. In retrospect, both of them got it wrong.

From here on it is very difficult to escape the conclusion that Boycott was, as Mosey puts it, skulking in his tent like Achilles, brooding over the captaincy. That the selectors should not have seen the potential for the problem to arise in the first place is unfortunate; that they had previously been similarly blind to Cowdrey's mounting angst shows a sad record of insensitivity. That they should not have sought some way to reach out to Boycott during the rest of the summer, to find out what was troubling him, and to do their best to bring him back into the fold (perhaps offering him in advance the vice-captaincy in Australia) was more than unfortunate – it was tragic. It was to cost England the services of their best batsman for over three years, and to cost Boycott perhaps the best three years of his Test career.

The story of the rest of the tour against India is quickly told, as neither of the remaining two Test matches had any great relevance as sporting contests.

At Lord's England won by an innings and 268 runs, India being bowled out for just 42 in their second innings. There were centuries for Amiss, Denness and Greig in England's massive 629 all out.

At Edgbaston England won by an innings again, with David Lloyd, Boycott's replacement, scoring 214, and Denness another century. This was a deeply disappointing series, with India showing none of the fight they had displayed so impressively in 1971, and fielding perhaps the friendliest bowling attack seen in England in modern times. It was certainly little suited to the classic 'English seamer' conditions exploited so well by Old, Arnold and Hendrick.

England had learned little, except that all their batsmen could score runs against undemanding bowling, and that all their bowlers could take wickets against batsmen showing for the most part a sad lack of fight.

Pakistan, it was thought, would be different. For one thing they did have some decent faster bowlers in Asif Masood, Sarfraz Nawaz and Imran Khan, though the latter two had not yet grown into the great bowlers they would be in their maturity. For another, England had been made all too well aware in 1971 of just how effective Pakistan's batting could be. So it was to prove.

In the first match, in seamer-friendly conditions at Headingley, Pakistan made 285, largely thanks to Sarfraz, whom nobody had suspected of batting pretensions, contributing a robust 50 at number ten. England were then held by Pakistan's seamers to just 183; only Lloyd, Greig and Knott offered any serious resistance. Now it was Pakistan's turn to struggle against Old, Hendrick and Arnold, this time totalling just 179, leaving England 282 to win, a tall order on this pitch and in cloudy conditions.

England began badly, losing both openers to stumble to 22-2. However, Edrich, Denness and Fletcher then dug in. With wickets continuing to fall, however, England finished the fourth day at 238-6. Frustratingly, the whole of the final day was lost to rain, leaving each side able to claim a moral victory. In truth, though, England were probably lucky to escape. Fletcher was batting with Old, with only Underwood, Arnold and Hendrick to come, Pakistan were bowling well (Sarfraz in particular), and conditions were far from easy.

This had been a good match for Sarfraz, who had been discovered playing in a park in Lahore by Roger Prideaux while on Cowdrey's ill-fated tour of Pakistan in 1969. Then captaining Northants, Prideaux both requested and received by telegram permission to sign him on the spot as an overseas player.[112]

The second match at Lord's was also badly affected by the weather. It seemed that heavy rain before the game had somehow seeped under the covers, because after lunch on the first day the sun came out, and the drying pitch started taking excessive turn, as had happened at the Oval in 1968. Underwood, in 'Deadly' mode, bowled Zaheer at 91-2. With Greig switching to his offcutters at the other end, Pakistan lost their last nine wickets for 39 runs, Underwood finishing with 5-20.

England were reduced to 118-6 by more accurate Pakistani bowling, but were now indebted to a stand between Knott and Old which saw them finish on 270.

The next day more heavy rain fell; again some seemed to have seeped under the covers, though again this was not immediately apparent, as Pakistan were at one stage 191-3. However, as the pitch started drying, Underwood prompted almost as dramatic a collapse as in the first innings, Pakistan losing their last six wickets for 34 runs.

Now it was England's turn to feel aggrieved, as once again rain robbed the game of the whole of its last day, leaving them just 60 runs short of victory. Given the circumstances, though, a draw was undoubtedly the fairest result. Pakistan made a formal protest to Lord's about the state of the covering,

---

[112] *Beating the Bat* op cit

criticism which Lord's, in a predictably pompous press statement, seemed to accept (they had little choice).

The match at the Oval was a high-scoring draw, with Pakistan's batting firing on all cylinders to score 600-7 declared, Zaheer Abbas showing his class with 240. England replied with 545, including big centuries from Amiss and Fletcher, plus another good score (65 this time) from Old, raising hopes, sadly to remain unfulfilled, of him progressing into a genuine all-rounder. On the last afternoon, England reduced Pakistan to 94-4, but the match was long since dead.

So the summer had been one of two halves. Against an inept Indian side England had triumphed. Against a challenging Pakistani one they had struggled. Nowhere was this contrast more sharply expressed than in the batting performance of their captain. Against India he had scored 299. Against Pakistan he had scored 91.

From Australia, as the England selectors sat down to choose the touring party to defend the Ashes, came news that Dennis Lillee was making Herculean efforts to get himself fit again, but these were only half-believed. A man with a fractured spine does not suddenly become a fast bowler again.

It soon became clear that England would travel to Australia missing their best batsman (Boycott) and their best bowler (Snow). Boycott's replacement was Brian Luckhurst. Snow's continued omission from the side seemed to be on the grounds that he was 'difficult'. Perhaps the selectors did not want to burden Denness with having to deal with such a mercurial character.

Denness and Edrich had already been named as captain and vice-captain. The other batsmen were Amiss, Fletcher, Lloyd and Luckhurst. Greig was the sole recognised all-rounder, Knott and Taylor the wicketkeepers. There was a surprise recall for Peter Lever, whom many had thought most unfortunate to be overlooked for so long, alongside Arnold, Old, Hendrick and Willis. The spin department provided another surprise. Alongside Derek Underwood was Fred Titmus, who had played his last Test match in 1968 before having four of his toes mangled by a boat propeller. While the return of the ever popular Titmus was warmly welcomed, one wonders at the logic. If Titmus had (as many believed) remained the best offspinner in England once he returned to county cricket after his dreadful injury, why had he not been on previous tours in preference to Pocock, particularly since he was still something of an all-rounder (though his batting had fallen off in recent years) while Pocock was not?

The balance of the side prompts questions too. Six specialist batsmen allowed little scope for injury or loss of form, while two of the five specialist seamers were always likely to play little cricket, barring injuries. With Arnold known to be much less effective in non-English conditions, and Old prone to niggling injuries, a quartet of Snow, Lever, Willis and Hendrick would have had a better feel to it. Over Greig too, there hung a question mark. The balance of the team seemed to suggest that he would need to play in almost every game, with consequent risk of injury or exhaustion; in the event, only Denness, Amiss and Fletcher (none of whom had to bowl as well as bat) would play in more tour matches.

From Australia was now starting to come talk of a bowler called Thomson. Perhaps some of the English batsmen such as Edrich, Luckhurst and Fletcher thought back to Illingworth's tour and assumed this referred to Alan 'Froggy' Thomson, who had not troubled them unduly. If so, they were to be quickly disabused. As *The Guardian* would later point out, Froggy Thomson ran up more quickly than he bowled, whereas Jeff Thomson was the other way round.

CHAPTER 20

THE 1974–75 ASHES

England's first encounter with Jeff Thomson came during a warm-up match against Queensland prior to the first Test in Brisbane. Thomson bowled fast, but rather loosely, though occasionally accurately enough to cause significant problems, especially to Amiss, who looked ill at ease, and fell to Thomson in each innings. In view of what was subsequently to occur, it is only fair to note that when Queensland batted Willis bowled several bouncers, one of which hit Geoff Dymock, Thomson's opening bowling partner, on the shoulder.

A few days later the first Test began. There indeed was Dennis Lillee, back in the Australian side and apparently restored to full health. Partnering him was Jeff Thomson. In support was Max Walker, plus the legspin of Terry Jenner. Ross Edwards was back in the side, as too was his namesake Wally Edwards, who was being tried out as an opening partner for Ian Redpath.

For England, Old had succumbed to one of his niggling strains, while Arnold had not found his touch, so their three remaining seamers, Willis, Hendrick, and Lever, took to the field supported by Greig and Underwood.

David Lloyd was also injured, so Luckhurst opened with Amiss, and Edrich batted at number three.

Australia won the toss and batted, quickly losing both their openers to Willis and Hendrick, the former having bowled several bouncers at Redpath before bowling him with a full length delivery. A long, gritty stand by the Chappell brothers then rescued Australia. However, England continued to bowl tightly and, once these two were parted, wickets fell regularly to leave Australia 229-8. Frustratingly for England, though, the last two wickets put on exactly 80 runs, with Max Walker in particular looking stylish and composed. In the end it took a run-out of Thomson by Denness to bring the proceedings to a close. Lillee was dismissed by Tony Greig with a fast-medium bouncer that he top-edged to Alan Knott. As he left the field, he said something to Greig, perhaps enquiring how he was enjoying his time in Australia.

Sure enough, when England batted, they were greeted by a barrage of sharply lifting deliveries. Lillee was bowling authentic bouncers, but Thomson, generating furious pace from his trademark slingy action, was frequently getting the ball to rear alarmingly from not far short of a length. In the space of his first four overs he dismissed both England openers. Denness and Fletcher soon followed to Walker and Lillee. That England achieved any sort of total at all was due almost entirely to Tony Greig, who launched a ferocious counter-attack, hitting boundary after boundary. He was ninth man out, shortly after coming to his century, and England were all out for 265.

There was just time before the end of the third day for England to take two wickets: Wally Edwards, who was finding Test cricket something of a struggle, and the Australian captain. At 51-2 the game was nicely poised going into the rest day. Australia were only just over a hundred in front, with eight wickets in hand.

Eight wickets quickly became seven when Willis bowled Redpath soon after play resumed, but from this point on the game ran steadily away from England. Runs all down the order from the younger Chappell, Ross Edwards, Walters and Marsh enabled Australia to declare late in the evening leaving England 333 to win. England survived the brief remaining period of play, which was briefer than it might otherwise have been. In doubtful light, Thomson bowled three successive bouncers at Amiss, whereupon the umpires took the players off the field.

England began the final day with fine intentions of saving the game and even, with another Greig firework display, forcing a win, but these aspirations were quickly simply swept away. First Luckhurst offered a tame edge to slip off Lillee, then England were destroyed by a ferocious spell of bowling from Jeff Thomson, both Edrich and Amiss (who again fell twice to Thomson) finishing the game with broken fingers into the bargain. The bowling had been fierce and hostile, and the English batsmen had seemed to have no real answer to it. They managed only 166 runs, exactly half the total required.

As a somewhat shell-shocked England team flew across Australia to Perth, their original selection of only six specialist batsmen had required only a few weeks to be shown up for the gamble it was. With two of the six injured, they were already in need of a replacement. So it was that Mike Denness made his historic phone call to Colin Cowdrey.

For Cowdrey, Denness must have sounded like a voice from beyond the grave. Both he and everyone else had assumed his Test career to be well and truly over nearly three years ago. Yet without any hesitation he murmured that he would be delighted to help out, exactly as he might have done had he been asked to bring a spare table to a bridge supper, and went upstairs to pack his kit.

It was a mark of England's desperation that just four days after stepping off the plane from England, and not having played any first-class cricket for some months, Cowdrey found himself pitched straight into the second Test match alongside his old West Indies vice-captain, Fred Titmus. Surely neither could have expected ever to play another Test match, let alone in company with each other. England might have wanted to give their older statesman more time to acclimatise, but were left with little choice, both Edrich and Amiss being *hors de combat*.

So it was that Lloyd and Luckhurst found themselves opening for England after Denness had won the toss. They fared better than Amiss and Luckhurst had in either innings at Brisbane, putting on 44 before

Luckhurst was out, having already sustained a badly bruised hand, at which Cowdrey came in to bat, to a generous reception from the crowd. Finding himself at the non-striker's end at the beginning of the next over, he introduced himself to a startled Jeff Thomson, saying urbanely 'hello, we haven't met, have we? I'm Cowdrey.' Thomson, who had been banned for life from Australian Rules football for punching a referee on the jaw, was unused to such cocktail party niceties.

Until well into the afternoon Lloyd and Cowdrey progressed steadily, if slowly. Then with the score at 99 Cowdrey, who was moving well across to the off to get into line to the faster bowlers, tried too much of a good thing and was bowled around his legs by Thomson. Now the floodgates opened and England were dismissed for 208 on what looked a good batting wicket, only Knott reaching 50.

When Australia batted, centuries from Ross Edwards and Doug Walters saw them to 481, England's bowlers all struggling; already the final outcome was clear. This was first hastened by Jeff Thomson, who had been wayward in the first innings but now found his line and length to take five wickets, then delayed by Fred Titmus, who top-scored with 61. As with Cowdrey, his old-fashioned technique of getting right across behind the line of the ball contrasted with the looser methods employed by some of his teammates; the two 41-year-olds were giving the younger men a lesson in basic batsmanship. Watching the old-timers from the commentary box, Christopher Martin-Jenkins was moved to wonder whether Brian Close might not have been another useful addition to the England party.[113]

When Australia batted again they needed just 21 to win, which gave just enough time for Wally Edwards to be lbw to Arnold for a duck. Australia's win was convincing, built around their two centurions and Thomson, who skittled Greig, Denness and Fletcher in quick succession to shatter England's second innings.

So England went to Melbourne for the traditional Boxing Day Test already two down in the series, and with the press, both British and Australian, openly speculating about Denness's future. Strengthened by the return of

---

[113] *Assault on the Ashes* op. cit.

Amiss and Edrich from injury, they also rejigged their bowling, with Old and Arnold making way for Hendrick and Underwood.

England again batted first and made 242, Edrich and Cowdrey coming to the rescue after a poor start, and gamely battling a combination of vicious short-pitched bowling from Thomson and high-class pace and swing from Lillee. Once both were out at 110, Denness failed again, and Greig was run out. Only another plucky 50 from Knott enabled England to post a respectable total.

Tragedy struck England in the sixth over of Australia's reply when Hendrick pulled up in agony from a torn thigh muscle; he was out of the match and out of the tour. This was a major disaster as England had gone into the game with only two specialist seamers, so Greig, bowling his fast-medium, had to deputise as opening bowler and both Titmus and Underwood had to do a lot of bowling. Bob Willis rose to the occasion, extracting pace and bounce much as Thomson had done, and restricting Australia to 241.

England then briefly threatened to take the game by the scruff of the neck as Amiss and Lloyd put on 115 for the first wicket, but four quick wickets from Lillee and Thomson saw them collapse to 165-6, after which they were indebted to an attacking 60 from Tony Greig to get them to 244.

The three innings to date of 242, 241 and 244 respectively seemed to indicate pretty conclusively what a par score on this pitch was. With Australia needing 246 to win, a tight finish beckoned. The prospects for each of the three possible results fluctuated wildly during the final day. Eventually Marsh and Lillee, needing 55 to win from the last 15 overs, decided, a trifle puzzlingly, first to put the shutters up against the spinners and then, when Denness took the new ball, to launch a final frenzied assault which very nearly saw Australia home. They finished 11 runs short, but with England needing just another two wickets, honours may be said to have been even. Certainly the crowd had enjoyed a thrilling day.

Denness's awful individual run had continued, however, with him scoring just ten runs in the match, and dropping a vital catch on the last day which might have won the match. Before the Sydney Test match he took the courageous decision to drop himself from the team. It was the first time that any England captain had ever stood down openly admitting loss of form or lack of ability. Edrich, as vice-captain, stepped into his shoes.

Geoff Arnold took five wickets after Ian Chappell won the toss and chose to bat, but this did not prevent Australia from building a match-winning total of 405. Remarkably nobody scored a century, which demonstrates that runs were contributed all down the order, including 80 from newcomer Rick McCosker, replacing the hapless Wally Edwards. The innings was marred by some childish behaviour by Lillee, who objected to being hit on the elbow by a ball from Tony Greig, whereupon Greig was warned for intimidatory bowling. The irony of the situation, with Greig being a medium pacer, and Lillee one half of a combination which had consistently bowled short and aggressively all series, did not console England.

England were then all out for 295, which was much better than it might have been. At one stage they were 180-6 and only another fighting innings from Knott, and brave contributions from Titmus and Underwood, saved them from humiliation. Both Lillee and Thomson subjected the batsmen to a barrage of short-pitched bowling and several were hit, including Cowdrey. The umpire eventually warned both bowlers, but only unofficially and far too late. This did not stop Lillee from later hitting Underwood with another bouncer, for which he was again warned, but again unofficially.

Australia then went after runs with a view to a declaration, ably enabled by Greg Chappell, who scored a sparkling 144, and Ian Redpath, who contributed 105. During their innings Tony Greig completed his Test career double of 1,000 runs and 100 wickets. In fact, he rather overdid things, since he had scored 2,000 runs by the time he took his hundredth wicket, a feat then only achieved by three other England players (Rhodes, Bailey and Illingworth) and he did so in fewer matches than any of them.

England needed to bat for more than a day to save the match, but failed, undone this time as much by the able offspin of Ashley Mallett as by the aggression of Lillee and Thomson. The two fast bowlers were influential beyond the four wickets which they took, however. Cowdrey was hit by Thomson, Edrich was hit and had his ribs broken by Lillee, and

Fletcher was hit dangerously on the head by Thomson, and returned to the pavilion white and shaken. Remember that this was a time before helmets. If Fletcher's glove had not taken some of the pace off the ball first, then it is quite possible that cricket may have witnessed its first fatality that day in Sydney.

With their victory Australia won back the Ashes, but given the viciousness of Lillee and Thomson's bowling, it was a hollow victory. These were two great bowlers, both at their peak, and quite capable of bowling England out without resorting to terror tactics. It was this series, and this match in particular, which finally brought home to many people that, for some bowlers in the world, hitting and hurting a batsman was now at least as satisfying as taking his wicket.

Denness returned from his sabbatical for the fifth Test in Adelaide, and banished some of his personal demons with a sound 50, top-scoring in England's first innings total of 172. Australia had, however, already made 304, despite Derek Underwood taking seven wickets, and went on to win comfortably even without Jeff Thomson, who was unable to bowl at all in the second innings because of a shoulder injury. The highlight of the match for England was a fine century from Alan Knott in a losing cause in the second innings. Remarkably, this was only the second time that a wicketkeeper had made a century in Ashes Test matches, and Kent had also supplied the other one: Les Ames in 1934.

So England were now four–nil down in the series as they returned to Melbourne for the sixth and final Test with at least the encouragement that they would not have to face Thomson, whose shoulder had not recovered. They brought Peter Lever back into the side in place of Bob Willis, who was out with sore knees. Lever was angry, feeling that he had been marginalised by the rest of the party, not playing in any of the last four Tests.

At Brisbane he had bowled fast and short, and come away with no wickets. At Melbourne he reverted to type, bowling lusty fast-medium and pitching the ball up, as he had on that magic day at the Oval against the Rest of the World in 1970, and with similar results. He took 6-38, as Australia were bowled out for 152. There was a nasty incident along the way, though, when Greg Chappell was hit on the head by Lever, though it is unclear whether this was a genuine bouncer or a ball which kicked off a damp spot.

152 was never going to be enough, and was shortly to look a mockery. Dennis Lillee hurt his foot and was able to bowl only six overs when England batted and, without Thomson, and with the wicket taking no appreciable turn, Australia's attack suddenly appeared threadbare. Although Max Walker bowled magnificently to take eight wickets, Mike Denness and Keith Fletcher, the shackles of short-pitched fast bowling having been removed, both made superb centuries: 188 and 146 respectively. Incidentally this was, at the age of 33, Denness's highest score in first-class cricket, which gives some indication that his batting at county level was sound, but hardly extraordinary.

England reached the unusual riches of 529 and, hard though Australia fought, including a century by Greg Chappell, they were always going to be unable to make good their first innings collapse. England, in the absence of Lillee and Thomson, won by an innings.

Denness's century revealed little that was not already known or suspected. He was a good player of fast-medium bowling but looked horribly exposed against truly fast deliveries. It was, however, a reprieve, especially when coupled with another big century and an undefeated 50 in the following two Test matches in New Zealand. Taken together, would this be enough to give the selectors an excuse to persevere with him as captain?

Before that decision was taken, however, an incident occurred which seemed to many, at the time and since, both to epitomise everything that had gone horribly wrong with cricket and also to offer a turning point, an opportunity, if they wanted to take it, for players, umpires and administrators alike to pull back from the abyss which threatened to destroy the game. Sadly that opportunity would go unused, with tragic consequences to be shortly explored.

As the fourth day of the first Test against New Zealand drew to a close, the Kiwis' last pair was at the crease and facing obvious defeat. They still needed 83 runs to make England bat again and, with a whole day's play remaining, only one result was possible. Geoff Howarth, batsman brother of Hedley, was shepherding Ewan Chatfield, New Zealand's number eleven who had made a duck in the first innings, but was now providing unexpected resistance. Peter Lever felt that the time had come to test Chatfield with a bouncer, and duly produced one which struck the batsman a sickening blow on the head; he collapsed, poleaxed, to the ground and lay motionless.

He had in fact died. His heart had stopped, and he had a fractured skull. For good measure he had swallowed his tongue. Realising that no doctor was available, Bernard Thomas, England's long-standing physio, ran onto the ground with an ambulanceman. As Chatfield lay dead on the pitch, they worked quickly to disentangle his tongue and give him cardiac massage and mouth-to-mouth resuscitation. As Peter Lever knelt on the ground, sobbing uncontrollably and being comforted by some of his teammates, Chatfield's rescuers brought him back to life, got him onto a stretcher, into an ambulance and off to hospital. Miraculously, he would make a full recovery.

Three times in as many matches a batsman had been hit on the head by a fast bowler, and only by a miracle had cricket not been confronted by its first death at the wicket. In retrospect it seems incredible that the various participants in this supposedly most gentlemanly of sports did not simply get together, offer up thanks that a tragedy had been narrowly and fortuitously avoided, and resolve to end all this nonsense straight away. The fact that they did not is perhaps evidence that the game had already become so brutalised that nobody any more saw the thuggish maiming of a batsman as unacceptable.

Yes, there had been incidents in the past. Bouncers were as old as the game itself. In 1962 Charlie Griffith had inflicted Chatfield-type injuries on Nari Contractor who, unlike Chatfield, did not make a full and swift recovery; he was in a coma for six days and, unsurprisingly, never played cricket again. Later Griffith would attack England's batsmen, famously injuring Cowdrey and Underwood. To add to the controversy, it was alleged that he 'chucked' his bouncer – photographic evidence appeared to bear this out. In 1970–71 Snow had bowled short-pitched deliveries in Australia, as had Willis on the current tour.

Yet this was different. This was systematic rather than occasional, and injuries were inflicted intentionally, or at least recklessly, as both Lillee and Thomson openly acknowledged. This was a return to the Bodyline of 1932–33, that most controversial series of all, the last time that bowlers (English then) had aimed deliberately and consistently at the batsman himself.

Writing in 1975, presciently in view of what would shortly transpire, Christopher Martin-Jenkins said:

It seems clear that if Test cricket is to remain a reasonably chivalrous exercise, a fair challenge between bat and ball worth watching and playing, the *excessive* use of bouncers has got to be curbed ... [the umpires] who stood throughout the series were occasionally weak in not implementing the law firmly enough ... It is easy, however, to criticise the umpires. Cricket should be played not at the discretion of the umpires, but of the players. This has always been one of the great hallmarks of cricket, indeed the one characteristic which sets the game apart from others. It should be played toughly but fairly, and the tradition of cricket, its spirit, ought to indicate to players what is fair without their having to be told by the umpires.

The italics are Martin-Jenkins' own, and go to the heart of the matter. A short pitched delivery when bowled occasionally is a legitimate weapon. It keeps the batsman honest, as the Americans say, preventing, or at least deterring, him from simply pushing forward to every ball. As soon as it rises to chest level, it forces the batsman to decide whether to play it defensively, hook, or duck, a decision that must be taken in a fraction of a second and therefore understandably often leads to the batsman getting in a tangle and offering a catch. But, and this is such an important point that the reader will hopefully forgive the use of a conjunction to begin a sentence, it is bowled with that end in mind, not in the hope of causing the batsman serious injury. Nor is it bowled systematically ball after ball.

During the Bodyline series England had rightly been roundly condemned for using tactics which were against the spirit of the game. Against the spirit, but not the law, at least not then. In the wake of Jardine's tactics, the laws had been changed, first to allow a maximum of two fielders behind square on the legside, reducing the effectiveness of the 'leg trap', and second to ban the use of persistent intimidatory bowling. So Lillee and Thomson were not only contravening the spirit of the game but also the laws. In the failure of umpires to enforce those laws, and in the failure of governing bodies to give them guidance and support, can be seen the proximate cause of the descent of cricket into barbarism. The proximate cause, but not the root cause. That lay in the sudden and collective failure of moral judgment on the part of bowlers and captains. As Christopher Martin-Jenkins says, the spirit of cricket 'ought to indicate to players what is fair without their having to be told by the umpires'.

CHAPTER 21

THE 1975 ASHES

Cricketing folklore has it that the barrage of bouncers encountered on Denness's Ashes tour prematurely ended the careers of a whole generation of English batsmen – the cricketing equivalent of the First World War. Of course this is an exaggeration, but not an excessive one.

David Lloyd, a fine player with an unbeaten double century to his credit, never played another Test match. Nor did Brian Luckhurst, who scored four Test centuries and had been one of the outstanding batsmen on Illingworth's Ashes tour. More crucially for the future of the team, Denness's shortcomings against fast bowling had been ruthlessly exposed. Never before had an England captain felt forced to drop himself.

Edrich and Amiss had both been injured by a combination of fierce bowling and obsolete batting gloves which had proved unfit for purpose and were now being hurriedly redesigned. Yet the psychological damage lingered, and was perhaps more serious. Amiss would later admit to having been mentally scarred by Lillee and Thomson.[114] Edrich, having

---

[114] Dennis Amiss, *In Search of Runs*, Stanley Paul, London, 1976

courageously resisted another assault in 1976, would drop out of Test cricket, explaining that he had become tired of being used as 'a target man'. One can only sympathise with his views.

With Titmus and Cowdrey returned to pasture with thanks for their courage and endeavour, and the schedule of international cricket still apparently not adjusting to the absence of South Africa, Australia were due in England that summer for a four-Test series (shortened for the convenience of the World Cup, in an ominous sign of the growing tyranny of limited overs cricket), and the England selectors were faced with some tough decisions. The batting in particular was clearly in need of urgent overhaul, with only Greig and Knott having scored centuries against Lillee and Thomson. Even more pressing was the problem of the captaincy.

Treating the latter problem by simply ignoring it, the selectors decided to atone for the mistake of giving the captaincy to Denness by repeating it. With this issue now having been resolutely addressed, they moved on to consider the batting. The traditional MCC match gave a couple of clues as to their thinking, as both Graham Gooch and Bob Woolmer were included, but then so were Lloyd and Cowdrey. Gooch would in fact be brought into the side for the first Test, while Woolmer would have to wait a while. There was also a welcome return for Snow, who would partner Arnold and Old in the absence through injury of Willis.

Denness was faced with a tricky decision at Edgbaston when he won the toss. The skies were grey, and rain was forecast for later in the match. Doubtless reflecting that the conditions might prove ideal for Geoff Arnold, Denness put Australia in to bat. While it is difficult to criticise such a move, it was perhaps tactically reasonable, but strategically suspect. It set the wrong tone, suggesting that the English batsmen were keen to delay their reintroduction to Lillee and Thomson for as long as possible.

It became steadily apparent that Denness's gamble had failed. Rick McCosker and new partner Alan Turner put on 80 for the first wicket, and despite a flurry of wickets in the middle of the innings, a typically pugilistic 61 from Rod Marsh took Australia to 359 all out on the second day.

England's reply had lasted only one over when it was halted abruptly by a thunderstorm. When it resumed, they faced a single session of nearly three hours in poor light (with time added on for stoppages) against Lillee and Thomson.

They must have breathed a sigh of relief when Thomson proved so wayward that Ian Chappell took him off after only two overs, which had included five wides, and banished him to the outfield. If they had seen this as an escape, however, they were quickly disabused, for on in his place came Max Walker.

In all the media attention which Lillee and Thomson had commanded during the winter, the fact that Walker had enjoyed an outstanding series had been largely overlooked. He had taken 23 wickets and, a consistent irritant to England in the lower order, had come third in the batting averages to boot. With his fast-medium swing he was a classic English-style seamer, and now proved able to exploit the conditions in a way the more experienced Arnold and Old had not. Once Lillee had dismissed Amiss, Walker simply tore the heart out of England's middle order, dispatching Fletcher, Denness, Gooch and Greig in quick succession. At the end of the day England were already seven wickets down, and it took Australia less than half an hour to claim the remaining three the next morning. England were all out for 101 and asked to follow on.

Almost at once Amiss was hit a painful blow on the elbow by Lillee and forced to retire. He would later return, but to little avail. With Thomson now on target and taking five wickets, only Fletcher reached 50, and many of his runs came from edges through the slips. Eventually he got one edge too many and was caught by Walters. England were unable even to make Australia bat again, losing by an innings and 85 runs. The unfortunate Gooch bagged a pair on his Test debut.

Even the selectors were now forced to admit that this meant the end for Denness. As a captain, his decision to insert the opposition had probably cost England the match, and he had been widely criticised for only giving Underwood six overs on the first day. A big innings might still have saved him, but he had contributed only eleven runs in the whole game. Finally the selectors bowed to the inevitable, and turned to Tony Greig.

The new captain quickly made his presence felt in the selection process: into the side came David Steele of Northants and Bob Woolmer. There was also a recall for Barry Wood. The bespectacled Steele, prematurely grey and possessing a faintly apologetic air, seemed a most unlikely cricketer to face Lillee and Thomson. Woolmer was at this stage of his career playing as a medium-pace all-rounder. Wood had a proven technique against fast bowling.

Greig won the toss at Lord's and batted, but a familiar pattern soon emerged. Barry Wood went early, which brought Steele to the wicket, though somewhat slowly since he had never used the home dressing room before, and unfamiliarity with his surroundings coupled with big match nerves saw him descend one staircase too many to find himself in the rather splendid MCC gents toilet. Within minutes he was surveying the wreckage of the England innings at 49-4.

In company with Greig, Steele would now embark on the first of a series of performances which, over the space of only just over a year, would see him taken to the hearts of the English public in a way which perhaps no cricketer has been before or since, being elected BBC Sports Personality of the Year in 1975 by popular vote. Only Jim Laker had won it before. Only Ian Botham and Andrew Flintoff have since won it.

John Arlott memorably described Steele walking to the crease as 'a bank clerk going to war' and, as befitted Arlott's poetic leanings, it captured the emotion of the moment exactly. For men, the sight of this essentially ordinary and unassuming individual taking on seemingly impossible odds tugged at the heartstrings. In women, he aroused maternal instincts, leading them to wonder whether he had remembered his sandwiches and a clean handkerchief.

Arlott's description was apt. David Steele was exactly what that unforgettable phrase evoked. He was an archetypal wartime hero, who emerges briefly at a time of national danger to perform acts of great gallantry, and then returns uncomplainingly to civvy street to put his medals in a biscuit tin.

Lillee had bowled superbly, as he would throughout the match, to claim all four wickets to fall, but Thomson was again struggling for consistency, sending down 22 no-balls on the first day. With Steele pushing resolutely forward, and occasionally swivelling to pull a short ball to leg, and Greig taking on the bowling in his own style, the complexion of the match began to change.

Steele would finally be dismissed by a rare straight delivery from Thomson, having batted two and a half hours for 50. Greig, Knott and Woolmer batted in more breezy style to take England to 315 all out, scored at nearly four an over. From a seemingly hopeless position when Greig had come in, England were now back in the game.

The next day the old firm of Snow and Lever bowled Australia out for 268, built around 99 from Ross Edwards and an unexpected 73 not out from Dennis Lillee, which saved his team from potential embarrassment at 133-8.

In their second innings England batted as though inspired by the exploits of Steele and Greig in the first. A magnificent 175 from Edrich enabled Greig to declare at 436-7, by which time Ian Chappell had resorted to the bowling of himself and Doug Walters. Lillee, Thomson and Walker had bowled 99 overs between them, and taken just two wickets.

Australia would bat out more than a day to secure a draw, but it seemed that England had turned the corner: the cause can be traced to the change of captain. Like Brian Close, Greig was a truly inspirational captain who led by example. The dramatic turnaround in England's fortunes when he took over is no coincidence. Ray Illingworth called Greig 'one of the most imposing and influential captains in the history of English cricket'.[115]

Even Greig could not solve England's perennial middle-order problem, though, so Amiss and Gooch were dropped to make way at Headingley for local boy Jackie Hampshire and yet another recall for Keith Fletcher. Has any England batsman ever been given more chances than Keith Fletcher? Only Hick and Ramprakash come to mind as possibilities.

The Headingley Test match would pass into history for all the wrong reasons, though there was no sign of this as England batted first and made a solid but uncomfortable 288 with fifties from Edrich, Steele and Greig. 'Uncomfortable' because the left-arm Gary Gilmour found excellent late swing to take 6-85.

---

[115] 'Why does Greig get a raw deal?' op. cit.

When Australia batted it was therefore expected that Chris Old might produce a similar performance, if he could only find the right line and length. In the event, though, it was Phil Edmonds, on his Test debut, who was the destroyer, taking five wickets. Without taking anything away from this splendid performance, at least three of his victims contributed to their own downfall, and Derek Underwood also bowled well at the other end, unluckily finishing with only one wicket.

With Australia all out for 135, England pressed home their advantage, making 291, which set Australia 445 to win, but allowing plenty of time to do so. Steele was unfortunate to miss out on a century, falling to Gilmour on 92.

When Australia came out to bat it quickly became apparent that, despite the huge target, they were determined to go for it. When the fourth day finished, Australia still needed another 225 to win with seven wickets in hand. With McCosker batting beautifully, the game was set up for an exciting finish.

The next morning it emerged that during the night the pitch had been vandalised as a protest against the recent conviction of a professional criminal called George Davis for bank robbery, and the game was abandoned as no further play was possible. For the record, Davis's conviction was later overturned, though he was convicted of two subsequent offences, to both of which he pleaded guilty.

It is interesting to speculate what might have occurred had the game been played out. Australia were chasing a massive score, but only about the same as New Zealand had achieved at Trent Bridge in 1973. Probably England would have won, but whatever the case the revival in their fortunes had continued.

For the final match at the Oval, England changed their middle order yet again, discarding both Fletcher and Hampshire after just one game, and bringing in Roope and Woolmer, the latter to play this time primarily as a batsman.

They needed to win to square the series but by the end of the first day it was already clear this was not going to happen – Australia were 280-1. They would bat until nearly the end of the second day, finally declaring at 532.

England's bowling was disappointing, particularly Edmonds after his fine display at Headingley.

After two days of sunshine, the skies darkened on Saturday and, amidst stoppages for rain and bad light, Walker again found conditions to his liking and the Australian seam trio dismissed England for 191; only Steele provided any prolonged resistance.

Following on, England needed to bat for a long time and score a lot of runs to save the game. This the newly resilient team duly did, the first seven batsmen averaging over four hours each at the crease. Chief among them was Woolmer, who batted for over eight hours to make 149.

So England ended the series on the losing side, but had good grounds for cautious optimism. Steele and Woolmer seemed to offer some sort of solution to their middle-order batting woes. Phil Edmonds had emerged as a spinner of promise for the future. Greig seemed to have instilled a new fighting spirit into the side, just as Close had done back in 1966.

There was now a hiatus in English cricket, since there was no overseas tour planned for that winter. However, in distant parts of the world, a chain of events was set in motion which would have profound implications for the very future of the game itself.

Rohan Kanhai had finally retired from Test cricket, handing over the captaincy of the West Indies team to an enthusiastic but inexperienced Clive Lloyd. The winter of 1975–76 saw Lloyd leading quite a young side to Australia, where they experienced the same sort of suffering inflicted on England twelve months earlier. Of the six Test matches, Australia won five, the one exception featuring heroic performances by Roy Fredericks, Clive Lloyd and Andy Roberts.

While the naturally talented West Indian batting line-up did not subside as tamely as England's had done, the fact that they scored only half as many centuries in the series as their opponents tells its own story, as does the fact that apart from Lloyd himself only Keith Boyce, who was playing primarily as a bowler, averaged over 40. That a batting side containing the likes of Fredericks, Rowe, Richards and Kallicharran could be tamed, speaks to something special having happened.

The something special was a sustained barrage of short-pitched intimidatory bowling, just as had been faced by England. Again, batsmen were hit. Fortunately nobody was seriously injured, but morale suffered. Viv Richards volunteered to open in the last two matches in place of Gordon Greenidge, believing his teammate's nerve had gone. For once a good turn was rewarded; he scored a century in one match and fell just short in the other, having already scored a 50 in the first innings.

The West Indies also encountered some similar umpiring, which did not help team spirit. After one particularly questionable decision a young bowler called Michael Holding sat down on the pitch and wept in frustration.

The readiness of the West Indies batsmen to carry the fight to Lillee and Thomson also did little to help *esprit de corps*, since they were regularly out hooking, and violent arguments broke out between those who felt they should eschew the shot, and those who wished to persist with it. The young captain could only watch and despair as his side fell apart around him.

There were, however, quiet moments when he could have a beer with his friend, Viv Richards, and in one of these conversations he mused on what might happen if a side had four fast bowlers to bowl aggressively at the batsmen, rather than only two as Australia did.[116] A dangerous seed had been sown. Growing into a poisonous creeper, it would wrap itself around the game of cricket and do its best to squeeze the life out of it.

West Indies then went home to a series against India. West Indies won the first match and drew the second. In the third, India scored 406 to win in the fourth innings, making the West Indian attack, which included only two fast bowlers but three spinners, look innocuous. Lloyd had had enough. The fourth and final match in Jamaica was to prove frighteningly different.

After bowling conventionally on the first day, a four-man pace attack, led by Michael Holding and Wayne Daniel, unleashed on the Indian batsmen the same sort of attack to which the West Indies had been subjected by Lillee and Thomson. The result was carnage.

Two batsmen were forced to retire to hospital, one (Gaekwad, who

---

[116] David Tossell, *Grovel! The Story and Legacy of the Summer of 1976*, Know the Score Books, Worthing, 2007

played in glasses) hit on the head and another (Patel) in the mouth. Viswanath broke a finger while giving a catch. Both Armanath and Viswanath were caught while fending off head-high balls. With Holding bowling round the wicket, as Larwood had often done in 1932–33, it was Bodyline without the leg trap. Gavaskar, having received four bouncers in one over, walked down the wicket to enquire why the umpire was doing nothing about it, but received no explanation. Finally Bedi, captaining the side, declared in protest. Never one to mince his words, he complained later to the press that West Indies were waging war, not playing cricket.

When the West Indies adopted similar tactics in the second innings, Bedi simply declared again, even though in so doing he was effectively forfeiting the match. When he was told the rules did not provide for this situation, he instructed the scorers to list all the remaining Indian batsmen as 'absent hurt'. When West Indies batted again to score the dozen runs which they needed to win, Bedi stayed pointedly in the dressing room.

It was a brave and principled stand which, like all brave and principled stands, was destined to come to nothing. India flew home and lodged a formal complaint with their cricket board about West Indies' behaviour. This too came to nothing. If only others had possessed the courage to follow Bedi's example, the game of cricket might yet have been saved. When even his own cricket board refused to support him by complaining formally to the ICC, it was clear that the sport had passed the point of no return. The dark ages had arrived.

CHAPTER 22

AT HOME TO
THE WEST INDIES

Sadly Tony Greig had been doing his homework on what had happened to the West Indies over the winter. 'Sadly' for two reasons. First, his analysis led him to make a most unfortunate public pronouncement. Second, perhaps because his research had overlooked the disgraceful scenes in Jamaica, he failed to foresee the possible consequences which this pronouncement might have.

Being interviewed by the media, he correctly identified that the West Indies team and its performance had recently been volatile, not least in the recent series in Australia, and that when they were good they were very good, but when they were down 'they grovel'. 'I intend to make them grovel', he finished. Inspirational words, perhaps, but there was always the danger that it would be the West Indian team, and their many supporters in England, whom they would inspire the most, as indeed would prove to be the case. By the end of the summer, they had even become the subject of a reggae song in the pop charts.

In the heightened racial tensions in Britain at the time, which would see riots in Brixton in 1980 and Toxteth in 1981, leading to the Scarman Enquiry, it was perhaps not the wisest language for a blond-haired white

242

South African to use in respect of a black West Indian cricket team. However Greig had intended the words (and he had surely uttered them innocently and spontaneously), the West Indians certainly saw them as an affront, an affront which they were determined to avenge.

The West Indies touring party of 1976 included three genuinely quick bowlers: Roberts, Daniel and Holding, plus another, Julien, who could still produce a quick bouncer when he needed to. The veteran Vanburn Holder could provide the West Indian equivalent of Max Walker if called upon. It was not long before they were in action.

The traditional MCC match against the tourists saw a side packed with batting and captained by Richard Gilliatt. Dennis Amiss was recalled to try to reclaim his place in England's opening partnership. In the continued absence of Boycott, it was widely felt that he now possessed the best technique of any English batsman. Mike Brearley was chosen as his opening partner and the match also featured a young Derek Randall.

When it came time for the MCC to bat, Amiss soon misjudged the length of a ball from Holding, largely because of the extreme pace at which it was delivered, and ducked into it. Again, it was a miracle that cricket did not witness its first fatality. Bleeding profusely from behind his ear, and with blood running all over his cricket whites, Amiss was helped, semi-conscious, from the field. Richard Gilliatt was so appalled at the sight that he sent in a bowler, Phil Carrick of Yorkshire, to protect the remaining batsmen. Perhaps he thought that the West Indies would be chivalrous enough not to bowl short at him. They weren't, but he did manage to hang on for a while with Brearley. Later his only real memory would be of Brearley greeting him on his arrival at the wicket, Amiss's blood clearly visible on the grass, with the immortal line from *Beyond The Fringe*, 'the time has come, Perkins, for a useless sacrifice'.

John Woodcock wrote in *The Times*: 'bouncers, and the terror that springs from them, must be kept in check … [Amiss's injury] was another reminder to the umpires that the first-class game … will soon have a death on its hands.'[117]

---

[117] Quoted in *Grovel!* op. cit.

Amiss's injury was a massive blow, practically as well as psychologically: practically because England had been hoping he might fill one of the opening berths; psychologically because he was thought to have a sound technique against fast bowling.

With Amiss out of the reckoning for the foreseeable future, Brearley was preferred as Edrich's opening partner, thus gaining his first cap. The last ever selection by England of someone who had played as an amateur under the old system was one of two notable aspects of the team selection. The other, though it had been widely trailed in the press and by Greig himself, was the recall of Brian Close.

The West Indies themselves were flabbergasted. They had been sceptical whether even Edrich would be chosen, at the age of 39. Now here was an England team featuring a 45-year-old who had last played Test cricket nine years previously. The press, predictably, loved it. It was a hugely romantic decision, redolent of Close striding down the wicket to Hall and Griffith back in 1963, and taking a battering on the body for his pains. Romantic, yes, but would it work?

West Indies meantime had selection problems of their own when Michael Holding went down with suspected glandular fever and had to be hospitalised. This scuppered Lloyd's plan to play four fast bowlers but he decided to stick as closely to it as he could, preferring Holder to a spinner.

When West Indies won the toss and batted, Greig chose to set fairly defensive fields from the start in an effort to slow West Indies' scoring rate. These tactics were partially successful, but could not stop Viv Richards from scoring 232, and his team 494. The introduction of Underwood was strangely delayed until quite late in the innings, but he made an immediate impact, taking four wickets, including the vital ones of Richards, Kallicharran and Lloyd.

When England began their reply on the Saturday they quickly lost Brearley for a duck, but Steele and Edrich then spent nearly three hours together in bringing up 98. Steele would go on to a hugely popular century, well supported by Woolmer, as England scored 332. Brian Close survived just three overs.

West Indies then blazed a whirlwind 176-5, Richards again leading the way to set England a target of 339, but with time having been lost through rain and bad light there were now only about two sessions to go; the old stagers Edrich and Close safely batted out the draw, Close batting for over three hours and seeming to vindicate his selection.

For the second Test at Lord's, England lost a key player, while West Indies gained one and lost one. John Edrich, who had batted for almost eight hours in the first match, pulled a muscle and was replaced by Barry Wood. Michael Holding returned from glandular fever, but Viv Richards, his tour room-mate, succumbed to it. Such was West Indies' confidence in their batting that they replaced him with a specialist spinner, Raphick Jumadeen. England also altered the balance of their team, bringing in a spinner (Pocock) for a seamer (Hendrick).

England batted first and lost two quick wickets: Wood and Steele. This time it was Brearley and Close who dug in against the West Indian bowlers. Each would bat for almost three and a half hours, Close being struck repeatedly on the body, but after they departed only Woolmer seemed to be able to resist. England finished on precisely 250.

The fabled West Indies batting machine for once failed to work properly. Despite good knocks from Greenidge and Lloyd, the rest collapsed tamely against superb bowling by Snow and Underwood, resulting in an unexpected first innings lead for England of 68.

In their second innings England were again indebted to Close, and this time to Steele, who resumed normal service with 64, ground out over four and a half hours. Their total of 254 set West Indies 323 to win. Incidentally, during the England innings Clive Lloyd showed another facet of the 'four fast bowler' approach which would be cynically exploited over the coming years: the ability to slow the over-rate down to about twelve an hour. Of course Cowdrey had employed similar tactics back in 1968, so England were hardly in a position to criticise.

West Indies seemed unable to decide whether to go for the runs or not, alternately attacking and defending. In the end, the match finished with the whole England team gathered round the bat, still needing four wickets to win. Close warned Steele to be ready to catch a rebound off his head at short leg, but sadly for this narrative no such trademark Close dismissal was to occur.

A flurry of illness and injuries before the Old Trafford Test match would see Brian Close and John Edrich opening the batting for England, and Hendrick and debutant Mike Selvey the bowling. Frank Hayes came into the side to bat down the order. Richards came back for West Indies, but Lloyd used the absence of Holder through illness to keep a spinner, Padmore this time, in the side.

Even at the time, asking Close to open seemed a strange and unfair thing to do. He had never been a regular opener, having done so only occasionally as a stand-in. As if that was not bad enough, there was general agreement that the Old Trafford square was a mess (a fact which Lancashire vehemently and angrily denied) and the pitch not fit for Test cricket.

Mike Selvey, on debut, exploited the seam movement and variable bounce in the pitch to take four wickets, and West Indies were at one time 26-4 before a good stand between Greenidge, who scored a superb century, and Collis King pulled them around. Even so, they could manage only 211. England were then summarily dispatched for 71 by a combination of bouncers and yorkers. Particularly dangerous deliveries were bowled at Pocock and Underwood, balls which would only a few years previously have been received with outrage, but now seemed to be accepted with resignation by the batsmen, and ignored by the umpires.

Gordon Greenidge now made his second century of the match, signalling his belated arrival as one of the game's great opening batsmen. Some years later he would win a game single-handedly on this same ground with a double century on the last day, coming to it with a six. This time too, the crowd were treated to a real spectacle, with Richards also batting imperiously for a century at the other end.

The 552 which England were set to win, with over two days to go, was academic. However, what the crowd and the watching television viewers were now to witness over the remaining hour and 20 minutes of the day's play would shame the game of cricket, and the reputation of Clive Lloyd and the West Indian team, for ever. Pat 'Percy' Pocock, who was playing in the match, describes the events of that evening session as 'the most appalling and unforgivable that ever I saw in all my years in first-class cricket.'[118]

Making no attempt at all to bowl at the stumps, Holding, Daniel and Roberts directed ball after ball at the batsmen's bodies. In good light and on a sound pitch it would have been disgraceful, unsporting, and against the laws of cricket. In poor light, and on a treacherous pitch, it was vicious, premeditated violence. Being outside the laws of cricket it was also illegal, and had either Close or Edrich been killed then a prosecution for manslaughter could well have been brought against captain and bowler.

As for the captain, he stood impassively at slip while Close and Edrich ducked, weaved and were hit, Close repeatedly. One ball seemed to most observers obviously to break a rib, and set Close shaking involuntarily before, squaring his jaw, he took guard again. Mike Selvey remembers:

'These two old boys, England's oldest opening pair, refusing to get out. I can't speak too highly of Closey that night ... what we saw then was an extremely brave man. He went up massively in my esteem, as did John Edrich.'[119]

As for the umpires, they delivered just one official warning, to Holding, who showed his contempt for it by immediately bowling another short-pitched delivery which hit Close in the ribs again. He then stalked back past the umpire (Bill Alley), as if daring him to do anything about it; he didn't, of course.

Ironically, the Australian Alley had in his time himself been a fearless player of fast bowling, despite having been hit on the head while batting, an injury which forced him to retire from his (undefeated) career as a middleweight boxer after 28 fights as he was unable to get his medical certificate renewed. Sadly, on this evening his courage failed him. This was doubly unfortunate since the other umpire, Lloyd Budd, was standing in his first Test, and looking to Alley to give him a lead.

An excuse proffered on behalf of the umpires, both that evening and

---

[118] Pat Pocock, *Percy*, Clifford Frost, London, 1987
[119] *Grovel!* op. cit.

generally during the dark ages, is that they were reluctant to intervene because they feared they would not be supported by the authorities if they did so. This may well have been founded in truth.

ICC proved over the years completely unable to do anything about the situation because the West Indies and their allies simply voted down any proposals to clarify the laws on intimidatory bowling. One is forced to wonder, though, why the MCC did nothing. Then, as now, they were responsible for the laws of cricket, and could quite simply have introduced specific wording to deal with this unacceptable behaviour. Similarly, one wonders why the TCCB did not simply cancel the rest of the series and state that they would not play the West Indies again, either at home or abroad, unless and until they agreed to toe the line. West Indian cricket was at that time almost totally dependent financially on tours of England to fill their coffers, and could not long have withstood such a tactic, particularly if other countries (India?) had joined England in a more general boycott.

Even if true, however, such an argument does not exonerate the umpires, no matter how much one might sympathise with their plight. As Simon Wiesenthal said, in order for evil to flourish, all that is necessary is for good men to do nothing. Pocock says simply that it was 'the biggest umpiring disgrace I have ever seen'.[120]

As for the captain, it is difficult to find words to describe his behaviour. To wish to win by playing the game hard but fairly is one thing. To place the wish to win above respect for both the spirit and the laws of the game is quite another. For the record, Lloyd would later say (1) that it was for the umpires, not the captain, to intervene if they felt the bowling was against the rules and (2) that it was England's fault in picking old men that Close and Edrich were hit so often. If that sounds both callous and cynical, it is because it is. Let us remind ourselves of what Christopher Martin-Jenkins had written the previous year:

Cricket should be played not at the discretion of the umpires, but of the players. This has always been one of the great hallmarks of cricket,

---

[120] *Percy* op. cit.

indeed the one characteristic which sets the game apart from others. It should be played toughly but fairly, and the tradition of cricket, its spirit, ought to indicate to players what is fair without their having to be told by the umpires.[121]

Lloyd 0, Martin-Jenkins 1.

Many watching this cricketing GBH were shocked, appalled and sickened. Several journalists wrote of the obvious danger of someone being killed if such behaviour was allowed to continue. It would be comforting to be able to record that even at this late juncture the cricketing authorities stepped in to put an end to this madness. Comforting, but false. The MCC, the TCCB, and the ICC, it seemed, were prepared to see someone get killed rather than rock the political boat. Clive Lloyd had put the establishment to the test and found it wanting. That he should subsequently have become an international match referee brings to mind the explanation by Tom Lehrer that he gave up writing satirical songs after Henry Kissinger won the Nobel Peace Prize because he felt that satire had nothing left to say.

In fairness to the TCCB, they *did* take resolute action. They fined Tony Greig for suggesting to the press that the pitch was sub-standard. Those who have read this far will perhaps no longer find it surprising that under the warped moral code of the English cricket establishment they should punish someone for telling the truth, but not for breaking the laws of cricket. Perhaps Close and Edrich were doubly fortunate not to have been more seriously injured; if they had been, they might have been fined for time-wasting.

Though the result of the game now seemed academic, as it had to Bishen Bedi in Jamaica, one should report for completeness that, predictably, England fell a long way short of their target the next day, blown away by Andy Roberts. Brian Close would bat for nearly three hours in total in making 20, savouring his last Test innings to the full, though clearly restricted in his movements. He had refused to go to hospital overnight with his broken ribs, preferring whisky and strapping.

---

[121] *Assault on the Ashes* op. cit.

In contrast to the pitch at Old Trafford, the last two Tests took place on good batting surfaces. For Headingley, England tried their fourth opening partnership in four Tests (the Oval would make it five out of five), promoting Steele and Woolmer, awarding first caps to Peter Willey and Chris Balderstone (a First Division footballer), and recalling Frank Hayes; Edrich, Close and Gooch missed out.

Neither Edrich nor Close would ever play Test cricket again. Edrich has a fair claim to be reckoned one of England's best opening batsmen, with a Test average of 43.54 and a triple century to his credit. Close's contribution to the game has already been acknowledged. For anyone who saw it, the image of them ducking, weaving and being hit on that infamous evening at Old Trafford will surely live in the memory, like a scene from some black and white film in which the middle-aged sergeant and the reprobate released from the guardroom bravely sacrifice themselves holding the pass against a rampaging enemy, so that the young lads in their platoon can make good their escape. Fittingly, but ironically since they were now both discarded, Edrich and Close would finish the series in first and second place respectively in the batting averages.[122]

At close of play on the first day at Headingley, the good news for England was that West Indies had lost nine wickets. The bad news was that they had made 437 runs at over five an over, both Greenidge and Fredericks making big-hitting centuries. Only one result now seemed possible, though England recovered well, making 387 with centuries from Greig and Knott, and Bob Willis then taking five wickets to bowl West Indies out in their second innings for 196. A target of 260, though modest, proved beyond them, as they were bowled out by the West Indies pace quartet. Tony Greig was once again the hero for England, with 76 not out.

At the Oval England brought back Dennis Amiss to form their fifth opening partnership of the summer with Bob Woolmer, thus ending the Test career of Frank Hayes, the golden-haired wonderkid who had burst onto the scene with a century on debut, but then made less than 140 runs in his other 16 Test innings.

---

[122] Amiss was not included, since he played in only one match.

In fact, no less than seven English cricketers would play their last Test in this series: Balderstone, Close, Edrich, Hayes, Snow, Steele, and Ward.

Amiss made a triumphant return at the Oval, but joined that select band of batsmen who have made a double century but still ended up on the losing side, a feat emulated by Paul Collingwood at Adelaide in 2006, though Brian Lara, as so often, tops the list, scoring both a double century and a century at Colombo in 2001 but still losing to Sri Lanka.

The reasons here were twofold. First a majestic 291 by Viv Richards, one of the great all-time Test innings. Then hostility and persistence combined by Michael Holding gave him fourteen wickets in the match on a lifeless wicket, one of the great all-time bowling performances. Greig, when he was bowled by a Holding yorker in the second innings, having lasted just four deliveries, gave a mock grovel to the largely West Indian crowd, underlining that, for him at least, his remark had never been intended that seriously.

The featherbed wicket at the Oval, produced partly by one of the longest heatwaves in British history, had drawn the sting of the West Indian attack. Forced to bowl conventionally, Holding had done so and underlined the fact that he was one of the best fast bowlers ever to play the game. Yet this should not obscure the fact that this series marked a dramatic turning point in the game of cricket, demonstrating two things in particular.

It demonstrated beyond all doubt that within the last few years a new breed of captain and fast bowler were prepared deliberately (or at least recklessly) to inflict serious injury on batsmen, and dare the authorities to do something about it. Unfortunately it also demonstrated beyond all doubt that the authorities were either unwilling or unable to rise to the challenge. Knowing, or at least suspecting this, the umpires did nothing.

In the case of the ICC, international consensus proved impossible. With only six members (until the admission of Sri Lanka in 1981) after the expulsion of South Africa, West Indies only ever needed to get two other members to vote with them to create deadlock. In any event Australia, to whom England had traditionally looked for support, were not keen on seeing the activities of Lillee and Thomson, their most potent weapons, curbed.

The case of the TCCB is more difficult to understand. They could simply have refused to play any more Tests against West Indies, at least in the absence of playing conditions which clearly defined intimidatory bowling, and enforced a minimum number of overs a day, backed up, say, by a penalty of five runs for every over remaining unbowled at close of play.

Whatever the reason for their inaction, there could no longer be any doubt that cricket had now been fully exposed to the modern era, and brutalised in the process. Once again, however, trouble was brewing on the other side of the world which would shortly present the cricketing establishment with perhaps its greatest challenge ever; a challenge which, perhaps predictably, it would comprehensively mishandle.

CHAPTER 23

THE DAWN OF A NEW ERA

Proponents of chaos theory sometimes argue that the beating of a butterfly's wings can cause a hurricane on the other side of the world. The butterfly effect simply suggests that a seemingly insignificant occurrence can, through an infinite and unpredictable chain of cause and effect, have significant consequences. For all you Star Trek fans out there, this is in fact the theoretical rationale for the Prime Directive.

The butterfly effect can be seen at work one day in 1908 when, according to legend, a young man in Tasmania finds a dollar bill on the ground at a racetrack. He picks it up and puts it on a rank outsider. The horse comes romping home, and he uses his winnings to pay his fare to the mainland and fulfil his dream of becoming a journalist.

His name was Robert Clyde Packer, and by the time he died on a cruise ship in 1934 he had amassed a considerable media empire; his achievements also included founding the Miss Australia beauty contest, which first ran in 1926. He had also played a bit part in the saga of the Bodyline tour, since he insisted that a young cricketing journalist called Don Bradman honour his newspaper contract, almost causing him to miss playing in the series (he missed the first Test in any event due to illness).

His son, Sir Frank Packer, expanded the empire still further, including a commercial television network, the most prominent part of which was Channel Nine, which went national, challenging directly the monopoly of ABC. When he died in 1974, the reins passed to his son Kerry who was both a keen cricket fan and a vigorous and aggressive businessman.

It is worth explaining by way of background that various factors were at work in Australian broadcasting at the time. The government had introduced a quota system requiring a certain amount of Australian-made content (a similar system used to operate in British cinemas, and still does in France), and, importantly, sportscasts of domestic events counted as Australian content, which was good news for those who were terminally bored with *Skippy the Bush Kangaroo*.

In 1976, when the ACB (Australian Cricket Board) invited bids for the next three years' TV rights to Australian home Test matches, Channel Nine made a knock-out bid of A$1.5 million. Packer was surprised to lose out to ABC, not least when it was announced that their winning bid had been about one eighth of Channel Nine's. To this day it is unclear why the ACB made this somewhat quixotic decision, though personal animosity to Packer, loyalty to ABC, and a fear that Channel Nine's saturation coverage would deter people from turning up to watch the matches live have all been suggested.

Packer, predictably, was furious, seeing this reverse as a personal snub. It was one which he was determined to avenge. Pouring petrol on the flames, the ACB also persuaded the TCCB to grant the Australian TV rights for the forthcoming 1977 Ashes series in England to ABC, despite there once again being a higher offer on the table from Channel Nine.

Meanwhile Tony Greig was leading England (or MCC, as they were still anachronistically dubbed when touring overseas) in India. The series was a personal triumph for Greig and undoubtedly his finest achievement as a captain. England beat India for the first time on Indian soil since the Second World War, becoming the first touring side to clinch a series in India by winning the first three Test matches. India then fought back to win the fourth Test, and the final one was drawn.

England took a new bowler with them on this tour, John Lever of Essex, who had a fine series as well as scoring a valuable 50 in the first Test. Having discarded David Steele somewhat ruthlessly after his heroics against Australian and West Indian fast bowlers, they also took two new batsmen, both of whom were also brilliant fielders: Graham Barlow of Middlesex and Derek Randall of Notts. Barlow would not make the grade in Test cricket, but Randall would become one of its best-loved participants.

It was a series during which, apart from moments of individual brilliance from the likes of Gavaskar, Amiss and Greig, the ball dominated the bat. For England, Lever, Willis, Underwood and Old all took their wickets at 20 or less. Underwood dispelled the myth peddled by some cricket writers that he was only effective in English conditions, and even then should be taken along in the team like an umbrella, in case it rained. He took 29 wickets, more than any other bowler on either side.

The winter then took a very unusual turn, since it had been decided to play a one-off Test match in Melbourne to mark exactly one hundred years since England and Australia had first played each other, though then the Melbourne Cricket Ground had been somewhat less famous, and used as a club ground by the local police force. So, instead of returning straight to England, Greig's team went first to Sri Lanka, which was still not a Test-playing nation, and then on to Australia.

The Centenary Test was a huge success, not only as a spectacle, but also as a game of cricket. The Queen and Prince Philip attended, and every player who had ever played in an Ashes Test was invited. All the former captains who were present led their respective teams onto the pitch. Eerily, as if scripted in advance, both the result and the winning margin would exactly reproduce the events of 1877.

Greig won the toss and put Australia in; because he was afraid of facing Lillee, they said; because he wanted England's seamers to have first use of helpful conditions, he said.

In the event, both views were probably correct. Accurate bowling from England restricted Australia to 138, a jarring note having been struck to the festivities when McCosker had his jaw broken by a ball from Willis. He would bravely return to bat in both innings, his face heavily strapped.

Lillee and Walker then responded by skittling England out for 95, with

Walker looking, if anything, even more dangerous than Lillee, with the ball moving around.

However, the weather then changed, and the rest of the game was conducted in batsman-friendly conditions. Australia made 419, built around a fine century from Rod Marsh, which would turn out to be a match-winning performance; his team were 187-5 when he came to the crease.

As befitted an exhibition match, England then went for the 463 they needed for victory, and very nearly got them. That they did so was thanks almost entirely to Derek Randall, who began the match as a virtual unknown and ended it as a national hero. His 174 that day would remain his highest Test score. Knocked over by one bouncer from Lillee, he turned what could have been an inelegant sprawl on the ground into what looked like a graceful gymnastic mat exercise. After ducking under another, he confronted the glaring bowler, stood to attention and doffed his cap.

Randall was a mass of contradictions. Walking with a shambling, round-shouldered gait which earned him the ironic nickname of 'Arkle' (a famous racehorse of the time), he was nonetheless an electrifying fielder – he and David Gower would shortly become a fearsome duo at midwicket and cover point. Moving into shots fluently and gracefully, he was nonetheless a dreadful fidget at the wicket. When he was good, he was very good, but when he was out of touch he looked awful.

His departure from Test cricket, when it came in 1984, had little to do with a lack of natural talent, but owed everything to a growing brittleness to the mental pressure of the international arena. He lacked the ability of a Boycott or a Barrington to survive and play a long innings even when out of touch, gradually playing himself back into form in the process.

If Derek Randall found himself popular in Australia, then so did Tony Greig. He had already stored himself up a stock of goodwill during Denness's disastrous tour, when he had stood out as a gutsy fighter on the losing side, a quality the Australians admired. Then, with England not having an overseas tour in 1975–76, he had spent the winter in Australia, playing cricket and appearing on television. So, he was already almost as well known there as he was in Britain.

Greig was said, a little unkindly by other cricketers, never to be without his briefcase, a charge that would later also be levelled at Phil Edmonds (he responded in appropriate fashion by founding a successful public company). It is certainly true that, with his penchant for appearing in advertisements and TV commercials, he had an eye to the main chance.

Yet why not? After all, cricketers had quite a short career and, with no equivalent of an occupational pension scheme, was it objectionable that they should try to earn as much as possible while they could in order to provide for their future? This was, after all, what the idea of a benefit season was for, towards the end of a player's career. Even so, no cricketer had ever become independently wealthy, at least not from cricket. Many an England cricketer found themselves running a pub in retirement, like Peter Parfitt, or a post office, like Fred Titmus.

During the fifties, cricketers and footballers had earned roughly the same amount of money, enabling many, such as a young Brian Close, to consider a joint career which would run all year round. This had all changed in the sixties. First, the Football Association scrapped its wage cap of £20 per week, and by the mid-sixties leading players were already earning at least five times that, a very considerable sum at the time. Second, quite quickly, in the space of only five to ten years, people simply stopped going to watch Championship cricket. As already discussed, this would lead to various enquiries into the state of the game, one outcome of which would be the introduction of various limited overs competitions.

Limited overs cricket, and the consequent increase in gate money and television dues, brought a lot more money into the game, saving some counties from bankruptcy and totally transforming the fortunes of some, such as Lancashire, who were consistently successful at the shorter forms of the game.

Yet none of this money trickled down to the players. As late as 1976, an England player would receive only £210 for a five-day home Test match, and about £3,000 for an overseas tour.[123] This latter amount was less than what Ray Illingworth reckoned he could earn in a winter selling fireworks;

---

[123] *Grovel!* op. cit.

it had also been a factor in Tom Graveney's departure from Test cricket. Many cricketers felt very keenly that they were underpaid relative (1) to other sportsmen and (2) to the gross income of their respective counties (this was before the days of central England contracts). Few felt this more keenly than the briefcase man, Tony Greig.

So, when Kerry Packer approached him with an idea as to how he could significantly increase his earnings, Greig listened attentively.

Packer's plan was audacious; nothing less than the creation of a world of cricket which would run parallel with the official one, mounting its own series of matches with its own contracted players. It would be called World Series Cricket, with the participants being paid much more than in the official version of the game. In a few seasons of WSC, a cricketer could expect to earn pretty much the same as he could during his entire career as an English county cricketer.

So supportive was Greig of this idea that he not only committed to it himself, but he also agreed to be Packer's recruiting agent, approaching other Test cricketers, particularly of course those in the England team. It must have been obvious to Greig that he was treading on dangerous ground here. It was hardly consistent with his role as captain of the England cricket team to be simultaneously soliciting them on behalf of a potentially competing organisation.

That summer, in 1977, the Australians were due to tour England. It would later emerge that most of them had already secretly signed with Packer, something of which the ACB were to take a dim view when the truth emerged. Emerge it duly did, and in somewhat ironic circumstances. One of their early tour matches was against Sussex, skippered by Greig. The game was ruined by rain, but while Greig was entertaining some of the Australian players, he heard that the story would break in the newspapers the next day. It remains unclear exactly how the two Australian journalists concerned sourced their material.

Greig was unprepared for the severity of the reaction. Words such as 'betrayal' were inevitably thrown around, and within a few days he had been dismissed as England captain. His successor was Mike Brearley, who would be England's last captain to have played as an amateur.

It says something for the state of English cricket at the time that there should have been no other obvious candidate. Fletcher could not even be certain of a place in the side. Boycott was still in self-imposed purdah, and in any event his flaws as a captain were by now self-evident. No other county captains had even as much claim to a place in the side as a player as Brearley did himself. None of the other senior players already in the side, such as Knott and Underwood, were apparently considered, perhaps because they were felt to lack the right credentials for the role.

Brearley's continuing position in the side had for some time looked increasingly curious. He had scored 340 runs in eight Tests at an average of just 24, and had never looked convincing as an international player. It is difficult not to compare his situation with that of Mike Denness a couple of years previously. Perhaps in the minds of the selectors he was the gentleman captain they really hankered after, rather than the brash, abrasive Greig. However, there were a couple of important differences between Brearley and Denness.

Brearley had been a young batsman of enormous promise. Captaining a representative under-25 tour of Pakistan in 1966–67, he scored both a double century and a triple century; Alan Knott, who was also on that tour, expressed the opinion that he had never seen a young batsman of higher quality. Why this early promise was never fulfilled remains something of a mystery, but a probable explanation is that his decision to pursue postgraduate studies at Cambridge robbed him of the formative years which would have laid the basis of a sound technique at the highest level. While he played occasionally for Middlesex during this time, much of his batting was for Cambridge (for whom he played for eight consecutive seasons), rarely against first choice bowlers; thus many of his games, while technically first-class, were actually more in the nature of second eleven fixtures. He did not become a full-time county cricketer until 1971, whereupon he was immediately appointed captain of Middlesex, but by now he was already 29, an age when many of his contemporaries would have been playing full-time for over ten years. His Middlesex opening partner, Mike (M.J.) Smith, for example, first played county cricket at the age of 17.

Brearley was also an all-time great captain, and wrote a seminal book on the subject, *The Art of Captaincy*. His academic career had increasingly tended towards psychology – he would in retirement become a qualified psychotherapist. Given this, it is hardly surprising that he was skilled in motivating his team, even including mercurial characters like Ian Botham. As Rodney Hogg would say in awe, Brearley 'has a degree in people'. He would, for example, famously make Bob Willis bowl uphill at Headingley in 1981 'to make him angry', and then unleash him from the other end, whereupon he demolished Australia.

Brearley was also an outstanding slip fielder, one of the best in the country; this was welcome in a side where close catching had in recent memory been an area of fallibility. He was also a stand-in wicketkeeper, though he was never called on in this capacity.

By the time the first Test started at Lord's there was already widespread speculation that all the players who had signed for Packer would be banned from first-class cricket with effect from the end of the English season. For the Australians, almost all of whom had signed, this produced visible anger and uneasiness. England were less affected, only Amiss, Woolmer, Knott, Underwood and Greig having signed (plus John Snow, whose Test career had ended). Woolmer, Amiss and Snow would in fact end up playing for the 'Cavaliers' in WSC, a team made up largely of back-ups and recently retired players, captained by Eddie Barlow.

A rain-affected match at Lord's was drawn, Bob Woolmer missing out on a century in each innings through a run-out.

He scored another century at Old Trafford, a match which England won comfortably largely as a result of his efforts with the bat, and Underwood's with the ball (he took 6-66 in the second innings), and which marked the Test debut of Ray Bright for Australia.

The third Test, at Trent Bridge, Nottingham, marked a significant event: the return from the wilderness of Geoff Boycott. The Yorkshireman would experience first tragedy and then triumph, ineptly running out the local boy Derek Randall, and then scoring a century in the first innings and an undefeated 80 in the second. A century alongside him in the first innings from Alan Knott established a dominant position; a young debutant called

Ian Botham took five wickets in the first innings. Rick McCosker's century in defeat was the only consolation for Australia.

With media attention centred firmly on Geoff Boycott's return, it became known that the great man intended to score his hundredth first-class century in the fourth Test at Headingley, his home ground. If successful he would become the first Englishman to do so. The plan nearly went awry before it started, when he was in danger of scoring it a few days early in a county match, but he dealt with this problem by retiring hurt. Thus, the stage was set.

In the event he rather overdid things, scoring 191 in England's one and only innings, cheered every run along the way by a loyal and enthusiastic Yorkshire crowd. A clearly dispirited Australia were then bowled out cheaply by Hendrick and Botham, and again by Willis and Hendrick when they followed on. It is difficult to overstate Boycott's achievement. He was only the eighteenth Englishman ever to score a hundred hundreds at all, and will almost certainly remain the only one ever to do so in a Test match on his home ground. He would finish his Test career in 1982 level with Hammond and Cowdrey at the top of the list of English centurions (22 each).

For the fifth and final Test at the Oval Australia, with life bans looming, brought Kim Hughes and Mick Malone into the side as they were the only members of the tour party who had not yet been capped. The medium-paced Malone would make the most of his only Test appearance by bowling unchanged for an entire day when play finally began on the Friday, save only for two overs before lunch. In the process, he took five for 63 and England were all out for 214. However, with much of Saturday also being washed out, this became effectively a three-day match and ended predictably in a draw. So, rather tamely, did Australia lose the Ashes.

With no result likely, and the knowledge that this would be the last Test match before WSC cast a cloud of uncertainty over the future, the game was played out in an air of unreality and anticlimax. It was notable for two milestones: Geoff Boycott reached 5,000 Test runs and Jeff Thomson reached 100 Test wickets. The latter feat was accomplished in just 22 Tests, exactly the same number which Dennis Lillee had taken to reach the milestone two years earlier. Interestingly, Stuart MacGill, but not Shane Warne, would later surpass them.

The TCCB now moved, as widely predicted, to ban all Packer signees from Test and county cricket. That such draconian action should be taken speaks to the moral outrage at what was felt somehow to be a betrayal of the game, but also to how deeply threatened the cricket establishment felt, not just in England this time but also in Australia. In England, the MCC and its shadow organisation the TCCB controlled every aspect of the game: to them it was simply unthinkable that any cricketer should flout their authority or, even worse, simply ignore it. In Australia, the continuing battle with Packer was clearly felt to be something personal, with ACB and ABC ranged together against this upstart who was trying to muscle in on their cosy little arrangement.

Packer counter-attacked by funding a legal challenge to TCCB in the High Court in London, brought by Greig, Snow and Procter. This was something which TCCB really should have foreseen, but appeared not to have done. It was obvious to any law student that they were at risk both for the tort (civil wrong) of inducing a breach of contract between two third parties, and for acting in restraint of trade. When the TCCB lost, and were ordered to pay their opponents' costs, the counties were secretly delighted. Not only would they be able to keep their star players but if, as seemed likely, TCCB refused to pick them for England, then in the absence of Test calls they would have their services all summer.

For the cricketing establishment, however, the court case marked their Suez. Whenever unruly, 'uncouth' professional cricketers had threatened to get out of line in the past they had always been able to strong-arm them into submission, usually behind the scenes. This time, like Eden, they had been forced into an open confrontation and publicly humiliated. Compromise, rather than confrontation, would have saved their face, and surely done less harm to the game which they professed to love and serve.

In time, compromise came, as was always inevitable. By 1979 the ACB, its finances desperately weakened, did a deal to award Packer the television rights he had always craved. For the Australian 1979–80 season Greg Chappell was appointed captain, and Packer players once again appeared in the baggy green. The English authorities, now isolated, were furious, believing that they had supported the ACB in its hour of need, only to be let down by them (much as Eden felt about the Americans after Suez, with just as little justification). Eventually they too tacitly admitted defeat, starting to pick Packer players like Alan Knott again from 1980 onwards.

In the meantime, their absence had allowed exciting young players such as Gower and Botham fully to establish themselves in the England side, and county plodders like Rose and Radley an unexpected taste of Test cricket.

In the same year, 1980, Brearley would give up the England captaincy to Ian Botham, dropping out of Test cricket in consequence. He would of course famously return at Headingley in 1981 in an attempt to revive English fortunes, only to find himself being forced to follow on, but that is another story, and one which has already been told.

EPILOGUE

Change came slowly to cricket, as it always has. The dark ages were finally brought to an end by a combination of a greatly belated (but nonetheless welcome) determination to tackle intimidatory bowling, and new minimum over-rate requirements, backed up by fines and disciplinary measures. By this time helmets had in any event become commonplace and had eliminated the danger of death, if not of serious injury.

At the same time, fortuitously, the game saw the emergence of perhaps the greatest spinners ever to play the game, and crowds were able to revel once again in the true subtlety of what is undoubtedly the greatest and noblest form of sporting contest in the world. Shane Warne played his first Test in 1992, as did Muttiah Muralitharan. It was touch and go, though. During the dark ages it felt as though spin would never again feature decisively in Test cricket.

World Series Cricket turned out ultimately to have been not such a bad thing after all. Though it survived for only a few seasons and probably lost money, it forced counties and countries to start paying their professional cricketers a more realistic share of the greatly increased amounts of money that were now coming into the game.

The D'Oliveira affair cast a long shadow. In its immediate aftermath Tom Cartwright, not a fanciful man, believed that his house was searched during a family holiday; opening drawers afterwards, it was as though their contents had moved around. Peter Hain, who had been an active participant in the Sheppard / Brearley protest movement and who led the 'Stop The Seventy Tour' campaign, would later go on to become an MP and a Labour minister, but not before he had been sent a letter bomb, which fortunately failed to explode, in 1972, and tried on trumped-up charges of bank robbery in 1976.

The former was widely believed to have emanated from BOSS, the South African security police, who are believed to have dealt with other dissidents around the world in a similar way but with more successfully explosive results. A visit to his parents' house by a mysterious South African of dubious background later brought intelligence that the robbery trial too was the result of BOSS action, and part of a concerted campaign to discredit him. By way of background, it should be explained that Hain's family were South African, and had been effectively hounded out of the country for their opposition to apartheid. One of Hain's teenage memories was of being woken in the middle of the night by BOSS searching his parents' home for incriminating papers.

In his book which he subsequently wrote on these remarkable events,[124] Hain points out that Prime Minister Harold Wilson subsequently complained to journalists about unauthorised activities by right-wing elements within MI5 at this time, particularly in respect of the Liberal Party, of which Hain was then a member and leader of its youth branch. Hain believes this hypothesis is also supported by some of the revelations which were later offered by Peter Wright of *Spycatcher* fame. Wilson was sufficiently concerned to suggest the setting up of a Royal Commission.

It now seems clear that for at least a year prior to the bank robbery charges, BOSS had been financing the printing and distribution of anti-

---

[124] Peter Hain, *A Putney Plot?* Spokesman Books, London, 1987

Liberal party publications alleging, among other things, that the Liberals were in collusion with Moscow. While we will never know the truth, it seems entirely possible that the robbery charges were indeed the result of collusion between BOSS and maverick elements within MI5, both of whom were aiming at the same target. Hain's mysterious visitor said that the crime had been committed by a BOSS agent known to bear a strong resemblance to Hain. It has also been suggested that it was committed by an independent operator, retained by BOSS.

Certainly it seems hard to believe that the prosecution could have been brought without some sort of pressure on and/or support for the police from behind the scenes; the story is too bizarre and the actions of the police too incomprehensible. For example, they failed initially to take Hain's fingerprints or to check his family's alibi evidence, both of which one would have thought to be fairly obvious basic steps in any investigation, despite him asking them to do so. He also answered their questions readily from the very first moments, and protested his innocence throughout. From reading the transcripts and summary of the evidence nearly 40 years on, it seems remarkable both that the case was brought and that the judge allowed it to go to the jury.

The issue of fingerprints was key for it was common ground that the robber, who was pursued through the streets while making his escape, dropping the stolen money in the process, was not wearing gloves. Yet Hain's fingerprints were not found on a single banknote. The alibi evidence provided by members of his respectable middle-class family was entirely disregarded. The only evidence offered by the police was from an identity parade, which was conducted only after the fact that Hain (whose face was constantly in the media) was a suspect in the case had been leaked to the press (and even then several eyewitnesses failed to pick him out). Much of this evidence was given by a group of schoolboys, who consistently got fundamental points wrong, such as where they had just had lunch, with whom, and what they had had to eat. A further member of the group, who was not called by the prosecution, flatly contradicted their evidence. Another eyewitness unearthed by the defence gave evidence that she had seen a man she had initially thought was Hain walking near the bank, but when she got up close to him she realised it wasn't, though he looked similar.

The prosecution case was basically that Hain, a well-known public figure, robbed a bank very close to his home, which he had previously been photographed picketing in an anti-apartheid protest. He wore neither a mask nor gloves, ran off while clutching stolen banknotes but magically without leaving any fingerprints on them, and made good his escape on foot, dropping the money as he did so. He then reappeared a few minutes later in a car without even having bothered to change his clothes to throw off suspicion, parked beside the very people who had just been chasing him, and went into a shop, crossing directly in front of them, to buy typewriter ribbons with which to type his PhD thesis.

Far from not allowing the case to go before the jury, the judge, Alan King-Hamilton, embarked upon a summing up so prejudiced that it was objected to during the trial not just by the defence (unusual enough) but also by the prosecution (almost unheard of). He suggested directly that Hain's family were lying, and that this could be used by the jury as corroboration of the schoolboys' testimony, and sought to explain inconsistencies in the prosecution evidence by suggesting possibilities of which no evidence had been given at all.

Fortunately for Hain, the jury resisted the best efforts of the English legal system to convict an innocent man. Some MPs called for the resignation of the director of public prosecutions which, needless to say, did not occur. The police closed their file and refused ever to seek out the true perpetrator of the crime. King-Hamilton retired from the bench three years later in what *The Daily Telegraph* called 'a whirlwind of controversy' after having castigated in very offensive terms a jury for failing to convict. *The Sunday Times* called it 'a disgraceful epitaph to an undistinguished judicial career'. He died in 2010 at the ripe old age of 105, his obituary noting that one of his many eccentricities on the bench was to keep the jury regularly updated on the Test score.

The Gentlemen

Colin Cowdrey died in 2000 having been made first a knight and then a peer; Barry Knight, who kept up a correspondence with him from his new home in Australia, said he often forgot how to address the envelope. He would later take as his second wife a daughter of the Duke of Norfolk, his manager and dinner host on the Australian tour of 1962-63. Two of his sons would play first-class cricket, one of them briefly captaining the England Test team.

S.C. 'Billy' Griffith died in 1993. His son Mike, who as we have already seen captained John Snow for a while at Sussex before being succeeded by Tony Greig, subsequently served as chairman of MCC's Cricket Committee.

Gubby Allen, the man who refused to bowl bodyline for Jardine, had already served as president of the MCC by the time of the events described in this book. In the latter part of his life, MCC provided a house for him next to Lord's with a personal gate into the ground, where a stand has been named after him. He insisted on being brought home from hospital in 1989 so that he could die within sight of the pavilion.

Doug Insole, the chairman of the most celebrated selection meeting ever held, went on to become president of the MCC and sat on various MCC committees. He politely declined to be interviewed for this book.

Peter May, another of the men at the centre of the D'Oliveira affair, died in 1994, also having been president of the MCC. In recognition of his contribution to the game, Surrey, whom he had captained during their era of greatness in the 1950s, elected him president posthumously, the only time the honour has been so awarded.

He would become chairman of selectors in 1982 and hold the position for seven years. In retrospect this was a mistake. His nature was not well suited to collaborative decision-making, and his behaviour became increasingly aloof and dictatorial. He had already attracted criticism for the manner of his sacking of Keith Fletcher (see below) by the time his tragic hubris finally culminated in the infamous 'summer of four captains' in 1988.

During the second Test, Mike Gatting was sacked as captain after an alleged incident with a barmaid. It is likely that May was looking for a chance to dismiss him anyway, after a controversial confrontation over the winter with Pakistani umpire Shakoor Rana. He was replaced by John Emburey.

After the third match, which England lost, Emburey was sacked and replaced by Peter May's godson, Chris Cowdrey. It is difficult to see this decision as having been prompted by anything other than favouritism, given Cowdrey's moderate Test match record. Perhaps significantly the selectors made seven changes in total, a move smacking of panic. England lost again, Cowdrey making five runs and taking no wickets.

Perhaps fortunately, Cowdrey was then injured playing for Kent, and this provided a convenient excuse for the selectors to make yet another change, this time bringing in Graham Gooch.

The following year the pendulum swung in yet another direction, with May appointing Gower in place of Gooch. By this time his decisions had become so aberrant that there was general recognition that enough was enough, and 1989 marked the end of his reign.

Ted Dexter succeeded Peter May as chairman of selectors, riding a motorbike between engagements, and later became president of the MCC.

Tony Lewis has also been president of the MCC, as well as chairman of Glamorgan, the Welsh Tourist Board, and the Welsh National Opera. He has just stepped down from the chairmanship of the World Cricket Committee, a position he held since 2006. As he says, he has performed every voluntary role in Glamorgan apart from cutting the grass.

Mike Brearley was also president of the MCC, ironically taking over from Doug Insole. He has been a prominent cricket writer, including authoring *The Art of Captaincy*, regarded by many as the finest book ever written on the subject. He practises as a professional psycotherapist and, his courage obviously not sufficiently tested by facing Joel Garner, is sometimes to be seen riding a bicycle around Swiss Cottage.

The Players

Fred Titmus died in early 2011, having been ill for some time. His record of having played first-class cricket in five different decades is most unlikely ever to be equalled. In retirement he ran a post office, but also served as an England selector between 1994 and 1996. Bizarrely, and for reasons which have never been explained, he was featured in a rock song in 1985 by the British band Half Man Half Biscuit. An internet entry describes their songs as 'satirical, sardonic and sometimes surreal'.

John Edrich is still going strong, despite having been diagnosed with leukaemia in 2000. He served first as an England selector and then as England's batting coach, and was appointed president of Surrey for the 2006-07 season. He, like Boycott, is a member of a very select club, having scored one hundred first-class hundreds.

John Snow, the 'cricket rebel', founded what became a very successful travel business when he ended his playing career in 1977, using his Packer earnings as his starting capital. He lives in Sussex with two pet donkeys. Sadly he never published any more poetry.

His opening partner 'Big Dave' Brown, who was surely unlucky not to play for England again after 1969, retired at the same time in 1977, having captained Warwickshire for the last two seasons. In 1982, Gladstone Small was called up in an emergency by England on the second day of a championship match. The first-class playing conditions had recently been changed to allow for a direct, full-playing substitute in such circumstances. Warwickshire were so depleted by injuries that they asked Brown, at the age of 40, to turn up and do his best. He duly became the first substitute in the history of the game to take a wicket as a bowler.

Tom Graveney would become the first professional cricketer ever to be president of the MCC in 2004. After retiring in 1970 he became a regular feature of BBC television's cricket coverage alongside Jim Laker and Peter West. He retains an encyclopaedic memory of the statistics of every match he ever played in.

Derek 'Deadly' Underwood would also become president of the MCC, immediately preceding Christopher Martin-Jenkins. He retired in 1987 though not before he had finally achieved his lifelong ambition of making a first-class century, which he eventually did at the age of 39, having gone is as a nightwatchman for Kent. For some time afterwards any unit of a hundred was known as a 'Derek' by investment bankers in the City of London.

EPILOGUE

As already noted, Ken Barrington died suddenly while managing the England tour of the West Indies in 1981. It was in Bridgetown, Barbados, where he had made his first Test century 21 years earlier.

At the time of writing, Basil D'Oliveira is in a nursing home suffering from severe Alzheimer's disease. However, before the condition claimed him he was able to return to his homeland to receive the recognition that was his due.

Tom Cartwright, whose principled stand was to torpedo the England selectors in 1968, ended up in Glamorgan (his wife was Welsh), where he continued to coach young cricketers in his retirement. One of them, Matt Windows, once rang the great man for advice but his wife answered, said 'we don't want any windows thank you', and put the phone down. Tom played his last game of cricket at the age of 70 at the famous Broadhalfpenny Down ground, and died following a heart attack in 2007.

Alan Knott lives contentedly in retirement in Cyprus.

Geoff Boycott, a controversial and enigmatic figure, did eventually get his wish of captaining England, when elevated during the winter of 1977-78 by injury to Mike Brearley. He retired in 1986, having been first sacked and then reinstated by Yorkshire, the latter as part of a protest campaign run by a 'Reform Group' of Yorkshire members which hopelessly split the club for some years. In the process he fell out with both Brian Close and Ray Illingworth.

In 2002 he was diagnosed with throat cancer from which, happily, he has apparently made a full recovery, resuming his career as a trenchant summariser with TMS, where his pregnant exchanges with Jonathan Agnew are eagerly awaited as a highlight of the day. 'Aggers', who once famously asked 'Sir Geoffrey' to endorse Mike Denness as an England captain, is yet to suffer the ultimate brush-off. Did Boycott but know it, he took more Test wickets than Agnew, and at a much better average.

Ray Illingworth captained Leicestershire until his retirement in 1978, winning the County Championship in 1975 as well as numerous one day competitions. He was largely responsible for having the potential of David Gower recognised by England. Illingworth, an old-style disciplinarian, once reprimanded Gower for being scruffily dressed, whereupon Gower came down to breakfast the next morning in a dinner jacket.

Perhaps surprisingly he, like Close, was reconciled with Yorkshire, taking up a post as cricket manager after ending his playing career with Leicestershire. Frustrated by their poor performance, he took to the pitch again at the age of 50 as captain to take Yorkshire to the Sunday League title. He subsequently became Chairman of the England selectors, and was for a while a one-man 'cricket supremo' in charge of the Test side. However, his man-management skills were not ideally suited to this role and it was generally seen as a relatively unsuccessful postscript to a fine playing career.

At the time of writing he had just been released from hospital to convalesce at home following a heart attack and therefore sadly was not available to interview for this book. Cricket lovers around the world will wish him a speedy recovery.

Mike Denness left Kent in 1976 and moved to Essex, enjoying a glorious Indian summer batting alongside Keith Fletcher. His subsequent career as a Test referee was sadly mired in controversy in 2001 when this most mild-mannered of men decided to sanction six Indian players for a variety of offences, including ball-tampering and excessive appealing, banning them all for one match. This did not go down well with the volatile Indian cricket board, who responded by playing all six in the next Test, in defiance of Denness's ruling.

Despite the matter being fanned by the popular press in India, with Denness even accused of being racist, the ICC for once stood firm, refusing to recognise the next match as an official Test. It was then found that Denness required cardiac surgery, and the ICC stood their next committee meeting over without reaching a conclusion. By general agreement, the matter was then dropped.

Tony Greig, the man with the briefcase, has what is generally reckoned a job for life with Channel Nine, where he has proved a successful and insightful commentator. The fact that he was an epileptic, and had suffered from the condition throughout his playing career, became public knowledge shortly before he emigrated from England in 1979.

Keith Fletcher, 'the Gnome', would go on to captain England briefly, before being sacked in somewhat controversial circumstances as half of his team defected to a rebel tour of South Africa in 1982. He would later serve as England manager between 1993 and 1995, which was not a successful period for the team.

His continual returns to the team despite disappointing performances were a testament to the paucity of good middle-order batsmen on offer, but even so he was surely lucky to play so many more matches than Parfitt, Hampshire and Sharpe, all of whom were better fielders (Parfitt was also a useful spinner). Fletcher would score only seven centuries in 59 Tests and only one, against the West Indies in Bridgetown in 1974, against an attack featuring world-class fast bowling.

Brian Luckhurst died of cancer in 2005, having held for some time the post of president of Kent. His batting against that wonderful Rest of the World side in 1970 will long be remembered by those who saw it.

Dennis Amiss retired in 1987. He served later as an England selector and then ran Warwickshire as its Chief Executive from 1994 until 2005. Like Boycott, Edrich and Cowdrey, he is a member of the 'hundred hundreds' club.

Finally, what of the two captains that day at Edgbaston in August 1967?

The Gentleman

M.J.K. Smith, England's last double international, was Chairman of Warwickshire for over ten years, and an ICC match referee until 1996. His son Neil would later captain Warwickshire and play one day cricket for England.

The Player

Brian Close ended his 30-year first-class career at the end of the 1977 season at the age of 46, and now lives in retirement in Shipley, having happily been reconciled with Yorkshire County Cricket Club. However, the word 'retirement' is relative when applied to Closey; in his seventies he is said to be still coaching, playing for and captaining the Yorkshire colts.

INDEX

INDEX